SIMONE WEIL FOR THE TWENTY-FIRST CENTURY

SIMONE WEIL

FOR THE TWENTY-FIRST CENTURY

ERIC O. SPRINGSTED

University of Notre Dame Press
Notre Dame, Indiana

University of Notre Dame Press
Notre Dame, Indiana 46556
undpress.nd.edu
Copyright © 2021 by the University of Notre Dame

All Rights Reserved

Published in the United States of America

Library of Congress Control Number: 2021931597

ISBN: 978-0-268-20021-3 (Hardback)
ISBN: 978-0-268-20022-0 (Paperback)
ISBN: 978-0-268-20020-6 (WebPDF)
ISBN: 978-0-268-20023-7 (Epub)

CONTENTS

Preface		vii
Acknowledgments		xv
Abbreviations for Weil's Works		xvii
A Brief Biography of Simone Weil		xix

PART I. PHILOSOPHICAL AND THEOLOGICAL THOUGHT

CHAPTER 1	A Thoughtful Life	3
CHAPTER 2	Mystery and Philosophy	17
CHAPTER 3	The Nature of Grace: Incarnation and Crucifixion in Weil's Thought	32
CHAPTER 4	Love and Intellect	50
CHAPTER 5	"I Dreamed I Saw St. Augustine . . ."	68
CHAPTER 6	Spiritual Apprenticeship	86
CHAPTER 7	A Sacramental Understanding of the World	105

PART II. SOCIAL AND POLITICAL THOUGHT

CHAPTER 8	Beyond the Personal: Weil's Critique of Maritain	121

CHAPTER 9	The Language of the Inner Life	132
CHAPTER 10	"Thou Hast Given Me Room": Weil's Retheologization of the Political	146
CHAPTER 11	The Need for Order and the Need for Roots: To Being through History	159
CHAPTER 12	A Theory of Culture: Inspiration and Its Outworkings	175
CHAPTER 13	Searching for a New Saint Benedict: Attention and the Formation of Community	194
CHAPTER 14	Moral Clarity in War	210
	Conclusion	225
	Notes	231
	Bibliography	251
	Index	259

PREFACE

This book is not an introduction to the life and thought of Simone Weil. I put my hand to that many years ago, and numerous other volumes do that job, too. Nor is this meant to be a work primarily for Weil scholars, although it will certainly be of interest and help to them. Many of them were of great help to me in thinking through these issues in the first place. Above all, this book is meant to present Weil's thinking in some depth, looking especially at her late essays and notebooks, with a very particular eye to what she has to say about thinking to those in the twenty-first century. In many cases, it challenges that thinking, as Weil challenged the thinking of her day. In other cases, it hopes to point out a way to go. Chiefly, it means to help in reading Weil at the depth she deserves to be read, and that is, consequently, to offer Weil as something like a polestar to help orient our thinking in a time when the spiritual, moral, and intellectual world has become, in Charles Taylor's word, "flattened."

Weil has been an orienting light to me for a long time. I began reading her in the 1970s. I was a divinity student at Princeton Theological Seminary and had the good fortune to take classes with Diogenes Allen. At the time, I was most interested in Plato. Allen had been working on Iris Murdoch and was just starting to read Weil because Murdoch owed much to her. He suggested I read Weil, since she had a lot of interesting things to say about Plato. That began a journey, and, I gratefully say, it was for many years a joint journey with Dick Allen. He and I with others formed the American Weil Society in 1981, and together we continued to talk about Weil and to write on her. Over the many years of the Society, the best part, as my colleague Larry Schmidt once put it, is that it has been such a good place to do work—not only on Weil, but also on many topics that are important to the life of the mind and the soul.

Weil has in that way guided my thinking about these issues. Because she oriented me in the way she did, I have read and appreciated a lot of other thinkers in new ways and made use of them. They make regular appearances in this volume—Augustine, Wittgenstein, and Taylor chief among them, but many others as well.

A polestar also keeps you on track. There are limits to the metaphor, so a thinker who can serve in this way is not always right and to be followed slavishly. There are things in Weil that I am concerned about because of what I think she has to offer. Her views on Judaism are complex; sometimes they are subtle and offer a challenge to how we think about identity, especially about religious election. But she rarely gives the Old Testament the same sort of break that she easily gives the Greeks. She gets caught up in clichés that she herself would be put off by in different circumstances. In her religious thinking, she generally refuses to think about the Resurrection, although she believes in the Resurrection of Jesus. She thinks it is a consolation that can distract. There is surely a point there, but it is hardly all of the story. But despite these concerns, I also think that having her as a guiding light made me more and not less aware of these problems with her. That is why I am willing to say, with some confidence, that she can be a highly valuable thinker for helping us to make our way through unclear times and muddied thought.

Because this is the book's main goal, it does not presume a prior extensive knowledge of Weil's life or thought. It does require the ability to pay attention to an argument, as much of the presentation is a matter of carefully working through Weil's numerous essays, especially her latest ones. It is an effort in philosophy and in theology, and I have used numerous other thinkers, early and late, to help sharpen the issues. As a help, though, I have added a brief Weil curriculum vitae for those who don't know much about her and would like at least some sense of the arc of her life. In the end, I hope that in carefully working through her thinking, the reader will come to understand something of Weil as a thinker, a rare and great mind and soul, but particularly as one not to be admired at a distance or as a historical figure alone, but rather as one to stir our thinking.

I have often been asked what exactly Weil's thinking has to offer. The short answer is her belief, and subsequent working out of the idea, that life and thinking and love come on many different levels. A flattened world is one in which those levels are reduced to fewer dimensions; often to only one. We live in a flattened world intellectually and spiritually. This is seen in the penchant of many scientists, economists, social thinkers, and even philosophers to some sort of reductionism, to single-principle explanations. But it is not just them. As Taylor has argued, even religious thinkers have used a sort of shortsighted pragmatism and social utility to justify and explain religious belief and action, undermining religion's higher goals for human beings. As a result, the world, which Weil thought was so multitiered, shrinks and loses one or more vital dimensions. There is no mystery that challenges us to think deeper and to patiently endure contradictions. There are no different aspects to the world that we have to learn to see. Thinking is overly literal; there is not the fine sense of analogy that Weil had. There is no soul and hence no tragedy—and probably no divine comedy, either. There is an obsession with the self, but no inner life and no attempt by philosophy to see philosophy as a matter of working on oneself. Weil's thinking challenges us on all those things still today.

I have divided the presentation into two parts. While a reader may pick and choose the order in which to read them, the chapters are meant to follow upon each other.

Part I deals with philosophical and theological issues. It begins with an account of Weil's life as a thinker, not only to characterize what kind of person she was as a thinker, but also to underline that, with Weil, it is important to understand not only what she thought but also how she thought. It shows what kind of moral and intellectual example she is. As such, it is concerned with her habits of thought and their integrity, as well as the very significant change in the way she approached thought in her later years, as she moved from a strict disciplining of the mind to a regime of attentiveness. Like Wittgenstein, she thought that philosophy is a matter of working on oneself. Chapter 1 provides a broad assessment of what this means. It is not just about understanding Weil. It draws on Pierre Hadot's work and on that of recent phenomenologists such as Michel Henry and Jean-Yves Lacoste. It brings together many of her concerns about the inner life and social life. Much of Weil's thought in the latter years of her short life is the result of her conversion experience and having come to understand in a very profound way just what transcendence is, and how it changes how we look at the world and our own lives. Chapter 2 then examines the notion of mystery and how it distinguishes religious and theological thinking from science, but, moreover, how it gives depth to life. For Weil, thinking was at its heart, a matter of thinking through a mystery. To show how this is so, this chapter draws on philosophers Michael Foster, Gabriel Marcel, and Charles Taylor. But, if we, in thinking, encounter mystery, what kind of mystery is it that we face? Chapter 3 argues that for Weil it was ultimately the mystery of Christ: Christ the Word, but most especially Christ crucified. While in the strictest sense Weil was not a theologian, there is, nonetheless, an inerasable theological commitment in her thinking, namely, the grace that is centered in Christ's cross. For Weil, the world of mystery is a world in which there is grace, and the Cross is absolutely central to her account. What this means is worked out in relation to American theologian Kathryn Tanner's *Christ the Key*. Chapter 4 then presents a central claim of the book, namely that there is a subtle but crucial orientation in Weil's thought that distinguishes her sharply from many other thinkers. While Weil made trenchant comments about not entering the Church because she felt that her intellectual vocation would be compromised by the Church's approach to philosophy, close examination shows it was *not* her position that the intellect is the chief of a human's faculties in dealing with matters of depth. Rather, love is. Like Augustine, she believed that doctrine was to be presented to be loved; the Church, by treating it as a belief much like other sorts of belief, presented an obstacle both to the heart and the mind. This is not simply a critique of the Church's position. It is crucial to understanding something that runs through all of Weil's later thought and how what she has to offer is not simply a critique or an alternative position to contemporary options, but rather a demand to recenter human thought. It is a challenge in general about how we think and how thinking involves us, the thinkers, especially in those cases when thought is related to love. It is a challenge to philosophy in general, but especially to Christian philosophy. Chapter 5 continues this theme by showing that in which her very deep appreciation of Plato, a hallmark of her thought, consists. This is very Augustinian as well, namely, that where philosophy is at its most important to us it demands an "inner turn." This is also to recognize Weil as an important contemporary voice in appreciating exactly what the Augustinian tradition has meant for having an inner life. Chapter 6 then treats Weil's understanding of spiritual growth and how we change from a self-centered life to one that ultimately sees the world as the work of God's love. This change requires an apprenticeship: it requires bodily practice but also attention, an interest in and love for what one is doing. Chapter 7 broadens the argument via an examination of Weil's essay "The Implicit Forms of the Love of God." Drawing a parallel with French theologian Henri de Lubac's work on nature and supernature, it argues that her understanding of the world and nature is one that sees the world as not only created, but also as something in which God's Spirit dwells. In this regard, the way we live in the world has the possibility of being like a sacrament, inviting our participation in the life of God and having the potential to change us. Thus, ultimately, her "inward turn" is not inward looking but a way of living responsibly in the world. This provides a transition to Part II, giving a philosophical and theological context to her social thought.

Part II moves to consider her late social and political thought, especially in such works as *The Need for Roots* and other writings from her last months while working in London. It was an intellectually fruitful time in her life, perhaps unlike any other. It opens, as seen in chapter 8, in what is also a biographical interaction, namely, Weil's abortive but very significant encounter with Jacques Maritain in America. By itself, this encounter might be of only minor interest. But, as it turns out, Weil's thinking about Maritain was very much at the heart of her very important and provocative essay "What Is Sacred in Every Human Being?" This essay involves a turn in her social thinking that gave all her last essays, the ones written in London, their distinctive themes. Chapter 9 shows what this turn involved by a further examination of her claims in "What Is Sacred in Every Human Being?," an examination carried out by putting Weil in conversation with American social philosopher Michael Sandel, especially his central argument in *What Money Can't Buy*. This conversation shows in concrete detail Weil's position that values do come in levels, and that much of the modern world and economy have attempted to flatten them to one level, which in the end destroys depth in human life. The upshot of her deepest intuitions about the values that affect our lives is found in such things as her putting obligations ahead of rights. It also caused her, as chapter 10 argues, to rethink the social spaces in which we live. Rejecting liberal assumptions about individual preferences for goods as being at the heart of social life, about how they need to be negotiated, Weil looks at political and social issues sub specie aeternitatis and thinks of them within a much broader cosmological context. This raises issues that were important twenty-five years or so ago, when concerns about religion in the public square were being raised, but that now seem to have been lost. Weil raises them for us again as a way of rethinking the morals of political and social life. This argument is further carried forward in chapter 11, in which two apparently contradictory claims that are central to *The Need for Roots*—that the human need for roots is our primary need, and then that the need for order is—are set out and then reconciled, noting that we need to draw on a larger sense of order, such as the order of the world, for order in social life, but that we can only do this by appropriating our own historical context and recovering what might be called a useable past. Her view is both cosmological and historical. Chapter 12 continues this theme, presenting an argument that Weil never fully drew out but asserted with some confidence from time to time. Weil thought that there is something like an original revelation given to each people of the earth, and that their cultures need to be seen as the outworkings of that revelation in history. The value of the thought, Weil believed, is that this should lead us to appreciate the value of other cultures but to also understand that what is valuable to us is hidden in the history of our own culture. We can't stand outside it. Ultimately, then, to appreciate other cultures, we need to grab hold of what is valuable in our own, for what, ultimately, is valuable in any culture is God's self-sacrificing love, in which all people are called to participate. Chapter 13 treats questions of social disintegration and malaise, both those that arose in Weil's context during World War II and our own. It is a situation that led Alasdair MacIntyre to call for a "new St. Benedict." Weil makes a similar claim in asking for a new type of sainthood. But, unlike conservative social and religious critic Rod Dreher, who has recently called for a "Benedict option," i.e., for Christians to withdraw from politics and culture altogether, for Weil this was a matter not of withdrawing but of building a community within the wreckage we are experiencing. These chapters, then, are about communities, their possibilities and our hopes for shaping them to let human beings flourish. But, as all well know, although its obviousness is resisted, we do not only build communities. We also fight wars, sometimes even to preserve communities. But what does that mean? Weil lived and wrote in a time of war, and some of her most profound writing was about war, especially her essay "The *Iliad*: Poem of Force." Chapter 14 treats the moral importance and relevance of this essay by examining the issue of how in war, when madness reigns, moral clarity is demanded and yet utterly elusive. It does so by engaging with an article by American theologian and Catholic George Weigel in *First Things,* written at the beginning of the American war with Iraq. Rather than seeing clarity as a matter of seeing the moral necessity of war, as Weigel wants, Weil thinks that Homer's clarity is a matter of not being overcome by the blinding effects of force; his ability to show love is exemplary, but rare. But it is that sort of clarity that is needed to keep one's soul in the darkness of force and violence.

ACKNOWLEDGMENTS

These essays owe a great deal to many colleagues over many years. Some of them invited and published earlier versions of what is here; all of them were supportive, listened, continually prodded, had their own ideas, and generally made Weil scholarship a collegial and rewarding enterprise. They are friends. I owe thanks to Robert Chenavier, Emmanuel Gabellieri, and Michel Narcy in France; Giulia Paola di Nicola and Attilio Danese in Italy; Mario von der Ruhr in Wales; Maria Clara Bingemer in Brazil; my many North American colleagues, especially Sophie Bourgault, Joan Dargan, Jane Doering, Tomeu Estelrich, Clare Fischer, Vance Morgan, Larry Schmidt, and Rebecca Rozelle-Stone; and our late colleagues Diogenes Allen, Martin Andic, Richard Bell, André-A. Devaux, Henry Le Roy Finch, D. Z. Phillips, and Peter Winch; and my good friend Nicolette Weil Schwartzman.

An early book of mine on Weil was dedicated to my wife and daughters. This one is now dedicated to the grandchildren, Holden, Sawyer, Madi, Hudson, August, and any more who may come. Their mothers learned what Weil was about; they all learned compassion, justice, service, and the importance of thoughtfulness. My wish is for the same thing for their children.

Earlier versions of the following chapters appeared in these publications. All have been revised for this volume.

> Chapter 2: "Mystery and Philosophy," in *The Relevance of the Radical: Simone Weil 100 Years Later*, ed. A. Rebecca Rozelle-Stone and Lucian Stone (New York: Crossroad, 2010).
>
> Chapter 4: "Amour et Intelligence," *Cahiers Simone Weil* 33, no. 3 (September 2010): 353–74.

Chapter 5: "I Dreamed I Saw St. Augustine . . . ," in *The Christian Platonism of Simone Weil*, ed. E. Jane Doering and Eric O. Springsted (Notre Dame, IN: University of Notre Dame Press, 2004).

Chapter 6: "Spiritual Apprenticeship," *Cahiers Simone Weil* 25 (December 2002): 325–44.

Chapter 7: "Formes de l'Amour Implicite de Dieu: Simone Weil et l'Interprétation du Monde comme Sacrement," in *Cahier L'Herne: Simone Weil*, ed. Emmanuel Gabellieri (Paris, Editions de L'Herne, 2014).

Chapter 8: "Beyond the Personal: Weil's Critique of Maritain," in *The Harvard Theological Review* 98, no. 2 (April 2005): 209–18.

Chapter 9: "The Language of the Inner Life," in *Simone Weil: Beyond Ideology?*, ed. Sophie Bourgault and Julie Daigle (New York: Bloomsbury Academic, 2021).

Chapter 10: "'Thou Hast Given Me Room': Simone Weil's Retheologization of the Political," *Cahiers Simone Weil* 20, no. 2 (June 1997): 87–98.

Chapter 11: "The Need for Order and the Need for Roots: To Being through History," *Cahiers Simone Weil* 17, no. 2 (June 1994): 177–93.

Chapter 12: "Théologie de la Culture Chez Simone Weil: Inspiration et Développements," in *Simone Weil*, ed. Chantal Delsol (Paris: Éditions Du Cerf, 2009).

Chapter 13: "A la Récherche d'un Nouveau St. Benoît: Attention et Formation d'une Communauté," in *Théophylon: Revue de Théologie et de Philosophie de l'Université Catholique de Lyon* 9, no. 2 (2004): 535–57.

ABBREVIATIONS FOR WEIL'S WORKS

FLN   *First and Last Notebooks*, ed. and trans. Richard Rees (London: Oxford University Press, 1970; Eugene, OR: Wipf & Stock, 2015).

FW   *Formative Writings 1929–1941*, ed. and trans. Dorothy Tuck McFarland and Wilhelmina Van Ness (Amherst: University of Massachusetts Press, 1987).

GTG   *Gateway to God*, ed. David Raper (New York: Crossroad, 1982).

IC   *Intimations of Christianity among the Ancient Greeks*, ed. and trans. Elisabeth Chase Geissbuhler (London: Routledge & Kegan Paul, 1957).

LPW   *Simone Weil: Late Philosophical Writings*, ed. and trans. Eric O. Springsted (Notre Dame, IN: University of Notre Dame Press, 2015).

NB   *The Notebooks of Simone Weil*, 2 vols., trans. Arthur Wills (London: Routledge & Kegan Paul, 1952).

NR   *The Need for Roots*, trans. Arthur Wills (New York: Harper & Row, 1971).

OC   *Oeuvres Complètes*, 7 vols. (Paris: Gallimard, 1988–). Citations are given in the format book.volume, page.

OL   *Oppression and Liberty* (Amherst: University of Massachusetts Press, 1973).

SE	*Selected Essays 1934–43*, ed. and trans. Richard Rees (London: Oxford University Press, 1962; Eugene, OR: Wipf & Stock, 2015).
SL	*Seventy Letters*, ed. and trans. Richard Rees (London: Oxford University Press, 1965; Eugene, OR: Wipf & Stock, 2015).
SNL	*On Science, Necessity and the Love of God*, ed. and trans. Richard Rees (London: Oxford University Press, 1968).
SWR	*The Simone Weil Reader*, ed. George Panichas (New York: David McKay, 1977).
SWW	*Simone Weil: Writings*, ed. Eric O. Springsted (Maryknoll, NY: Orbis Books, 1998).
WG	*Waiting for God*, trans. Emma Craufurd (New York: Harper & Row, 1973).

A BRIEF BIOGRAPHY OF SIMONE WEIL

Simone Weil was born February 3, 1909, in Paris, to Dr. Bernard and Mme. Selma Weil. Her older brother, André, was one of the twentieth century's greatest mathematicians. The family was of Jewish lineage but were free thinkers and thoroughly assimilated. Weil saw her intellectual heritage as French and Christian.

Weil was educated in the best French tradition, attending the lycées Fénelon and Henri IV and studying with well-known philosophers, such as René Le Senne and Émile Chartier (Alain). In 1931 she was one of the first women to graduate from the prestigious École Normale Supérieure. With the degree of *agrégé*, she was entitled to teach in the lycée system. At the same time, she continued her deep involvement in political and workers' movements, something that had begun in her earlier school days. As a student it had made her an irritant to some of her own teachers; as a teacher, she was an irritant to most of the administrators of the schools where she taught, and she tended to scandalize the bourgeois parents of her students, as she led marches of the unemployed and taught classes for workers in her free time.

After writing in 1934 an extensive study titled *Reflections Concerning the Causes of Liberty and Social Oppression*, she felt there was more to be known about the subject, something that could only be learned by coming into contact with it. She took a leave from teaching and worked in three Paris factories as a common piecework laborer in 1934 and 1935. The experience nearly broke her, as she discovered what she came to call "affliction." She was morally defeated, and as one who had never been strong, other than in her will, suffering from migraines most of her adult life, she was physically ground down by the experience. At this time she began withdrawing from active political involvement, at least with respect to official organizations and parties. In 1936 she went to fight for the Republicans in the Spanish Civil War, no matter that she was committed at this point to pacifism; she simply could not bear to be absent in a struggle for justice. Soon, a clumsy accident caused her evacuation, which likely saved her life as her regiment was wiped out two weeks later. The experience in Spain opened her eyes to the realities of war, just as war was breaking out over Europe as a whole.

It was during this time that she had three religious experiences, with the third, in 1938, being a sense of Christ's personal presence. It gave her a sense of how love could be present even in affliction. Although her experiences were unknown to many friends and colleagues, she began writing extensively on religious topics. This marks a turning point in her life and thought.

When the Germans invaded France in 1940, Weil and her parents were on the last train out of Paris, escaping to Vichy France. They remained in Marseille until 1942. For Weil this was an extremely productive period, and many of her most important religious and philosophical writings come from it. This was in good part due to her discussions with Father Jean-Marie Perrin, who raised the question of her baptism. For her part, she sought to convince him of the universality of grace, particularly through her many essays on the ancient Greeks. In the end, although she continued to explore the possibility of baptism, she explained to Perrin that she believed it would be a betrayal of her vocation to accept it—not only a betrayal of those who were outside the Church, with whom she identified, but, moreover, disobedience to God. During this period she also worked for the Resistance in distributing materials and as a laborer in the grape harvest in the Rhône valley. It was there that she became friends with the folk philosopher Gustave Thibon, who would later put together some of the notebook material she left in his care, edited to his own concerns and titled *Gravity and Grace*. It might be noted that Weil published very little in her lifetime, although the French *Oeuvres complètes* will run to sixteen volumes when finished.

In 1942 she left Marseille with her parents for New York. Her plan from the beginning was to get back to the occupied zone, hopefully to take on a dangerous mission for the war effort. In particular, she had devised a plan for frontline nurses, and she hoped to lead it. She enlisted help for its realization anywhere she could. She was in New York from June to November, writing, researching, and attending black churches in Harlem. In November she got permission to go to London to work with the Free French. She left, hoping that this was her route back to France. However, she contracted tuberculosis, likely by the time she embarked, although she was careful to keep that fact from the authorities.

While in London, she kept pressing for the realization of her nurses project. Instead, she was given the job of writing reports on issues that would have to be faced when the Germans were expelled from France and a new French government installed. Although she was not happy with the assignment, she produced an enormous amount of highly original material in a short time, including the book-length analysis that came to be known as *The Need for Roots*. She collapsed from overwork and illness in April 1943. Her remaining months were spent in the hospital and, finally, a tuberculosis sanitarium. Although her doctors thought recovery was possible, Weil, who never did eat much, found it difficult to eat and justified it by saying that she wouldn't eat more than the people in occupied France were getting. She died on August 24, 1943, and was buried in Ashford, Kent. The doctors, baffled by her choices, officially declared the death a suicide because she refused to eat and follow orders. The story is told that she was baptized in her last days by a friend. There is little reason to doubt the story, but what is to be made of it remains a matter of controversy, with no clear evidence as to what Weil's own thoughts might have been about it.

PART I

Philosophical and Theological Thought

CHAPTER ONE

A THOUGHTFUL LIFE

When I first encountered Simone Weil some forty-plus years ago, the public and scholarly recognition and reception of her was very different than it is now. For one thing, there was not a lot of secondary literature on her. What there was chiefly centered on her extraordinary life. People knew of her year of working in a factory, her participation in workers' and social causes, and also her death. Some thought it heroic; others saw it as madness. Everybody had an opinion about whether she was a saint, or a seriously disturbed young woman, or a Manichaean, or a terrible example for feminists, or a self-hating Jew. There wasn't really a lot that looked deeply at her thought, though. What there was tended to look for confirmation of already held suspicions, positive and negative, about her life. She would have been disturbed by this. She herself wrote that she hoped that people would not ignore her thought because of the inadequate vessel in which it was carried.

At the time I largely concurred. Work needed to be done on what she thought. It was profound and coherent. The life of a philosopher shouldn't overshadow her thought as was happening with her. So, with respect to her thinking, I more or less held to Heidegger's oft-quoted lack of interest in philosophical biographies. Notably, he opened a lecture series on Aristotle with this as the sum total of Aristotle's biography: "He was born at such and such a time, he worked, and he died." I am of a somewhat different mind now. Why I am certainly has something to do with being suspicious about Heidegger's biography, even though I think it is a mistake to see it as nothing but a full and direct reflection of his colossal self-absorption or his acceptance of National Socialism. You can find both in what he wrote, but that isn't the biggest problem that has bothered me about him. What concerns me is how his failure to be interested in biography—or character and moral responsibility, to be more precise—says something about what and how he thought philosophically and hence how he lived. It is in such a way that I think it is worth looking once again at Weil's thought and its connection with life and saying something about that connection in the beginning of a book on her thought. She may have not wanted to have people look at her life instead of her thought, but her thought had a lot to do with thinking about value and character. Even if she felt herself inadequate, in a phrase borrowed from American philosopher Stanley Cavell, she saw a need to write better than she was. It is worth asking what kind of thinker is like this and what she has to offer.

There are situational reasons for asking this now, too. Intellectual work on Weil's thought has progressed. Since her death in 1943, she has remained a constant fixture in the constellation of eminent twentieth-century thinkers. No chair in any university is dedicated to her (perhaps to her credit), yet she is regularly cited, usually favorably and with admiration, within scholarly and intellectual circles. She is admired by thinkers of depth. Over many years, her ideas have provoked the sort of thinking that she thought needs to be provoked. For younger thinkers, there are not now many like her to look to. But at the same time, I sometimes wonder if her thought has somehow become disembodied along the way. This is a reversal of early scholarly writing on her. If this has happened, I want to suggest that it has happened in a couple of ways. One, there may be a certain failure to be struck with her life, or to understand it at the same time that one is using her thought. People such as Weil have become increasingly rare, and dealing with them has become more and more baffling. Perhaps more to the point are her often absolute claims and her willingness to stake her life on them. Claims of this sort strike many people in a postmodern, post-truth world as being just too much. You can't talk that way, we are told. But if her way of talking is at all close to her way of thinking, then I suspect that anybody who says that you can't talk this way just doesn't get it. It is easier to set those absolute pronouncements to the side and round the edges off. Second, there is also a certain failure, probably due to the worship of the same idols of the contemporary theater, to take her thought on in a way that lets oneself as a reader really be challenged by it. I cite here a tendency of many scholars in commenting on Weil to take her thought on very thinly. For example, a lot of the references made to her or work done on her have discussed her almost entirely through the contextless snippets that her friend Gustave Thibon, not Weil herself, assembled in *Gravity and Grace*. There is not a lot of textual work on her essays, much less her extensive notebooks. The essays and notebooks show her in the course of her thinking; *Gravity and Grace* does not. Her essays are more than striking, but manipulable, bons mots. They are not oracles. There is also a tendency to take the edges off what she said and make her sound like us. Concepts that are central to her thought are dulled. "Attention" becomes simply "noticing," which she says it is not. "Affliction" becomes simply "suffering," albeit intense suffering, which she says it is not. So, this sort of approach is not only piecemeal in failing to hold Weil responsible for her thought as a whole; it also betokens our failure for knowing her well. She gets treated like an icon. She could be wildly paradoxical, but if we want to understand her and use her, we need to find out if she was responsible. Perhaps nobody is interested in that because no one is particularly interested in being held responsible for one's own thought, or for depth, wishing only to appear deep. That also is a feature of a postmodern world in which there are no longer souls and in which, therefore, there can be neither tragedy nor inner greatness.

So, what exactly does it mean to talk about her life as a *thoughtful* life? In the end, that is how she needs to be understood and judged. If by that one means a careful and prudent life, one lived out according to a plan, then, clearly, that wasn't her life. It is something else we are after. What we should be interested in here is how she lived her life as a thinker, as a philosopher, and what that might tell us about philosophy and about thinking, and ultimately about how to think about the lives we are living and how to live lives that are thoughtful. To be able to say something about that would be to say where and why she is an important thinker. And it is, I believe, to talk about it as she thought a life ought to be talked about.

No one invents or constructs her life out of whole cloth. One comes into the world with a certain body and is heir to a history. As that being interacts with the world, she becomes aware to herself as a someone of some specific personality and then chooses to interact again with the world. It is a dance, as it were, as Weil was to describe perception in the philosophy course she taught at the girls' lycée in Roanne.

There are certain qualities to anyone's person, though, that seem to be more or less consistent throughout life. They are not necessarily the essence of who one is; they can take different forms according to other aspects of one's character. However, there do seem to be certain consistent aspects of character that let us recognize someone across many changes. For Weil, two aspects of her character seem most evident, namely, her strong will and her righteous concern for others. The first could express itself negatively in willfulness and stubbornness. It could also express itself far more positively in concentration, self-discipline, perseverance—which is not the same thing as stubbornness—and loyalty. The latter aspect showed itself in Weil's concern to share and know the lives of others and in a rare openness and generosity. The two aspects together could do a lot for others; they could also at times lead to a self-destructive asceticism.

There is, of course, a third consistent outstanding factor in Weil's life: her intellect. When she compared it to her brilliant mathematician brother's mind, she was ashamed of its insufficiencies, although when one allows it its own way, it was just as brilliant. But to say that it can be allowed its own way is to acknowledge that intellect can also be an extremely malleable element of character. It can determine how other parts of the self are shaped; it can take very different forms itself, especially over the course of a life.

Intellect was important to Weil. She cared about it; she was taught to care about it. She competed with it, at least inwardly with her brother, but more or less at times with others. She, like her brother, could use it to be bitingly critical. But she was also insightful in far more constructive ways, and she valued intellect as part of a good life. She respected it in others and was contemptuous of those who failed to respect it. She was intellectually generous. Intellect was not just for an elite, and she loved teaching anybody who would listen. She was generous to her students, trying to open up horizons beyond examination preparation; she gave her time to teach workers both formally and informally. Those are ways of thinking in which we are most interested in her as a thinker. They come to shape her will and sense of righteousness, as well. So, in trying to see the way in which she may have led a thoughtful life, we are most interested in how she thought and how thought formed the rest of her life.

Something else was consistent over the course of her adult life, something that she had learned from her teacher, Alain, at the Lycée Henri IV. Alain had always insisted that in order to think well, one had to make contact with the object of one's thought. This explains something of her distinctive example, such as taking a year off from teaching in order to work in three factories. Although she had just completed a major work on the causes of liberty and social oppression, she wasn't satisfied. She needed to engage workers and labor itself. Her desire to be part of the action during World War II by being parachuted into occupied France in order to be a frontline nurse surely owes something to this habit of thought.

But, even as we see what is consistent in her life of thought, we also have to realize that there were changes in how she thought. Broadly speaking, there are two periods to her life as a thinker that roughly correspond to the time before and after her religious experiences. In the earlier one, her concern was chiefly with social and political events; in the later, her concerns were far more transcendent as she wrote and thought about religion and questions of value and character, although she by no means gave up her concern with social life. Her unparalleled biographer and friend, Simone Pétrement, observes that while she may not yet have been a believer after her religious experiences, "there had already occurred a certain change in her philosophical ideas."[1] But it is not just the content. It is also how she thought.

To an important extent, in both of these periods Weil did not just think; she thought about thinking, as a philosopher should. But this is not just about thinking in general, about anybody's thinking; an important subjective element must be recognized. Wittgenstein once suggested, "As is frequently the case in architecture, work on philosophy is actually closer to working on oneself. On one's own understanding. On the way one sees things. (And of what one demands of them.)"[2] In a very similar vein, Weil understood philosophical thinking not just as a tool, which one needs to learn how to use and which needs to be used in order to produce certain desired results. It is also a matter of working on oneself. She herself says as much: "Philosophy—search for wisdom—is a virtue. It is a matter of working on oneself. A transformation of being. (Turning *the whole soul*). Different than mathematics" (OC 6.1, 175).

The difference between the two periods of her life can be seen with respect to the notion of "working on oneself." There were two distinct approaches. Pétrement describes the difference broadly as a difference between the sort of philosophy Weil had learned from Alain, which she says is "voluntarist," i.e., about the will and willing, and a mystical philosophy that involves a certain sort of passivity or receptivity in the inner life. French Weil scholar Pascal David gives some important precision and detail to this.[3] David argues that the point of working on oneself is for Weil a matter of being able to give oneself to the truth. She argues that we need to turn around in order to do this, a point she frequently uses Plato's allegory of the cave to make. She also regularly uses the language of transformation. That is consistent over the two periods of her intellectual life. One needs to ask, then, *how* does this transformation take place? That is where the two periods diverge.

Initially, she describes this transformation as a matter of *dressage*, of discipline and training. In a text from 1934, written for herself, she gives a list of temptations to be resisted.

1. The temptation of idleness. Flight from real life with its limitations, and from time, the essential limitation. Not to attempt anything that makes one aware that one isn't God. . . .
2. The temptation of the *inner life* (all emotions that are not absorbed *immediately* by methodical thought and effective action). Put aside all actions that do not attain the *object*.
3. The temptation of domination. . . .

4. Temptation of self-sacrifice (subordination to any object whatsoever, not only everything that is subjective but the subject itself; this comes from not being able beforehand to make the separation).
5. Temptation of *perversity*. . . . If you want to be cured, you must first of all be conscious of them. . . . Then subject yourself to merciless control and correction.[4] (OC 6.1, 407)[5]

In the earlier Weil, discipline and training also go hand in hand with a very great concern with the notion of method as a way to approach problems of knowing. Method particularly is a matter of disciplining the *folle imagination*, the "foolish imagination," that distorts what we see and think. This sort of discipline was the concern of her diploma essay, *Science et Perception dans Descartes*, and it continued on through the first half of the 1930s. In this period, she sees philosophy as a matter of constructing thought according to discipline and a method.

However, by the time of the later notebooks, Weil sees this sort of discipline as being of limited value. As David puts it, what is important to Weil now is no longer a matter of training oneself but rather of letting oneself be trained or shaped. "The role of the will tends to fade as attention gains."[6] She says as much in a way that sharply defines the issue:

> If we place a fault fully recognized as such in actual contact with God himself it is certain that we shall never commit it again; that even if it isn't destroyed in us immediately it is bound to wither away like a plant whose roots have been severed. If we are capable of such an operation, it is certainly much to be preferred to the process of self-training, which laboriously cuts through the stem. (NB 445)

Or, as she describes the matter in the essay "Some Reflections on the Love of God," we must keep our eyes trained on God. This is a sort of spiritual immobility. The will must not be the source of what we do; it is to be used solely for the performance of obligations that call for an exercise of the will. After that, "there is one effort to be made, and by far the hardest of all, but it is not in the sphere of action. It is keeping one's gaze directed towards God" (SWW 81).

So, as Weil comes to see it, work on oneself is no longer a matter of self-formation or self-creation. It is a matter of attention, which is a way of being formed that depends on being revealed to. Philosophy, which she calls exclusively a matter of reflecting on values, thus needs to hold detachment as its chief value (LPW 33). This is not indifference or an artificial equality of all perceptions. It is a matter of being willing to accept reality even when it costs something, including some very dear things.

For Weil, this is not dreaminess or giving into the sort of temptation that she earlier described the inner life as, which is to say, to focus only on one's own inner states. It still requires changing one's readings of the world from egocentric ones to ones where one feels the world as a direct response to God's love. That, she is clear, takes an apprenticeship, and that requires the body.[7] It still involves discipline. Above all, it requires attention, which is to say, suspending one's own intentions and giving the object of attention a place within one's own self. She wanted her mind to be like water, "which is indifferent to the objects that fall into it: It does not weigh them; they weigh themselves after a certain time of oscillation" (WG 85).

This is the sort of thoughtful life Weil led, or at least sought to lead. But before giving a broader assessment of what this kind of thoughtful life means, and what it looks like, one question needs to be answered.

Surely an astute reader must wryly smile when reading the list that Weil wrote in 1934 of temptations to be resisted. For on that list is this: "Temptation of self-sacrifice." Self-sacrifice seems to be a hallmark of her life, sometimes of a kind that appears perverse. She told Father Perrin that when she thought of Christ on the Cross, she committed the sin of envy, although she recognized the problem in saying this (WG 83). Her so-called horrible prayer prays for the dissolution of all her faculties (SWW 88–89). Her disappointment in not being sent on a dangerous mission into occupied France and her seeming stubbornness in refusing to eat any more than she thought people there had to eat while she was suffering from tuberculosis both appear to confirm this.

Yet, the careful thinker will distinguish here between what may be troublesome about Weil's own choices and what is really a philosophical objection to an entire way of thinking, especially about what a human mind is meant for.

Weil was, in fact, successful on many fronts in resisting the temptation of self-sacrifice, if one means by that the temptation to be cannon fodder for large movements, where a few leaders, usually men, stand on the heap of bodies of those whose sacrifices made their power possible. At the time she wrote this note to herself, she would not sign petitions she had not written herself. She was tempted by the idea of revolution; she soon enough saw through it and refused to be a follower, often earning the sharp criticism of the comrades. She effectively quit being a part of political movements by the mid-1930s. She was a pacifist but was not afraid to change her mind. She *did* pitch herself into projects, especially those she came up with, such as the frontline nursing project. She never did anything halfway and pursued efforts often to her own hurt, especially if she thought they could benefit another person. She was intense, and she was not at all good at assessing risks, especially to herself.[8] She wanted to make a sacrifice for France, but so did a lot of soldiers. In the end, she does not seem guilty of desiring sacrifice for the sake of sacrifice alone, which is, indeed, perverse.

That she was not subject to this kind of perversity is confirmed by considering the full context of the texts that are usually pointed at in order to make the accusation. For example, "the horrible prayer" is not all that different from prayers that we have of Julian of Norwich. The "horribleness," too, needs to be set against the second part of the prayer, where the dissolution of her faculties is to allow her to be in "continuous conformity to [God's] will." In this state she prays, "May this mind, in fullest lucidity connect all ideas in perfect conformity with your truth" (SWW 88). Her sacrifice is for greater truth.

But it is at this point that the philosophical question is raised about this kind of wish. Isn't she asking for a lot? Isn't the wish for this sort of knowledge destructive and perhaps even fanatical? Isn't this wish not so much for human fulfillment, but rather something inhuman, considering its cost? And isn't she the perfect example that it is? The question is philosophical, and not merely rhetorical, because, upon reflection, the answer to all these questions is *not* obviously yes. It would appear to be so, *if* one assumes what liberal societies assume about the human being and her choices. Self-denial wherever the good is thought to be a matter of choice of the individual *would* be the radical and self-contradictory dissolution of the human being, and hence inhuman. Any way of thought that aspired to so much knowledge or goodness that it required this dissolution should be rethought on such an assumption. But, as British social critic Terry Eagleton has pointed out, "Sacrifice cannot be reduced to self-denial."[9] The rejection of sacrifice in the service of a great good is not necessarily self-destruction, even if it costs something.

To that point is Eagleton's further observation: "The most compelling version of sacrifice concerns the flourishing of the self, not its extinction. It involves a formidable release of energy, a transformation of the human subject and a turbulent transitus from death to life."[10] To get beyond the mediocre, something difficult may be required of us. To build anything great, some sacrifice may be required. Nietzsche thought so, although he detested the Christian and Platonic versions. Gandhi asserted that there "is no worship without sacrifice." Iris Murdoch, under Weil's influence and noting "the [current] identification of the true person with the empty choosing will,"[11] flatly claims that the problem in moral thinking is the big fat ego that stands between us and reality. Until it is vacated, we will not know the reality that only gives itself to loving attention. For Weil, that was everything. That is where she as a thinker continues to have a lot to say.

Weil, in seeking to know this way, often appears uncompromising and, perhaps, sometimes too much so. In talking of a transcendent good that is beyond the play of a world where good and evil compete and balance each other, she refuses to talk in terms where the good we should aim at is in any sense compensatory to the evils we suffer. She thinks such talk is a consolation that only feeds the ego and keeps us from truly seeing. But even when she does this, she gives a hint of a hope. She doesn't talk much of the Resurrection. Yet, she does without reservation say, "One must want to go towards reality; then, when one thinks one has found a corpse, one meets an angel who says: 'He is risen'" (SWW 66). She expresses an abiding hope also in the text titled "Prologue." This prose poem is an allegory of her own experience, and it was meant to serve as the prologue to a book of Pascal-like reflections. In it, she talks of an encounter with a stranger who tells her to follow and promises to teach her of things she cannot imagine. He does, and they share bread and wine. But then he tells her to leave. She departs and never tries to find the place again. She concludes plaintively, and, to some minds, with abnegating self-disparagement, "I know that he doesn't love me. How could he love me?" But she ends with profound hope: "And yet something deep within a particle of myself, can't help thinking, all the while trembling with fear, that perhaps, in spite of everything, he does love me" (SWW 32). Somehow, in accepting time and necessity, some kind of hope abides, even if it is not defined ahead of time. Along with attention is waiting *"en hupomenē,"* in patient endurance. That is how she viewed her intended book of thoughts.

So, let us return to consider more broadly the sort of thoughtful life Weil led. Thinking, as she came to practice it and to think about it, is not a method designed to produce some bit of knowledge. It is not a field. It also does not aim at systematic completeness. It does not try to smooth out contradictions or produce a system. It does not put thought out into the world and then take that thought as the object of reflection and refinement. Rather, having attention at its root, it does not think *about* things so much as it puts one into a new relation with things. Thought as attention is contemplative, but the more it is, the more, not the less, it is engaged and brings itself into relation with the rest of the world. Attention is open to an overflowing of thought that can never be contained within anything like a system. In fact, Weil was suspicious of thinkers such as Hegel who did aim at producing a system (LPW 35). Instead, as she puts it rather plainly, the real work of philosophy is a matter of asking what things mean. And asking that question is a matter of seeking salvation (LPW 42). The question that remains, then, is why this is at all admirable or exemplary.

While a contemplative life may appear at first blush to be a disengaged life, or at least one that is aloof, that sort of charge actually is leveled more accurately at a thinker such as Heidegger, who, in the end, by refusing the question of character, never really situated himself as a living being or engaged value. To be sure, he appreciated that thinking was, in some sense, thanking, a matter of gratitude.[12] But it is never quite clear how that worked in life itself, at least for him, in any responsible way. Weil, on the other hand, managed to recapture a sense of thinking and philosophy and life that is unified, a sense that ancient philosophy—and theology—had. In fact, in her essays on the Greeks, it is really this that she extols and not simply the sense that the Greeks had in front of their minds things that Christianity was later to reveal. Rather, in insisting on some sort of continuity between the two, she was looking at that continuity as a way of life and thinking. French philosopher Pierre Hadot made this point time and again by arguing that ancient philosophy was a way of life and that its doctrines were not so much systems as spiritual exercises. This, he noted, was something that early Christian philosophy continued. He argues, for example, that Augustine's trinitarian analogies are not a systematic exposition of the Trinity, a theory of how three persons can be one God, but "by making the soul turn inward upon itself, he wants to make it *experience* the fact that it is an image of the Trinity." As a result of recognizing this aspect of ancient philosophy, Christian and pagan, "Philosophy then appears in its original aspect: not as a theoretical world construct, but as a method for training people to live and to look at the world in a new way. It is an attempt to transform mankind."[13]

In a similar vein, French philosopher and theologian Jean-Yves Lacoste has suggested that theology, and the world itself, would benefit from recapturing the sense of philosophy that first inspired Christian theology and that early Christian thinking carried over from Greek philosophy. Theology as a field, to be sure, has to deal with traditions, concepts, arguments, and the like, and has to produce a field of knowledge. Anybody could do it with the proper training. But, he argues, it is something that also needs to be reunited with a philosophical sense of the thinker approaching God, wherein one does not just think *about* God but takes in the whole world. Theology in its more original sense puts the thinker in front of God, and it demands ways of thinking far different than those that produce a field of knowledge, using academic technology without personal engagement. Lacoste calls them "liturgical" ways, by which he means ways of thinking that spill over and are enacted in ways that can include, but are also beyond, those of standard intellectual practice. "Liturgical thinking" demands embodied thought; in this regard it can be done in many more ways than scientific thought can be. It needs different ways of working itself out. For example, Lacoste suggests, "Let us hasten to recall an obvious fact: [Paul's] theology is spelled out . . . is interwoven with prayer and argumentation. . . . The work of theological elaboration is already done in prayer and writing, too. Consequently, the motto *ora et labora* ought to be interpreted in another way than is suggested by a naive reading. It does not tell us that the monk and whoever follows his school should pray and *then* work, but rather they ought to pray and work together in the unity of a single work or *opus Dei*."[14] For this reason, Lacoste also argues that some kind of reunion of philosophy and theology is important now because it makes the human place in the universe, and the relation between Creator and creature, a live issue. Theology as a field does not necessarily do that; it frequently doesn't. Talking about God can get in the way of loving God. We need to find a way of connecting it in a living way with its object.

Let me cite one further thinker in order to say what is at stake in what I suggest, namely, that Weil insists on a sort of thinking that unifies the thinker and her life, putting oneself in the place one should responsibly occupy in the world. French phenomenologist Michel Henry has argued for a contemplative self in a largely Augustinian mode. What is at stake for him is that in modern—that is to say, Cartesian—ways of thinking, the self inevitably becomes a "duplicitous self," one that both sees and is seen even to itself. Because it is forced to see itself within worldly categories, at least according to standard scientific phenomenology, this self can be alienated from itself. It is the "duplicitous self" whose power is a Nietzschean sort of will to power. It exists in worldly self-assertion. Its transcendent roots are excluded and obscured. Thus, Henry has held out for a deeper contemplative self, a self that finds the eternal at its root.[15]

Joseph Rivera, in his comprehensive study of Henry, says that Henry was looking for "a contemplative self, especially enunciated in an Augustinian idiom . . . [that] aims to advance a corrective over against the duplicitous self. Contemplating eternity instructs the saint to occupy a theological position; a stance that is temporal, but that carries with it an attitude that desires the eternal. The logos of contemplation all at once unifies personal identity around the exchange between the subjective pole and the exterior, transcendent height of God's eternity."[16] He adds,

> The economy of contemplation creates the conditions for a radical unity between interior and exterior fields of display to take root. It affirms them both as meaningful realities for human life, a structure that works within. . . . Contemplation is a structure of experience, of selfhood that . . . affirms the economy of creaturehood, so that to see God in a life of contemplation is to situate oneself in correspondence between creatures and God; finding its locus in mutuality between myself and others, between myself and the world, between myself and God, contemplation, then, 'Cannot properly be a prostration before a power outside us; it is a being present to ourselves *in* our world with acceptance and trust.'"[17]

So, given this chorus, what does it mean to say of Weil that she led a thoughtful life? What kind of thoughtful life did she lead, and why should we care? It means to say that, for her, life should be lived as a matter of love, and that love gives itself to a sort of thinking that welcomes the world into itself and unites the inner and outer, and that positions itself as receptive to both the eternal and to what is in time; it is to be a mediator. It is important because it challenges a world where thinking and selves have become increasingly self-assertive and flat, less related to other selves, where value and truth are chiefly instrumental. It is a world in which thought and love do not intertwine as they once did for great souls such as Homer or Plato, or for Saint John. To see this about her is hopefully to see her in a new light, one that may illuminate how thinking could be done differently in a world of alienated and fragmented selves, selves that too often succeed by gaining the world and losing their souls.

CHAPTER TWO

MYSTERY AND PHILOSOPHY

How does one who thinks that philosophy is a matter of working on one's self change her view from believing that this is done by thinking methodically, or by strict intellectual discipline, to the view that it is done by attention and waiting to be revealed to? It is not something that one just *decides*. It would seem, rather, to be because one has seen something; it is because the world looks different and calls for a different response. In Weil's case, this was a result of her surprising conversion in 1937 at Solesmes Abbey. One way of putting what was impressed on her mind, as in the case of so many others like her, was that she became convinced that there is at the center of the world, in a very positive sense, a mystery. But how does one think in the face of a mystery? Much modern philosophy rejects mystery as something that defies thought. Invoking it is a matter of obfuscation. But not all philosophers have done so. A number have seen saying something about the importance of mystery as an important task.

One was Michael Foster, a philosopher noted for his work on theology and science. In 1955 he delivered a set of lectures at the University of Edinburgh that was subsequently published under the title *Mystery and Philosophy*.[1] The book became a classic for many philosophers who believed that religion was important to human life and thinking, but who justifiably felt themselves beleaguered by analytic philosophy, the dominant way of doing philosophy in the English-speaking world. Analytic philosophy in itself was not antireligious, although it was decidedly anti-metaphysical, and numerous analytic philosophers failed to see the difference between the two. But in the same year that Foster gave his lectures, an important new book was published: *New Essays in Philosophical Theology*.[2] Using analytic philosophy, this book set the philosophical case against theism for the next twenty years.[3] Some alternative vision was needed, and *Mystery and Philosophy* helped provide it. It did so not by taking on any specific case made against religion; instead, it exposed the deep assumptions of analytic philosophy that misunderstood biblical religion and were ultimately incompatible with it. Even though the intellectual climate has changed since then, these assumptions might fairly be said to still haunt both philosophy and science, including friends of religion.

They were, indeed, assumptions and not a philosophical doctrine. But they were all the more pernicious because it was so easy to overlook the freight that they carried. Foster pointed at two of them. First was "a demand for a certain kind of clarity";[4] second was the assumption "that all thinking, and therefore all philosophical thinking, consists in solving problems."[5] The issue is not that clarity is bad, or that one should not solve problems, but rather "the belief that nothing is really puzzling and that therefore there cannot be anything unclear that we legitimately want to say."[6] In short, analysis assumed that there was no mystery in philosophy, and whatever passed by that name was simply a problem that could be solved with due diligence and rendered clear by analysis.

Foster was not the first, nor was he the only one, to notice the problem. In fact, he explicitly drew on the eminent French philosopher Gabriel Marcel. Marcel, first in *Being and Having* (1949) and then in his Gifford Lectures, *The Mystery of Being* (1949–50), made the crucial distinction between a mystery and a problem. The latter is capable of solution—it is a sort of puzzle; the former is not capable of solution but gives itself infinitely. Moreover, Marcel argued, the response to a mystery is something that involves the whole person; as the ancients might have said, it involved the heart. Foster, using Marcel's work, then put his finger on the importance of the distinction for unveiling a whole approach to philosophy. For most analytic philosophers, mysteries were due either to a lack of knowledge or to unclear thinking. They believed that science would fix the first and philosophy the second. The goal of both disciplines was the same for "the goal towards which both the scientist and philosopher are working is a state in which there will be no more mystery."[7]

Why is this a problem? It is certainly not the case that analysis of terms, concepts, and arguments is bad. Theology is itself a sort of analysis. Still, it proceeds upon different assumptions, and those assumptions were being dismissed out of hand. In particular, the assumptions of analytic philosophy "exclude Revelation as a source of truth *ab initio*."[8] They do so because revelation, at least as it has been understood biblically, is a matter of God speaking, not in the sense of communicating factual information that could, in principle, be gotten by science or linguistic therapy, but in the sense that God communicates Himself and His Holiness. The appropriate response to *that* is repentance, an opening up of oneself in order to listen further. This is what mystery is about; it is not something to be solved, it is not a set of facts, but something that keeps giving itself. And, it requires a response. This is not only the biblical worldview; ancient Greeks such as Plato had it, too. Truth was something that revealed itself. Achieving this required contemplation and the attitude of wonder from thinkers. *Theoria* is looking and gazing, not a closing of the case. Analytic philosophy unconcernedly blows past all of this.

The upshot of this argument was Foster's distinction between mystery as a theological category and clarity as a philosophical one. He argued that the thought worlds of science and the Bible were different. Neither should be reduced to the other, and one did not have to choose between the two; one needed to recognize the importance of both to human thinking. So, if one took the difference seriously, it was necessary to recognize that "part of us is captured by our Lord."[9] Foster proposed that in the future "the basic question will be not what is rational and what empirical, but what is human and what divine; what is in man's power to discover and what can be revealed only by God."[10]

This general position is one that can be immensely helpful for understanding Weil's thinking. She herself made explicit appeals to mystery and even gave a helpful and penetrating definition of what should count as a mystery.[11] For this reason, grasping Foster's point can be helpful to understanding Weil's thinking on this issue as well as setting a general context for the relevance of her use of the concept of mystery. But it is not just her *use* of the concept of mystery. That use is brought into play because her thinking as a whole involves seeing the world as a mystery. Therefore, understanding what a mystery is and what is at stake in thinking that mysteries exist helps us see what sort of questions she is tackling, and that they do have connections with what other philosophers have thought. However, Foster's distinctions are only a first step, helpfully clarifying as they are. Weil went a lot farther than Foster did in treating the concept of mystery. Where and how she did are important not only to understanding her but also to truly having a sense of what it means to live surrounded by the divine mystery. For Weil did not set philosophical clarity and theological mystery against each other (as Foster also did not) nor side by side in human life (as Foster did). Rather, she thought that if we were involved in mystery in any significant sense, we were involved in mystery at *all* points in life, even though we might not always recognize it. This affected the way she thought of philosophy, and, as a result, she ultimately saw the nature of philosophical thought quite differently than any number of thinkers have in the modern period. Its point for her was not ultimately to clarify things, although it does that, too. Real philosophy was something undertaken with a sense of wonder, as Plato thought, and with an explicit recognition of mystery. It drives beyond rationality toward an explicit divine encounter, effecting the transformation of the human by the divine.

If this is the case, then there are two additional conclusions that need to be drawn, ones that Weil herself drew. The first concerns the role of philosophy in a life that is surrounded by a divine mystery, and the second is a certain conception of life itself. In both of these lies a great deal of Weil's radical challenge to contemporary thought. For there is a great contrast between a world that has no mystery and one that exists within the divine mystery. A world without mystery, or one where mystery is not acknowledged, is a world where technique and mastery dominate and where contemplation and wonder retreat. It is essentially a flat world; there is little texture and no concern for the importance of aesthetic form, or concern for beauty as having anything to do with truth. Goodness is deduced from common principles and is rarely a matter of striving for anything transcending. Charles Taylor, quoting Oscar

Wilde, has talked about this "flatness of modern civilization which sees 'the final triumph of the Hollow Men, who, knowing the price of everything and the value of nothing, had lost the ability to *feel* or *think* deeply about anything.'"[12] On the other hand, the acknowledgment of mystery, at least the mystery of the good, involves us in all those things. Life within an embracing mystery that balances contraries and does not obliterate them has to recognize the importance of beauty and a striving for a nonevident and often hidden good. If there is such a mystery, then it is at least philistinism to try to eliminate it; at worst, it is the manifestation of a single-minded pursuit of technique and power.

The most obvious place to begin, then, is by looking at how Weil treats explicit theological mysteries. In numerous places, she writes of "the mysteries of the faith," which she equates with dogmas.[13] However, it is equally apparent that she is no propositionalist with respect to theological mysteries. (This will be further developed in chapter 4.) She is adamant that mysteries are beyond what the intellect can affirm or deny. For example, she notes that "the dogmas of faith are not things to be affirmed. They are things to be regarded from a certain distance with attention, respect and love" (GTG 113). They "are not of the order of truth but above it. The only part of the human soul which is capable of any real contact with them is the faculty of supernatural love" (GTG 112). Like Foster and Marcel, she thinks that mysteries need to be approached and dealt with in a significantly different way than, say, the way that analytic, or Scholastic, or neo-Scholastic philosophy, or even the current effort of "analytic theology," have tried to deal with propositions. Even if there is information involved, mysteries are not primarily informational; there is something existential about them; above all, they engage us and draw us into involvement with them. That is where their relevance and importance lies. Demanding propositional clarity about them often mistakes how they function in our lives, including our intellectual lives; demanding adherence to them as truths similar to geometrical truths is illegitimate.

Weil's very definition of a mystery underlines this sense of a living engagement. She argues that we only have hold of a legitimate mystery when, after an intellectually rigorous search, we come to an impasse and a contradiction, but, also, where it would seem wrong to solve the contradiction in favor of one side or the other, "the suppression of one term makes the other term meaningless and that to pose one term necessarily involves posing the other" (SWW 110). Far from demanding more work to solve the apparent contradiction, that intellectual impasse needs attention; it then acts "like a lever . . . [and] carries thought beyond the impasse, to the other side of the unopenable door, beyond the domain of intelligence and above it" (SWW 110; FLN 131). Mysteries in this sense engage love and not speculation (see chapter 4).

Weil's definition of mystery is not simply internal to her own thinking. It is theologically very helpful and should be seen as being rooted in the actual living of religious life. Consider a doctrine, a mystery, such as the Trinity: there is one God only, yet in three distinct persons. What we know about how that doctrine arose in the early Church is that, on the one hand, there was the strict monotheism of Judaism, which was also the Church's, and on the other hand, there was also the very early tendency to talk about Jesus in terms that normally belonged to God. For example, there was the practice of calling Jesus "Lord," a title normally belonging to God. Moreover, there were practices, such as praying to Jesus, that seemed to make him equivalent to the one and only God, and there were sayings ascribed to him that made him equal to God. He was thought to reveal God perfectly. But how can all this divinity attaching to Jesus be possible if there is only one God? The early Church, of course, recognized the issue, and any number of people tried to solve what seemed to be the contradiction. Those solutions became the history of heresy, which favors one end of the contradiction over the other and tries to resolve it rationally. Whenever there has been failure, it usually was the result of trying to make things too clear; the solution ends up losing a light found in the practice of worshiping one God, and Jesus Christ as his only begotten Son, God of God, light of light, true God of true God. For example, were one to solve the mystery, as the heretic Arius did, by suggesting that there are three persons, but that two of them, the Son and the Spirit, are not God, then one can no longer claim that God became a man and died for us; God remains at a distance, having sent a substitute to help us out. As Gregory of Nazianzus observed of the related Eunomian heresy, by trying to say more through defining the divine nature rationally, the Eunomians actually kept one from saying as much as one could. In this sense, the Nicene Creed, then, is ultimately rooted in protecting the grammar of the mystery that is rooted in the actual life of the Christian community; its only creativity was that of explicitly writing that grammar in order to protect it. Solving the contradiction leads to less light, not more.

In Weil's writings, mysteries have a sense of being end points to thought. Thought drives toward them and, then, in front of them, gives way to attention and love. But this is also where Weil begins to enter into a much broader sense of mystery, one that does not put contemporary philosophy at its side, but one that demands a very different way of doing philosophy. This happens first with respect to philosophical method, which she thinks ought to reflect the mystery whose appreciation is its goal; second, it determines that the value of philosophy is how it engages a thinker with questions of value.

Mystery involves being enlightened from gazing at what lies behind two contradictory lines of thought. It is no surprise, therefore, once again to discover that Weil thinks that contemplating contradiction lies at the very heart of doing philosophy. She asserts, "Method of investigation: as soon as we have thought something, try to see in what way the contrary is true" (NB 121). This, of course, is always a good idea, since it at least allows one to develop a critical facility. But there is more to it than that for Weil. Borrowing a suggestion Plato makes in the *Republic*, she thinks that one needs to think about contradiction because it is what ultimately will allow one to emerge from a point of view. It allows us to move from a limited perspective on reality to one that is far more inclusive. Here she makes extensive and frequent use of an example taken from Greek mathematics. When ancient Greek mathematicians discovered that certain types of lines—for example, the diagonals of right-angled triangles—had no common measure with the lengths of the sides of those triangles, they were in a quandary because they thought of numbers as proportions between lengths. But in this case there could be no possible exact proportion, at least, not as long as they thought of numbers consisting only of what we call rational numbers. However, Eudoxus in time discovered that both irrational numbers (the diagonals) and rational numbers could be incorporated into a system of real numbers that included both rationals and irrationals.[14] This "Eudoxean system" Weil thought could be carried through equally well in "psychological and spiritual matters" (NB 162). Weil's distinctive treatments of "necessity" and "reading" are both related to this method. For example, Weil's discussions of "necessity" analyze the concept as having at least three different levels: brute necessity; the mathematical tissue of invariant relations of force; and, finally, what is "persuaded by Goodness" and obedient to God.[15] Each of these, furthermore, is related to a level of reading, the way by which value impresses us as we read the world also at three different levels: at the level of individual pleasure and pain; at a second level where individual preference is left behind and one reaches a sort of Stoic acceptance of all that happens—amor fati; and then, finally, where all that happens in the world is felt, as it were, as something belonging intimately and lovingly to one's own self. There is a hierarchy to these concepts, and Weil presumes that one moves up through them through contemplating the contradictions at lower levels.

To leave it at this, however, might well leave one with the impression that Weil is engaged in a sort of idealist, Hegelian project whereby apparent oppositions and antitheses in thought are reconciled and synthesized in a higher unity. For her, that sort of approach works best in a limited, piecemeal way that describes individual growth and even historical, cultural workings out of ideas. However, for Weil there is no ultimate synthesis, at least not on any level that is accessible to the intellect or realizable in history. Mystery is the end point of thought, as it is its beginning; it is what one casts one's gaze on, and it is what one lovingly accepts when one *cannot* go any farther. Mystery is most apparent in the face of a well-developed intellectual pluralism. Mystery dawns as one appreciates more and more the diverse roads of thought that one takes.

Weil points out that "all philosophical thought contains [contradictions]" (LPW 35). It does not eliminate them, and it does not, therefore, try to construct systems. At best, such systems are poetry;[16] at their worst, "these systems are below even the level of conjecture, for conjectures are at least inferior thoughts, and these systems are not thoughts" (LPW 36). Wittgenstein, in a similar frame of mind, described this attempt to eliminate contradiction and find answers to all philosophical questions a "sickness" and an "obsession" that was at the heart of the enterprise of philosophy. Weil on that score would have no disagreement. The philosophers of any worth are those who maintain the contradictions and do not try to solve them.

A further comparison with Wittgenstein is apt at this point to get a better sense of what Weil is driving at. Wittgenstein famously ended his *Tractatus Logico-Philosophicus* with the comment "Whereof we cannot speak, thereof we must be silent." On one interpretation of this comment, Wittgenstein was thinking of something like the ethical or religious, even something like the mysterious givenness of the world, as what cannot be put into propositions; we must therefore be silent about it. Wittgenstein himself tended not to talk directly about these things as such, at least not in any way that sought to *explain* them. He was ever careful to avoid what seemed to be the impossibility of drawing a line in language between the sayable and the unsayable. The respect for the distinction lay somewhere else. While Weil occasionally violates this warning and is quite willing to talk directly about mysteries in terms that make her look like a classical metaphysician—a dangerous tendency because it allows mysteries to be invoked in ways to justify most anything—the fact of the matter is that she really is close to Wittgenstein on this issue. Her point about mysteries is that the intellect in encountering them can go no further than to acknowledge that two contradictory lines of thought are both correct, and then to carry out thought under the shadow of its incompleteness. Mystery enters into the human realm somewhere else, namely, in love and attention. Indeed, her greatest complaint about the Roman Catholic Church's approach to faith was that it made it a matter of intellectual belief. The dogmas, the mysteries of the Church she thought were not so much matters for the intellect as things meant to be gazed on with love. She says quite plainly, "The mysteries of faith are not a proper object for the intelligence considered as a faculty permitting affirmation or denial. They are not of the order of truth, but above it. The only part of the human soul which is capable of any real contact with them is the faculty of supernatural love. It alone, therefore, is capable of an adherence in regard to them" (GTG 118). Thus, Weil, although she talks about mysteries, does not think she is in any sense capturing them in doing so, and certainly not in language. But that one cannot capture or define them does not leave the concept of mystery as vacuous or fuzzy beyond use. In fact, Weil thinks that we can have a very definite sense of when someone has given him- or herself to a mystery. One's encounter with them is seen in the light that they shed on everything else.

This "light that they shed on everything else" can be described in a couple of different ways. First is the image of a balance that Weil often uses. The supernatural, or a mystery, if you will, is not an item among others that is ever put into balance with other things. It is not on the balance at all. Rather, it is something like the fulcrum of the balance; it is what is outside the system of equilibrium that puts everything else in that system into equilibrium. In this sense, the person who has actually encountered mystery is not revealed by his or her knowledgeable words about mystery; there is no right or wrong description, and a fool or a liar might be able to say as much and as well. Rather, the person's encounter is seen in the way that he or she balances everything else, in the way of putting things into relation with each other.

Just what this means can be seen in a second way of illustrating how Weil thinks of a mystery, namely, how one thinks and acts in the world. In a series of striking images she puts this enlightenment by mystery in these ways:

> A bride's friends do not go into the nuptial chamber; but when she is seen to be pregnant they know that she has lost her virginity.
>
> There is no fire in a cooked dish, but one knows that it has been on the fire. . . .
>
> It is not the way a man talks about God, but the way he talks about the things of this world that best shows whether his soul has passed through the fire of the love of God. In this matter no deception is possible. There are false imitations of the love of God, but not of the transformation it effects in the soul, because one has no idea of this transformation except by passing through it oneself. . . .
>
> According to the conception of human life expressed in the acts and words of a man I know . . . whether he sees life from a point in this world or from above in heaven. . . .

The value of a religious or, more generally, a spiritual way of life is appreciated by the amount of illumination thrown upon the things of this world. (SWW 108; FLN 145–46)

One's engagement with a mystery or with the supernatural is something that belongs to one's habits of the heart; it is something written in our way of being. It is in that respect something that is seen only insofar as it is incarnated and lived with in the flesh.

It now starts to become clearer why the concept of mystery is so important and how relevant it is. The concept of mystery, and philosophy's engagement with it, is not a matter of a position or an argument. It is not an assertion of a fact, say, that there is a God, to be argued for or against. The question that mystery poses is ultimately asked and answered somewhere other than in the intellect, although our reasoning plays an important role in the process. One cannot be intellectually careless. But, in the end, the concept of mystery chiefly concerns the very question of depth and meaning and goodness in life and is, despite being displayed and represented by arguments, something that lies at the very heart of the human being's activity as a living being. It is, perhaps even better put, what the question of depth and meaning and goodness is *in* human life, a question that stands behind all the rest of our subsequent reasoning.

How this is so may be seen by looking briefly at Weil's essay "Some Reflections on the Concept of Value" (SWW 29–36). (Let it be assumed, rather uncontroversially, I would hope, that what is being called here depth and meaning and goodness is translatable for the greater part into what one may call the concept of value.) At the outset of the essay she claims that "the concept of value is at the center of philosophy. All reflection bearing on the notion of value and on the hierarchy of values is philosophical; all efforts of thought bearing on anything other than value are, if one examines them closely, foreign to philosophy" (LPW 30). Leaving aside here the issue of who is really a philosopher and who isn't, we can simply concentrate on what Weil lays out as to how we think about value and what all it involves.

Philosophizing about value, trying to get clear on what is valuable and what is not, is very different than the pursuit of any other kind of knowledge and involves certain deep problems. On the one hand, it is a matter of finding a means of judging between values, as the search for knowledge in other areas is also finding a means for judging. It requires comparing and contrasting different values. But this is to assume that we can take a distanced, cool, and hypothetical attitude to value. The problem is that we can't be indifferent here; "a value is something that one admits unconditionally. At the moment when it directs our actions, our system of values is not accepted with conditions or provisionally or reflectively; it is purely and simply accepted" (LPW 30). Thus, Weil contends, with a hint of paradox, that values are "unknowable." This is simply to say that everything else that we know, and therefore knowledge itself, is "hypothetical," or, we might say, contingent; it depends on its links to other demonstrations and other facts that are themselves not necessary. So, if that is what "knowable" means, then values are not knowable. We take them in very differently.

Yet, Weil goes on, one ought not to take away from this that they are irrational or mere emotional statements of idiosyncratic preference, as English positivist philosopher A. J. Ayer tried to claim was the case with ethics because ethics could not be shown to fit the epistemological principles of positivism. "One cannot give up on knowing them, for giving up would mean giving up on believing in them, which is impossible, because human life always has a direction" (LPW 30). The result? "At the center of human life is a contradiction" (LPW 30), a contradiction that is at the heart of the philosophical enterprise, that is, the search for value. The contradiction is that, on the one hand, we need, as searchers, not to be prejudiced in our search, and, on the other hand, that we are searching at all means that we have committed to some value and stand on it absolutely. (If we did not think it absolute with a claim on us, it would not really be a value for us. If we really thought it were better than what we currently accept, we would make it ours. The price of doing otherwise would be to destroy moral thinking, for we would then deliberately choose the worse over the better—because we thought it was better!)

So how do we approach value? How do we change from the worse to the better? If philosophy were simply a matter of presenting arguments and devising ethical systems, we probably would have little hope of it doing anything for us on this score. For the most part, it would simply be rather sophisticated advocacy, or poetics, or mere sophistry. So, even though we do not give up on reason or argument, a very different sort of attitude is required, a different sort of reflection, one that demands *detachment*. This detachment is radical, and it is a radical openness. "Detachment is a renunciation of all possible ends without exception, a renunciation which puts a void in the place of the future just as the imminent approach of death does" (LPW 33).

For numerous reasons, Weil sees this detachment as something that borders on the miraculous, and as a matter of grace. For example, it has to be the supreme value, but in order to be that, all other values must already be set aside. But what at least is clear is that philosophy, as Weil wants to take it, namely, as a search for transforming value, is not an accumulation of knowledge but a radical disposition to knowledge. It is a matter of attention, which she famously defines as demanding detachment and availability. It is a willingness to live with the contradictions of life and not to force them, just as Wittgenstein argued that we should not force the grammar of one way of speaking about the world upon another. What the world is, is in all the ways we have spoken about it, and we should not choose one grammar over another. That restraint is not logical; it is moral, for it is a matter of respecting what is given to us. We are to gaze upon the world and wait upon it in order to be transformed, in order to move from the worse to the better, from the mediocre to the excellent, from the nice to the good. As Foster argues with respect to the somewhat narrower question of biblical revelation, what is required here is an attitude that lets us be spoken to and an attitude where our listening takes into our hearts what we hear and lets it change and transform us. Any other attitude is simply moving within the confines of our own reading.

Some of the ways in which the concept of mystery is important in the contemporary world have already been suggested. Our obsession with technique and method and the resulting flatness, the monodimensional aspect this obsession gives to life, are reason enough to take the concept of mystery seriously in philosophical life. Our desire to understand in order to control gives many more. And even more can be said. But, in concluding, I want to confine myself to saying something more about this idea of transformation, of moving toward greater depth and meaning. In doing so, just as I relied on one philosopher, Michael Foster, to introduce the issues surrounding the concept of mystery, I will now rely on another to help illustrate this issue of depth and locate it.

In his recent *A Secular Age*, Charles Taylor examined from just about every perspective possible what it means to say that we live in a secular age. In the end, it is not a matter of saying that belief and the religious have actually disappeared. However, belief can now no longer be assumed; we live in a world in which religion is questioned as a matter of course. We—and that includes most religious people—no longer think that it cannot be questioned. Even if we are of the committed faithful, we are not surprised and shocked by our friends and relatives who might think differently. A good part of Taylor's case is dedicated to explaining how this has come about. In part, it is because science has, indeed, contested claims that are important to religion. But science, Taylor argues, is not the only thing responsible for the secular turn of mind. Religions themselves have contributed more and more to it as they have defended themselves against criticism by moving in a more and more immanentist direction. They have bought the viewpoint of religion's critics and ceased to look to their own original, transcendent and transforming core. For example, one well-rehearsed way of defending Christianity is to talk about its civilizing effects, of what it has contributed to the culture. In short, to talk about it largely as a form of crowd control. Taylor points out that whenever this happens, the transcendent aspect, the really deep moral challenge of biblical religion, is lost. Or, as he names it, spirituality becomes "excarnated," "the steady disembodying of spiritual life, so that it is less and less carried in deeply meaningful bodily forms, and lies more and more 'in the head.'"[17] The challenge to any deep transformation of life is lost; in "identifying the Christian life with a life lived in conformity with the norms of our civilization, we lost sight of the further, greater transformation which Christian faith holds out, the raising of the human life to the divine (theiosis)."[18]

Often, when people first encounter Weil, they do so with respect to her extraordinary biography. The more I consider Taylor's comments, the more I have come to realize how important the extraordinary and even bizarre elements of Weil's life are for showing the depth of her life. They indicate, as Susan Sontag suggested many years ago, a seriousness about life that is sadly lacking in a monodimensional world. Sontag suggested, though, that while admiring this seriousness, we did not need to follow her example.[19] In numerous particulars, perhaps not. In a lot of different ways there probably was, as they say in the American Southwest, a kick in Weil's gallop. But that should not blind us to the fact that her own thinking was not "excarnated"; it really was an example of living a philosophical life. The philosophical life, which is what a serious life lived in world surrounded by mystery is, is always an extraordinary life, and one that will never fit into the common unexamined goals set out by a method. A serious life, a philosophical life, is revealing of the great depth and goodness that is open to the human spirit, if only it will let itself be spoken to, and if only it will look attentively.

CHAPTER THREE

THE NATURE OF GRACE
Incarnation and Crucifixion in Weil's Thought

To acknowledge mystery is to face depth in the world, a world of meaning at several levels. It is to be willing to stand in wonder of what is and be awed. It is also to have to face the negative mysteries of evil. One is no longer the center of the world. At this point of mystery, religion and science can even intersect for a while. That is a lot. But in the case of Simone Weil, there is also a very specific theological center to the world's mystery that goes beyond simply a sense of wonder and awe. That center involves a deliberate gift; it involves *grace*. This gives her thought a very specific direction and shape.

What, exactly, is at stake here? It is to see that there is a theological center to Weil's thought and that it has a specific *act* of God at that center. For her, this act is *key* to the world, human and natural. Whether one approaches this act from the vantage point of creation, or from that of the Incarnation or the Passion, it has the quality, as eminent French Weil scholar Emmanuel Gabellieri has stressed, of a *gift*.[1] This is to say that grace is a gift given, not merely that there is a gift-like quality to the universe or to certain aspects of human life. To be sure, for Weil that gift is found in qualities located in the universe and is not separate from them. Nevertheless, her account stresses that grace is what made the universe what it is.

The claim that there is an act that constitutes grace at the center of Weil's thought is easily demonstrated, textually at least, and it is easy to see where it comes from. It is deeply embedded in her account of creation and redemption, for that account is centered on the act of God not only becoming incarnate but actually dying. For Weil, while the creation is presented as an act of renunciation on God's part, a withdrawal so that something else might exist, as she also makes very clear that withdrawal involves a separation and rending in God as the Son is crucified on time and space.[2] That might be simply a symbolic way of talking that only has rhetorical force. But, as is especially clear in the essay "The Love of God and Affliction" (SWW 41–70), Weil's account of the Crucifixion and its ability to contain and use the otherwise soul-destroying phenomenon of affliction within God's love depends upon Christ's actually suffering in the flesh the full force of necessity. She then refracts this very concrete account to give her account of creation and nature more generally. For, by Christ's suffering necessity and still continuing to love even in absence, he sets the limits of necessity, she claims. And so necessity is persuaded by goodness, and, by his cross, Christ becomes the mediator between humans and God, not only in the specifically theological account of Christian faith, but cosmically. For Weil, the saving effect of Christ's cross is further extended whereby, in a Platonic scheme, one participates in God in any number of sacramental acts, or implicit loves of God, wherein by our participation in Christ's kenotic self-emptying we are spiritually and morally remade. Christ's incarnation and death also give rise to a set of *metaxu*, intermediaries, by which human beings, who are creatures and fully subject to necessity, can lead lives permeated at many different levels by grace, a grace that not only imitates and participates in Christ's kenosis figuratively but also is ultimately dependent on God's act.[3]

Despite the fact that the texts of Weil's writings pretty clearly insist that Christ has to be actually incarnate and has to suffer necessity fully, and that there is a specific act of grace, not everyone has seen this to be true of Weil's thought. Some have recognized the account of that act but see it as mainly anthropological and symbolic. Therein also lies the difference between a theological center and a nontheological one. The great Roman Catholic theologian Hans Urs von Balthasar got the theological issue right, although he was not right about Weil. He argues, citing Weil specifically as one of those "who have sought to interpret the Cross anthropologically or ontologically, in a pre-Christian way," that "Then the crucified Christ becomes a symbol, denser perhaps than the rest of reality put together, but a symbol all the same. And he is thereby subordinated to what is universal, whether the latter engulfs him as law or as the absolute freedom of man. Here theology is transcended, and is replaced by anthropology."[4]

Jacques Cabaud, in his early work on Weil, simply stated that "There is no necessity for the Incarnation of the Word. Christ has become an example, a paradigm, a living doctrine, but he is not the source or the necessary condition of salvation."[5]

Much more recently, American Weil scholar Inese Radzins has gone further. She argues that Weil means to *de-emphasize* the Cross. Radzins does not argue for what might be called an accidental position wherein, for Weil, Christ's incarnation really is not necessary, or where Weil's approach is strictly anthropological because her views on the Incarnation and Cross are just the ultimate rhetorical expressions of her direction of argument. She argues that Weil *deliberately* chose *not* to take and to understand the Incarnation, and by extension the Passion, as an act of God giving grace to a world of gravity. After saying, incoherently, that "incarnation for Weil was more cosmologic [*sic*] than Christological," she claims, "Displacing Christology in favor of a cosmological Christianity allowed Weil to locate truth in the cosmos, or universally, rather than in any particular event, religion or person. Incarnation is for Weil this Word/Truth of the eternal universe. She is clear that this Truth is not the earth, or human experience of the world, but rather the cosmos as the whole totality of what is."[6]

The accuracy of these claims, of course, with respect to Weil's writings needs to be argued textually; I do not believe that Weil's own texts support any of these interpretations. But, putting the textual question to the side for a moment, it is worth noting what is common to all of them, namely, that whatever else Weil had to say about the Incarnation, it gives way in the end to a philosophical universalism that she also wanted to espouse. This might be simply because that is the tendency of Weil's argument and her universalism thus runs away with her, as Balthasar seemed inclined to think. It could also be, as in Radzins's view, that Weil deliberately chose to take a strictly symbolic view of the Incarnation, arguing that it was the better view. In any case, all of them would seem to see philosophy pitted against theology in Weil, with Weil ultimately coming down on the side of philosophy. Insofar as they do, the position reiterates some old problems that the scandal of particularity of Christianity's incarnational claims cause. A quick read of Kierkegaard will say what they are. Basically, the problem is that truth is universal and cosmological; how can it be in an individual human being, other than as an example?

But it is simply *not* the case that philosophy *has* to oppose a universal truth being revealed in a particular act. Philosophy has to deal with a world that has been effected by the incarnational act and take it as a whole. In this regard, Peter Winch's *Simone Weil: "The Just Balance,"* which remains the best philosophical work on Weil in English, is salutary.[7] Winch had no intention of deciding, or even taking a position, on the factuality of things such as the Incarnation, and he did not think it was the business of philosophy to do so. He claimed that he was giving a "secular" account; he simply wanted to see how far he could go in its terms. He had no intention of saying that the secular was the *only* way to go or that such an account as he gave even excluded the religious as a fact of human life; nor did he try to paint human life as it might look if one denied or excluded the religious. Instead, Winch gives an account of the supernatural that allows it to be situated within a way of thinking and living, within the given of human existence. Thus, as he locates it within the subject's activity, he claims that the concept of the "supernatural" as Weil used it is something like an epistemological concept. That is, in fact, a very accurate description of how Weil uses this concept, not to *justify* an attitude or way of being but rather to describe. Winch thought it simply outside the bounds of philosophy to try to justify, or to deny, a ground for a concept such as the supernatural; that is the sort of metaphysics that belongs to philosophy gone bad. The concept's use is not to point to an outside something, but rather "to express a connection between various attitudes, interests, strivings, aspirations, which are all part of our natural history."[8] But just because the concept of the supernatural as Weil uses it is part of our natural history—that is, that it needs to be understood within the lives we lead as creatures of flesh and blood, mind and spirit—it does not mean that "naturalism" is the case. The world that philosophy encounters is a given world. How it got that way is not the business of philosophy to get outside the world to decide. At least, Winch didn't think it was.

The positive point here is that philosophy, if it is sufficiently attentive and contemplative, can deal with a world of mystery if it is faithful to what is in front of it. In fact, this is precisely how Weil herself understood the task of philosophy. There is no philosophical need to dissolve the particular in favor of the universal, as long as one does not try to make a system out of the effort, and if one is willing to accept the contradictions that are signs of mystery—and Weil was. There is no reason why a particular revelation could not be the source of a universal truth. So, that still leaves the possibility of a genuinely theological account wide open.

There will, of course, always be a tension. Weil was willing to live with it; she even found it vital and creative. It is to her credit that in her treatment of the issue she steered away from the temptation of making faith in God a strictly intellectual problem, recognizing that the theological task is elsewhere. That task is, for example, to give an account of grace that is the story of grace received, and that, therefore, sets the lived context for what one can say about the nature of grace and for a life lived according to it. It is a matter of using what, say, Christianity puts forth as God's self-revelation to be the living context of a gracious life. Theological claims can and ought to be, as Wittgenstein saw, the grammar of a life that outlines a *distinctive* way of life with virtues and goods that are not recognized in any other context. If that is the case, then theology gives us reason to pursue something more than just gracious living. For example, if grace is the result of a divine act, then it would mean that a life of gratitude and a life of prayer and of worship are both at the heart of living graciously and of having a truly good life. The very understanding of truth in this case is deepened and even more demanding. It may even be the case that one tries to see for theological reasons how and where God's truth can be understood universally.

We can now see the issue that is at stake. To say that there is a theological center to Weil's thought is to say that she puts an act of God, upon which grace depends, at the center of her account of human fulfillment and of the universe in which we can be fulfilled. Indeed, for Weil the recognition of the centrality of the Incarnation and Cross is to see the "Lamb slain from the foundation of the universe," which determines the form of the world.

The question now is just what exactly this claim and this account might mean if it is something more than speculation. The questions that need to be answered are why and how the Incarnation and Passion are the keys to her account. In good part that depends upon seeing what she is saying as a theologically coherent whole and how it is an account of how the human person is engaged in living in a distinctive way, a way that reads the world as a gift.

One way to show that is by a comparison. One can first consider a recognized theological account that makes an act of God central to its account of grace and see how Weil's account compares. Thus, I want to consider American theologian Kathryn Tanner's recent *Christ the Key*. In part, Tanner is an appropriate choice because there are a number of similarities between her account of the Incarnation and Cross and Weil's. These similarities can indicate where Weil may have something to say within present theological discussions. But, for our purposes here, it is more important that Tanner is able to show what it means to give a theological account where the Incarnation is the key, and where it makes a difference, and what sorts of questions it answers. Then, we can ask if Weil in her account does anything like this.

Tanner wants to investigate what it means to say that humans beings are the *imago Dei*, the image of God. She sees them as being so by virtue of their participation in the divine being. In borrowing the hoary Platonic category of participation, as Weil also did, she takes participation to mean that a being draws, or is given, from another both power and qualities from that other that it does not possess by virtue of its own nature. This lets it share a likeness, strongly or weakly, with that other in which it participates. Thus, she argues, human beings can be said, initially, to be in God's image in both a strong and weak sense. Weakly, we participate in God's nature in the way that all of nature does, that is, by our simple existence. "Creatures participate in God by leading a derived life . . . a life derived from a God who does not derive from another as they do."⁹ We may well be the highest of all nature, but at this level the image is still a weak one. Still, insofar as we do image God even weakly here, we have from God at least the capacity to receive God, a capacity that Tanner sees in an expansive openness that allows for the presence of God and in human mutability and plasticity that allows us to change and act even beyond our created nature. This allows a second, much stronger sense of participation that can be given to humans. In this much stronger sense, creatures are in the image of God when they receive "what is beyond themselves—the divine image itself—and are considered the image of God themselves primarily for that reason. They would image God, not by imitating God, but in virtue of the gift to them of what remains alien to them, the very perfection of the divine image that they are not, now having become their own."¹⁰

This gift is the incarnate Word, for in the incarnate Word, when God is united to humanity, the very nature of humanity changes. Humanity, which in the weak sense images God and which in this sense can receive the image of God, now receives God in a fuller way and can be filled with God. In this stronger sense of the image, humans have and show this image by what they now can strive for and strive to be. In this second, stronger sense, humans then do not try to image God on their own and within the narrow limits of their own nature, "but instead, when drawing near to the divine image, so near as to become one with it. . . . Humans have the image of God only by clinging to what they are not—that divine image itself—becoming attached to it not merely physically but in every way possible for them—ideally with purity of attention, full commitment, and intense love."¹¹

On Tanner's account, then, it is because of the Incarnation that human beings are in the image of God. As Athanasius famously asserted, "God became man so that man might become God." Because God became a man, human beings are now in the image of God. Tanner then argues, "We can be knit into the Word as never before in virtue of the fact that the Word has *us* in a new way and that means that we can have the Word too in a new way, beyond what was possible for us simply as Spirit-filled creatures."¹² What is that way? It is by participating in God in a new way. This above all means that we have a new and close relationship with God, as Christ did, and which is not possible except by God's own gift and self-revelation. This means having new desires that are given by the divine gift. But it also is in the way that we engage the world—as Christ did. We develop our relation to the Word precisely in how we engage and even look at the world in which we live and are a part. Here the effect of the Incarnation is not even limited to human beings or human self-understanding. Being in the image of God is being in God's image as a human being, as a creature, for where humans are in God's image is in their likeness to the Incarnate God. And to be a human being is to be a creature of body and soul. As creatures then, like Christ, humans can be filled with God's Spirit. But, as such, the Incarnation then raises us, not out of the existence we have as beings of body and spirit, but within the physical existence we have. By extension, then, because of the Incarnation, we must see that the created world itself, the world of matter, is capable of being filled with Spirit. In this way, human beings show in their materiality that the material world itself "can be made over in God's image."[13]

This is a theological account of the nature of human beings and what they are oriented toward. What is important to note about it as a theological account, compressed as it is, is how it balances nature and grace. It seeks to see each with the integrity proper to each and yet shows how they are also deeply related. On the one hand, then, this is a decidedly externalist account, insofar as grace is given from the outside; as Tanner succinctly notes, "'by grace,' then, means 'not by nature.'"[14] Human beings *receive* from God the gift of fellowship with God and the possibility of imaging God by a power that is beyond their created nature. This is from the Word becoming flesh. On the other hand, this is a remarkably materialist account, that is, it remains centered in the material existence of human beings and their nature as creatures of flesh and blood. Grace here does not cancel out nature; indeed, it completes it insofar as human nature was created to enjoy God. Grace, although unnatural, does not take us out of the world. But neither is nature self-sufficient, making grace something simply superadded onto nature. On Tanner's account, human nature is made to share in fellowship with God and to reach for possibilities in love and faith of which it is not naturally capable. Human nature is frustrated by living strictly by nature, and sin is above all the frustration of our failing to let ourselves be completed. This completion of our nature only occurs as we leave ourselves open to the divine gift. She notes, "Our nature is perfected and completed, ironically, by making us act unnaturally, in a divine rather than human way."[15] So the nature we encounter in ourselves is not simply created nature; it is nature that has been joined to the divine Word and has possibilities that need to be seen as realistically fulfilled in the divine. A human being does not encounter nature or grace separately, but rather encounters nature that has been transfigured by grace.

What is significant is that, although grace is given from without, it is given through an act in the world, namely, the Incarnation. By focusing on this act, this account also gives a mechanism by which grace operates. None of this happens simply by God saying so or waving a metaphysical hand. This account is not a matter of metaphysical speculation to be shaved closely by Ockham, really reducible to nature itself. It begins in an act, understood as a divine act, and then carries out its effects as lived by those who experience this act as a grace. So, while grace is a gift, one given from without, Tanner notes that it operates within us. She argues, "We are justified, then, not simply because what has happened independently of us is imputed to us but because what [Christ] has achieved becomes ours through him. Through him, we participate, indeed, in both the justification and sanctification of humanity that has taken place in him."[16] The gift gives our capacity to be open to God a new, expanded capacity to receive God the way that Jesus received the Word, and it also gives us new desires. It teaches us to live by dependence on another. In this regard, faith is a matter of openness to being moved by the divine Spirit. But even though we are new selves, we still remain creatures. We are fulfilled and transformed by this gift, not cancelled out. What we therefore can become depends upon this gift. Quoting Calvin, Tanner observes, "We possess [the righteousness that we have in Christ] only because we are partakers of Christ."[17] The act and its intended consequences are located firmly within the realm of human experience.[18]

While the heart of Tanner's account is deliberately centered in the Incarnation, some of her considerations of the Cross should also be noted. They are particularly illustrative of what she is doing, especially insofar as they show in what way the action of Christ's crucifixion may be considered to give an actual grace. They are also helpful in shedding light on Weil's account, for which the Cross is central.

For Tanner, the grace that redeems and lifts up fallen humanity comes through the act of the Incarnation, of God uniting flesh to God, and thus of being united to humanity. It is not the Cross; or, rather, the Cross for her needs to be considered as the continuation of the Incarnation. In decentralizing the Cross in this way, Tanner is responding to, and taking for her own, several sorts of criticisms of atonement theory. Particularly, she is concerned about the mechanism of many atonement theories that require the Cross as a sacrifice to overcome sin, most notably those theories that take the Cross to be a propitiation whereby God's anger at sin is appeased, or God's honor restored, or those where Christ is a substitute victim for sinners. These theories remain curiously external to the one whose life is supposed to be changed. She is also concerned to take seriously feminist criticisms that have objected to the very notion of sacrifice as calling for subservience and the glorification of degradation. However, in taking on all these critiques of traditional atonement theories, Tanner by no means dismisses the Cross as unimportant or as irrelevant to salvation. Rather, her understanding of the value of the Cross is based on the Incarnation and its unity of natural humanity and the divine Word. What she wants therefore to emphasize about the Cross is the continuing "happy exchange" of humanity and the divine Word that begins in the Incarnation. The battle against sin is fought by means of the Incarnation. For "humanity is taken to the Word in the Incarnation in order to receive from the Word what saves it."[19] The Cross here does have an important role, for if the Word is to assume humanity as humanity is, it must assume humanity as it suffers.

> If the powers of the Word are to reach humanity suffering under the forces of sin and death, the Word must assume, become one with, a life of that sort, as Jesus goes through suffering and abjection to the cross. The idea that Jesus must be obedient unto death, humiliated on the cross, in order to be exalted means only that—not that Jesus is exalted, resurrected as a

reward. It simply means . . . that the Word must take on humanity as we know it in all its horrors if the powers of the Word are to be translated to that humanity in a saving way.[20]

If Christ had not suffered to the extent he did, one could say, as Gregory of Nazianzus did in a related context, that "what is not assumed is not saved."

For Tanner, Christ's suffering is not vicarious or a substitute for humanity's suffering. Nor does it pay a penalty; it should not be considered under forensic terms. Christ suffers and dies not because this suffering was *required*, but because that suffering and death are the result of an act in which he pays the cost of doing what is right. The Cross is the result of God's seeking to give life, not take it in order for God to be satisfied by the paying of a penalty. Thus, suffering is not valuable for its own sake, a view that she thinks should address feminist concerns. Suffering happens; what is of import is *how* the incarnate Word suffers, not that he suffers. His blood sanctifies human life and makes it possible; it is life-giving, as, for example, the Gospel of John stresses, because the Word is attached now to suffering.

> Here is a God who works unswervingly for our good, who puts no value on self-sacrifice for the good, a god of gift-giving abundance struggling against the forces of sin and death in the greatest possible solidarity with us—that of incarnation. Contrary to a great deal of feminist and womanist theology, there is something saving about the cross here, but there is nothing saving about suffering, death, or victimhood, in and of itself.[21]

Let us briefly review the formal structure of Tanner's theological account in order to use it to shed light on Weil's account of grace. It involves four elements: 1) grace is external, for 2) it involves an act in the world on God's part; 3) it provides a mechanism by which grace flows from that act and which penetrates and affects the humanity that receives grace; and 4) it addresses the question of the relation of nature and grace. Any account that has these elements and relates them coherently, whether or not it consciously means to be a contribution to theology, *is* a theological account and needs to be taken seriously as such. Such is the case with Weil. Even if she is not a theologian per se, she has given what needs to be given in a theological account. One would misread her if one ignored or denied the theological account within her work.

There are some notable differences between Weil's and Tanner's accounts of how grace occurs, namely, where they locate the specific act of God from which grace flows. It is worth recognizing what those differences are, as they can help us focus on why exactly Weil's account needs to be understood theologically and not mythologically or symbolically. Where the two accounts diverge can be seen as matters of perspective and not matters of difference on where the central act of grace lies, or that there even is one. Indeed, in this regard they may well be seen as mutually reinforcing. That is helpful for something of such broad import as the Cross, for if it can be seen from only one perspective and described in only one way, it may well be illusory or a philosophical sleight of hand. But where a common form of value exists, it would quite normally be capable of being seen in differing ways, as long as no key point is contradicted.

Weil's account of the act of grace and how it is played out in the world differs from Tanner's chiefly in the fact that Weil begins in the Cross and not the Incarnation. The Cross is the heart of the matter for her, insofar as the way that she describes the Passion includes the Incarnation and the Creation, and they are patterned on it. The value of each might be said to come from its ultimate participation in the Crucifixion.

This beginning point is not an arbitrary choice. For Tanner, the Cross is a continuation of the Incarnation, insofar as it is the divine Word's taking on human flesh and the human condition all the way to the end of suffering. The Cross's meaning depends upon what she has already said about the Incarnation. For Weil, it is less the case that Christ identifies with the human condition; it is far more the case that Christ *defines* it and its possibilities. Christ in suffering affliction, suffers and consents to the full weight of necessity. It is because he does, and yet continues to love God the Father who is absent and on the other side of creation, that it is possible for human beings who participate in his Cross to say yes to necessity and live. The broad consequences of the Cross are that by Christ's consent to necessity, and, hence, through his active love, Christ sets the limits of what necessity may do to the human soul. Perhaps a much better way to put it would be to say that Christ opens the way to love and faith precisely at the extreme where love cannot be fulfilled within the immanent world; by opening this *via* in the extreme case of suffering, he also provides the pattern in less extreme settings. In so doing, Christ then gives a certain vital form to the world of necessity. This is the act by which "necessity is persuaded by goodness" (Plato) as she, in fact, uses the Cross to describe this process when writing of the *Timaeus*. In the end, Weil sees what is going on in the Crucifixion as something more than just the possibility of surviving affliction; she sees it as the establishment of a non-natural, eternal love within creation. Christ's act opens up the spiritual possibilities and horizons of the human being. It gives human beings, beings of flesh and blood and creatures made of necessity, a goodness that necessity cannot provide. Christ gives them the possibility of spirit. For Weil, although this sort of account of the Cross would have to assume the Incarnation to work—and thus it is not opposed to Tanner's account—the difference between her account of Christ and Tanner's is a difference between a Christ who came to share humanity's nature and, in doing so, give it access to God (Tanner), and a Christ who in sharing humanity's nature gives its access to God by being the pioneer of faith (Weil). That important difference in emphasis may have an effect on what else one wants to go on and say. The accounts are not mutually exclusive, however.

It may be helpful to point out how Weil even came to think of things in this way. In her pre-factory thinking and writings, most notably "Reflections Concerning the Causes of Liberty and Social Oppression" (OL 37–124), Weil fully accepted the inevitable sufferings of human beings at the hands of the natural world. She thought, however, that human dignity and purpose could be kept intact by human beings seeing the necessity of that kind of suffering and thus consenting to it. They, in an important sense, remained on top of it. Her encounter with affliction in the factories, however, introduced her to something that by its very nature degraded and destroyed human beings and that therefore could not be consented to. It had no purpose, no immanently discoverable answer to why this occurred. That was what left her in pieces, body and soul, after the factory. But what she discovered in two of the places of her spiritual conversion, the Portuguese fishing village and Solesmes, was, she says, by virtue of Christ's presence to her in her suffering, an "understanding of the possibility of loving divine love in the midst of affliction" (WG 68). She discovered a love that was not defined by and did not come from the immanent world, and it could transform suffering. Christ's suffering on the Cross was for her the revelation of goodness in the midst of suffering and not just a good idea. As a result of the experience, an experience of grace given from outside immanent possibilities, she saw the world differently. Her thinking thus has good existential reason to be centered there.

But, if there is this divergence from Tanner, Tanner's account can help us see several important things about Weil's account. First, with respect to the Cross, as Tanner has suggested, it is not necessary to see the Cross as penal, nor is it necessary to see it as substitutionary. Nor should it be a matter of glorifying suffering for suffering's sake. This is as true of Weil's account as it is of Tanner's. Weil's actual account of the Cross does not insist on human possibilities being opened because suffering happened for its own sake. They are opened because Christ loved even in soul-destroying affliction. Jesus's suffering, for Weil, is, above all, as it is in Tanner, a consequence of living in the way that Jesus did. People like that tend to end up in affliction. Why? When they refuse to use force to define life, force is not resisted and is therefore laid on them; it runs them over. As a result, affliction has an accidental quality to it. Affliction is without purpose, it is blind, it does not give an answer to "why me?", and Christ as afflicted does not suffer it any differently than anybody else, other than he had no Christ to look to. "When Pity herself becomes affliction, where can she turn for help?" (SWW 64). Weil's claim that he was afflicted means that she intends us to understand that he, too, would have experienced the meaninglessness of an accident. But because of the way he suffers, that is, without denying his love of the absent Father, love, even in meaninglessness, is not defeated. This, Weil thinks, gives affliction a use—namely, the possibility of loving God fully and nakedly. What is otherwise the greatest destruction of human life now can, because of how Christ suffered it, open a human being to the full experience of divine love. Thus, what Tanner and Weil share in the way that they approach the Cross is seeing it as an act that is ultimately life-giving.

But here it is important to see *how* it is life-giving for Weil. To see that is to see both the mechanism by which grace operates and how Weil's account takes seriously, and does not glide over, the issue of nature and grace.

For Weil, grace, as it comes from Christ's suffering on the Cross the full weight of necessity, does not negate nature. Nor does grace come from an immanent possibility of nature or necessity. Necessity can produce affliction and human destruction; it cannot relieve it or give it any purpose or use. The great discovery in Weil's thinking is that nature is not sufficient;[22] affliction has, at least, the negative virtue of keeping us from thinking that it is. Rather, grace as it is given in Christ's continuing to love the Father, from whom he is separated by all of time and space, shapes, or, to use the Platonic term, persuades necessity to make it complicit in God's bringing the soul to life in God. This complicity is not the result of God being a chess master with respect to natural happenings, a God who arranges trials and sufferings to steer the faithful, to test them and to bring about character. Rather, because nature is not just what is other than God, but rather what is ordered by God's suffering of it, nature can suggest and witness to something beyond nature. As Weil was fond of quoting Kant, the beauty of the world is a promise.

But how does this happen? On the one hand, this is given for Weil in her theory of the *metaxu*.[23] The *metaxu*, which she sees as inscribed in nature, are bridges to and from transcendence. They are the possibilities of transcendence and participation in the divine that are present to creatures of spirit living in this world. They are places where transcendence can be encountered and where divinity has space to operate and expand in human life. In this, they give a sacramental sense to the things of the world in which we live. But they have that ability, not *ex opere operato*; rather, "it is necessary that a *metaxu draw the soul towards being*, that it call *for thought*" (LPW 69). A *metaxu* can "sustain the directing of the attention to God" (NB 596). This suggests what the mechanism of grace in the soul then is, as well as the way that Weil sees the soul participating in the divine as a creature of flesh and blood.

What above all marks the divine for the human, as Weil presents it, is that the divine does not ceaselessly expand and dominate. It does not give life in that way. Rather, it allows another to come into being by withdrawing. But this withdrawal is not a matter of avoidance; it is a suffering of the existence of the other. It is a consent to the life of another, and it is epitomized in Christ's full acceptance of necessity on the Cross. The soul that participates in Christ is the soul that acts as Christ did, that is, by self-emptying, an act that Weil is very clear is *not* given by nature, since necessity commands where it can and expands ceaselessly until checked. Thus, she argues, it is the way of those who participate in Christ; they do not command but rather consent to the life of another. They take it in, and, just as God gave room for a creation to exist, so they give room within themselves for others to exist—others such as the afflicted, the beauty of the world, and God himself. It is this way of living, I want to suggest, that Tanner calls a "derived life," one wherein we are in the image of God in the sense of strongly participating in God—whether or not we are even fully aware of it.

It is important to realize just how far this notion then goes in Weil's thinking. For the chief mechanism of grace, the chief means of human kenosis, as she sees it, comes in her understanding of attention. Attention as she describes it is a suspension of control and anticipation. But above all, it is an act of *disponibilité,* an act of welcoming and availability that gives room within one's soul to another. And that availability is what above all remakes the soul and changes it from a lifeless bit of matter to a creature of spirit, in God's image.

This chapter has shown that Weil's account of the Incarnation and Crucifixion is a coherent and foundational theological account in her writings. This has chiefly been a task of showing formally that it really is a theological account and needs to be treated as such. There is still a lot to discuss about what all is in that account. However, it will be helpful to offer some concluding comments about what sort of difference it makes to see that this sort of theological account is at the heart of her thinking and also to suggest where one might go with it.

The chief difference, I think, that acknowledging this account makes, has to do with a matter of depth. The human person on this account has a great and profound destiny, as Weil calls it in *The Need for Roots*. To talk about life standing on an act of supernatural grace and living it as participating in that act is not an explanation for certain virtues, nor a supernatural covering for natural insufficiencies. It is a bringing of humanity into the world in a way and at a depth far beyond where most of us are inclined to go. This account does not *explain* certain virtues, such as attention and compassion; it *demands* them of us, and it requires them because we are destined to know and love God beyond even the high degree of implicit love that she describes. Thus we are called to live graciously and into a mystery that absorbs us and might even consume us, if the key to it were anything other than an act of grace. As Tanner suggests, to see ourselves in the image of God is to see ahead of us a new set of desires, a new way of thinking and a new way of willing that depend upon our participation in the life and instruction of another.

But, I think, too, that in dealing with Weil, there are also tensions that need to be addressed. This first is seen in the fact that Weil did have a vision of grace and of how it is played out in the world, and she did want to see it played out universally. Her essays on the ancient Greeks and her research into folklore were a very conscious effort on her part to see the act of grace penetrating all times and places. If it didn't, she explicitly says, it would be impossible to excuse God for the existence of affliction. Humans need this act. Balthasar was entirely right to see that she wanted to make this act universally applicable and not limited to Christian confession. The problem—and she struggled long and hard with it—is how one moves from the very specific particularity of the Incarnation and Crucifixion, as she herself saw it, to the universal accessibility of grace. Her struggles involved, on the one hand, a fierce insistence that this act happen in the material world. She thought it a scurrilous attack when she heard it said that the gnostics, whom she liked, denied the bodily suffering of Christ (GTG 107–109). While she was quite wrong about the gnostics (they did deny it), in her objection she reveals where her treasure is on the issue.[24] The act cannot be mythological or symbolic only. On the other hand, this is also why she admits to considerations of avatarism, for she needed this act, and so she wanted to see it enacted in all cultures. She was not committed to avatarism but allowed that it was one way to a solution.

The second tension is the philosophical one that I mentioned much earlier. In reading the world as she did, she also tended to present in many of her writings a whole world, one in which she refused to separate nature and grace. When that happens, it becomes very easy for a reader to ignore her powerful concerns about the mystery and act of grace upon which the world rests. It is a distinct act, and grace is not just an aspect of the world itself.

But here an area of future investigation suggests itself, one that opens her theological account into a demand for a certain kind of philosophical investigation. Weil, perhaps more than any other thinker of our age, excepting perhaps Wittgenstein, saw the world as multivalent, as not flat, presenting to the thinker different faces. Thinking that through and not flattening all those differences and contours of the world is important to the way she writes philosophically. How she treats that multivalence allows for some very different ways of treating the relation of nature and grace. It also allows for different ways of treating philosophical and theological thinking, as they do not necessarily compete as accounts. Instead, they can be layered within each other and within the way we think. For example, for Weil these faces of the world are not just evident to us because nature and necessity are like a kaleidoscope, showing one color one moment and another the next. It is because reality is bound up with how we approach reality and how we put ourselves in relation to it. All those levels of reading, all those implicit and explicit loves of God, all the various *metaxu*, come about because objectivity and subjectivity are not neatly separable. This has long been recognized by numerous Eastern thinkers, but even many Western ones, too. Thus there is a hierarchy of readings, which in fact bespeaks a hierarchy of readers and a demand to be a certain kind of reader. That may well be the way that we need to go, and where Weil may well have a great deal left to offer.

CHAPTER FOUR

LOVE AND INTELLECT

Whenever Simone Weil is introduced, three métiers are usually ascribed to her: philosopher, mystic, and social critic. While rare, the combination is not unknown, especially in the linkage of philosophical thinker with mystical lover. There are a number of important examples of philosophers who were also mystically inclined, including Plato, Augustine, Plotinus, Nicholas of Cusa, Bonaventure, and John of the Cross. Many of them play roles in Weil's own work. Still, even if there is a tradition where mystical love and philosophical thought are linked, examples of it have become increasingly rare. After a century of positivism and then deconstructive irony, one finds few recent thinkers who add to the tradition, or who respect it, or who even know what it is. Being one of the few who belong to it is surely a large part of the appeal of a thinker such as Weil. She called for a new sort of saint, one of whom she thought the world was in much need, who is socially engaged and intellectually critical and, above all, loves deeply. She herself may be one of the few qualified candidates for the title.

What are those qualifications? First, Weil was above all else a thinker. She had an intellectual vocation, something she claimed with no hesitation. She thought that intellectual work was a worthy vocation. But she also did not see it as competing with the love that engages mystery—so much so that, while harshly critical of its modern versions, she even thought that science could be linked to mystical thought, if one heeded the Pythagoreans. She thought it could be an implicit love of God. So, while she was a philosopher, there can be no doubt about her mystical bent. The mystical experiences that led her thought to include spiritual and religious issues after 1937 are well described, and without doubt they were genuine and of prime importance to her. They influence not only what she thought but how she thought it after that point. She greatly respected and owed much in her philosophical writings to mystics such as Saint John of the Cross.

We have seen how her thinking admits a mystery and even a theological commitment. But how do these things line up with each other? How do they line up in her thinking, much less in how we are to understand philosophy and an intellectual vocation more broadly? Questions are regularly raised. On the one hand, her mystical bent has been blamed for what some see as an unreasonable, unrealistic, and illiberal set of prescriptions for social life in *The Need for Roots*. On the other hand, Peter Winch deeply respected and even admired her philosophical grapplings with religion, yet he also expressed grave concern with what he saw as her occasional rationalist streak. This was, he thought, a tendency to speculate and to run out that speculation to certain intellectually dangerous extremes, a tendency to stop looking and, based pretty much entirely on a chain of reasoning, start insisting.

If Weil is any kind of witness to a much-needed reformation of how we think, then how she thought about love and intellect, and how they function together, needs to be understood. In order to come to this understanding, we first need to sort out where the issue arises in her own life, how she describes it, and how she deals with it in her own thinking. That will relieve some of the apparent confusions. But once this is done, we find that a far more interesting sort of question arises, namely one about the role of the intellect in spiritual life. This is also a question of how and to what degree spiritual and intellectual life overlap—and don't overlap. Answering it can let us say something about philosophy and theology as human intellectual and spiritual exercises—that is, as spiritually something more than "second order discourse." It also has a great deal to do with how one believes doctrines proposed by the Church. It is there that we need to begin.

In the last year or so of her life, Weil wrote four texts that are surprisingly personal, given her penchant for avoiding first-person language in essays and even in her notebooks. The explanation for the personal references is simple, though, because three are letters and all of them deal with her personal struggles over the issue of baptism and becoming a part of the Church. These texts are letters four and five in *Waiting for God*, titled "Her Spiritual Autobiography" and "Her Intellectual Vocation" (WG 61–87); the unusual piece titled "Last Text" (GTG 62–65); and the somewhat infamous *Letter to a Priest* (LP; GTG 92–133). Because they are so highly personal, rarely have they been looked at with an eye for content other than her personal objections to becoming a part of the Church. Not many years ago, however, the late Canadian theologian André Naud did an admirable job of analyzing them with an eye toward developing a way of approaching Church doctrine.[1] Following his suggestion, we shall use these texts to see Weil's very positive ways of approaching the issue of doctrine; it is usually only the negative aspects of these texts that are noticed. However, for some obvious reasons, to do so we first need to treat her objections to the way that doctrine was presented to her. After all, Weil's point in each of them is to lay out her reasons for *not* becoming a part of the Church. So, before approaching the positive understanding, we need to begin with those reasons. There are two essential ones, and they are linked.

The first reason Weil refuses to join the Church is because of what she sees the Church requiring in faith, namely, total intellectual adherence. She is appalled by its condemnation of those who do not adhere to the propositions of faith as developed by the Church. Her objection is, as she succinctly put it, to the two little words *anathema sit*. What is the problem here? Chiefly she complains about the constraint put on intelligence. She states, plainly and without hesitation,

> Intellectual adherence is never owed to anything whatsoever. For it is never in any degree a voluntary thing. . . .

If one tries to bring about in oneself an intellectual adherence by the exercise of the will, what actually results is not an intellectual adherence, but suggestion. . . . And there necessarily appears, sooner or later, a compensatory phenomenon in the shape of doubts and "temptations against faith."

Nothing has contributed more towards weakening faith and encouraging unbelief than the mistaken conception of an obligation on the part of the intelligence. (LP 60–61; GTG 119–20)

She continues,

The jurisdiction of the Church in matters of faith is good in so far as it imposes on the intelligence a certain discipline of the attention. . . .

It is altogether bad in so far as it prevents the intelligence, in the investigation of truths which are the latter's proper concern, from making a completely free use of the light diffused in the soul by loving contemplation. (LP 61–62; GTG 120)

The second reason Weil gives for not joining the Church is a related one: namely, she believes herself to have an intellectual vocation. The demand for intellectual adherence is an issue that she takes personally. Giving into it would, in the first place, force her to give up on the degree of intellectual honesty that she believes is obligatory for her and demands that her thought "be indifferent to all ideas without exception." She thinks that her mind, with respect to ideas, ought to be like water, which is indifferent to the objects that fall into it. "It does not weigh them; they weigh themselves, after a certain time of oscillation" (WG 85). This is not simply a matter of general principle for Weil. As she notes in *Letter to a Priest*, the ideas that have already settled in her, especially those that led her to a high appreciation for many non-Christian ideas and to many unorthodox speculations, are ideas that have been condemned by the Church. She cannot give them up except by a sort of intellectual dishonesty. Thus, she concludes, her vocation must be to "be a Christian outside the Church" (LP 11; GTG 93). This is a matter both of intellectual honesty and, relatedly, moral solidarity with those outside the Church whose ideas she finds attractive and of genuine spirituality and that she wants to continue to entertain.

What are we to make of these objections? The initial impulse is to try to see them as rooted in one or more of three places. First, it may be the case that, rather Platonically, she sees the intellect as the spiritual faculty of human beings, and that it is not something that can be determined by force. The objection here, then, may be that the lower cannot determine the higher. The Church is forcing the issue as a social entity, and as a social entity with no deep access to truth, it is obscuring the issue of truth for the intellect. Here the objection would be about the nature of truth and the intellect's privileged access to it. The second way one might see her objections is as rooted in a position about the epistemological status of religious propositions akin to John Locke's "ethics of belief." This is to say that, lacking demonstrative certainty (in which case one would have knowledge and not belief), the degree or intensity of one's belief ought to be proportioned to the degree of likelihood that the evidence possesses; it is immoral to do otherwise. Thus, the Church cannot expect one to believe something wholeheartedly simply on its authority without proper evidence, which Weil does not see being provided or even possibly provided. So, she is here allowing herself a proper intellectual reservation and maintains her ethical integrity for doing so. Third, she may be a subscriber to John Stuart Mill's "marketplace of ideas" theory, in which a laissez-faire attitude to ideas is thought to let the best ones arise and dominate. The Church, by suppressing certain ideas, may be trying to say what the truth is without allowing real investigation into it.

All of these ways of taking Weil's objections have something in common: all see the intellect as the leading faculty, as it were, of the human being, the final court of appeal. It is there, though, that all of them all would be quite *wrong* as accounts of what Weil thought. For, despite her very high opinion of the intellect and intellectual work, Weil clearly did *not* think that the intellect is the highest faculty at all. It doesn't have anything directly to do with faith at all. She argues quite explicitly, "The mysteries of faith are not a proper object for the intelligence considered as a faculty permitting affirmation or denial. They are not of the order of truth, but above it. The only part of the human soul which is capable of any real contact with them is the faculty of supernatural love. It alone, therefore, is capable of an adherence in regard to them" (LP 57; GTG 118). It is attention and supernatural love only that give us access to the highest things. The intelligence—and Weil often crucially qualifies it as "the discursive intelligence"[2]—does not give that access. So, Weil clearly does not believe that in the realm of divine mysteries, the intelligence is the spiritual faculty, nor is she a subscriber to the ethics of belief as that is normally understood, that is, as ethics of respect for public evidence. Weil is quite clear that evidence is not at all the issue with respect to divine things. This has biographical support. In the letter known as her "spiritual autobiography," her movement from agnosticism to faith is, as she characterizes it, a matter of overcoming the problem of evidence as the determining issue of religious faith. She notes the effects of her experience of Christ himself coming down and taking possession of her: "In my arguments about the insolubility of the problem of God I had never foreseen the possibility of that, of a real contact, person to person, here below, between a human being and God" (WG 69). When she then goes on to admit, "I still half refused, not my love but my intelligence" (WG 69), she is *not* expressing the deepest sort of reservation. The intellectual reservation that remains does so at a level that is not the most important level. She is committed; she doesn't doubt what she has experienced. But her intellect has not fully grasped it yet.

Weil is making a fundamental distinction between attention, which is constituted by love, and the discursive intelligence. What sense does this distinction have? Throughout her writings she talks about it in various ways. Consider first how she talks about it with respect to language.

As we do so, however, let it be said at the outset that what Weil is ultimately after is a question of how one approaches a mystery. Or, perhaps better put, what she is after is something that calls into play the notion of mystery. Mysteries, of course, are beyond what the natural intelligence can grasp. But that does not mean, at least as far as Weil is concerned, that mysteries have to remain unspoken or entirely outside language. They do, though, call for a use of language quite different than the one called for when dealing with quotidian things. She is after a sort of intimacy that only love can really approach. So, she notes, "the language of the market place is not that of the nuptial chamber" (WG 79).

The force of this claim lies in the two different moral stances, the languages of the marketplace and the nuptial chamber.[3] The language of the marketplace is neutral and calculating, usually self-interested, although it is not always selfish or greedy. It captures and compares, plots strategy and chooses direction. The language of the nuptial chamber, however, invites; it is not self-assertive. It opens oneself to be impressed upon and revealed to. What Weil is pointing to can be seen in how she describes the difference between how we often talk to other people and how we (ought to) talk to God: "To implore a man is a desperate attempt to cause, by sheer intensity, one's own system of values to pass into the mind of the other person. To implore God is the reverse; it is an attempt to cause the divine values to pass into one's own soul" (NB 188).

To implore in this way is to open oneself up to the other. It is attention, in Weil's own distinctive definition of that term: an approach to another that does not fit him into a category, but which waits upon the self-disclosure of the other. It "consists of suspending our thought, leaving it detached, available, and ready to be penetrated by the object" (WG 111).

Attention has the flavor of altruism to it, or, better put, a sense of self-sacrifice, of kenosis, the self-emptying that allows an other sufficient room in which to exist. This moral sense is crucial to it. Because of this moral quality, attention and supernatural love have a capaciousness that the intelligence does not. Attention is what allows us to embrace a mystery that transcends our ability to conceptualize it—or, more accurately, it is what allows us to be embraced by a mystery. It is capacious in a way that intellect is not, insofar as it has to do with something like the holistic form that is conceptually more than the sum of the parts. She thinks that beauty, which can never be captured by an analysis of the parts, is often the entrance to and visible shape of the good that attention first puts us in relation to.

Intellect, however, operates with a different grammar and at a somewhat different level, especially with respect to its dependence on and stricter use of language to carry out its tasks of description, comparison, plotting, and the like. (The language of a lover is much more open and less restricted.) Because language functions within time and expresses relations, it is limited. For those who are deficient in the ability to use language, it can be void of content or nearly so. For those who are highly competent, it can be rich. It can deal with and express a wide range of relations. But, still, Weil goes on, "this relative richness is a miserable atrocity compared to the perfection that alone is desirable" (LPW 120). Pointedly, she claims,

> Even when it puts things well, a mind enclosed in language is in prison. Its limit is the number of relations that words can render present to it at the same time. It remains in ignorance of thoughts implying a greater number of relation; these thoughts are beyond language, unformulatable, no matter how perfectly rigorous and clear they may be and no matter how the relations that went into them were expressible in perfectly clear terms. Thus the mind moves in a closed space of partial truth, which can be more or less big, without ever being able to cast a glance on what is beyond it. . . .
>
> An intelligent man who is proud of his intelligence is like a prisoner who is proud of having a big cell. (LPW 120)

The context of this passage—namely, the discussion of justice that she is undertaking in the essay "What Is Sacred in Every Human Being?"—is also helpful for distinguishing between what attention grasps and how it grasps it, and the realm of the discursive intelligence. Whereas intelligence is limited to language and the relations it expresses and cannot see beyond what language gives it, attention is able to discern the afflicted and can hear their muted and inarticulate cries. It discerns a human being and gives her respect, it asks her consent to involve her and deal with her in our own plans, even where the accretions of personality have been stripped away from her: intelligence, articulacy, social standing, and where she has been forced outside the sphere of rights. Attention sees and loves what cannot be expressed or pinned down to a specific relation. Moreover, attention is creative, for it gives room for another to exist. It thus gives a deeper sort of justice than mere procedural justice based on rights can give. Whereas rights are often "asserted in a tone of contention" and leave the self thoroughly at the center of moral deliberations, attention sees and loves what cannot otherwise be seen. It moves us away from being the center. So, with respect to the intelligence and attention, the one calculates and the other loves. Supernatural love seems like a sort of madness to one who is committed to making calculations.

The distinction can be pushed in another direction as well, one that strengthens the fact that attention and intellect are different and not reducible one to the other. What we have called the increased capaciousness of attention is *not* a quantitative issue. Attention is *not* intellect raised to a higher degree. It is qualitatively different. Even when attention is dealing with matters that can appear to be in the jurisdiction of the intellect, a difference remains. For example, when dealing with the "knowledge of God" that Weil thinks is properly a matter of love and attention, she indicates that the real presence of God in the soul is not a certainty or knowledge that is built on an intellectual foundation. It does not need intellectual justification; its "proof" is somewhere else, in, say, the overall sense that one sees in the world and acts on as a result. Because it is, it would therefore be a conceptual mistake to provide, or to think that one has to provide, intellectual verification. In a notebook entry that we have already seen, Weil comments,

> The soul's attitude towards God is not a thing that can be verified, even by the soul itself, because God is elsewhere, in heaven, in secret. If one thinks to have verified it, there is really some earthly thing masquerading under the label of God. One can only verify whether the behavior of the soul as regards this world bears the mark of an experience of God.
>
> In the same way, a bride's friends do not go into the nuptial chamber; but when she is seen to be pregnant they know she has lost her virginity. (SWW 108; FLN 145)

Attention and the knowledge of God are not items of intellectual discernment, nor do they pertain to items in the world. They are a way of looking at the world. Thus "the Gospel contains a conception of human life, not a theology" (SWW 109; FLN 147), she claims. It is a light thrown upon the world. Once that light is cast, then the intellect may think the world.

There is an important corollary to this concerning the nature of faith itself. Faith is not, as in a Lockean ethics of belief, a proportioned opinion about a fact. It is above all a certainty as far as the soul is concerned—and yet it is not an intellectual certainty but an experimental one.[4] This is to say it is self-involving and not simply a belief or opinion "about" something. What Weil has in mind here is that faith does not opine the things of faith, even with great conviction, such as that God is good and God exists. Rather, in the person who has faith there is an unshakeable attitude toward God and God's good, an attitude of trust and reliance and desire. For Weil this plays out in numerous ways, but especially in the way we think of God's creation. To believe in God is a way of reading the world, of seeing, without fantasizing or speculating, that its web of necessity, which the intellect can lay out mathematically, is obedient to a goodness that transcends it. To read the world this way is to put oneself in it in a certain way. It is to see oneself as the object of love and the creation of goodness. Ultimately faith is even something that Weil thinks "creates the truth to which it adheres" (FLN 291). What she means is that to have faith in God's goodness, a goodness beyond the sort of good-and-evil mix of the natural world, is in fact to already experience a change that makes one better. It is to commit oneself and to so orient oneself as a whole toward that good that all the parts of the soul will submit themselves to it. Thus she claims, "The domain of faith is the domain of truths created by certainty. It is in this domain that faith is legitimate and is a virtue. A virtue creative of truth" (FLN 291). This domain of faith is not intellectual as such; it is a way of life, a conception of life that frames all other conceptions and gives them the space in which they are to function. It gives form to the intellect.

If this last point is not entirely clear, still, enough has been said to clarify her meaning when she says, in "The Last Text,"

> I believe in God, the Trinity, the Incarnation, redemption, the Eucharist, and the teachings of the gospel.
>
> When I say "I believe" I do not mean that I take over for myself what the Church says on these matters, affirming them as one might affirm empirical facts or geometrical theorems, but that, through love, I hold on to

the perfect, unseizable truth which these mysteries contain and that I try to open my soul to it so that its light may penetrate into me. (GTG 62)

For her to say that she believes in this way, and not in the way that one believes in a geometrical theorem, is to affirm a *stronger* sense of belief. It is *not* to qualify her faith by holding an intellectual reservation about it.

If it is now sufficiently clear what Weil means with respect to her own credo, then some of the things she says about belief in general in *Letter to a Priest* should also grow clearer. First, she is not simply refusing to admit the Church's authority because of its imperialism with respect to the intellect; she is also arguing that the Church is focusing on the wrong thing when it tries to prescribe to the intellect. Because it has focused on the wrong faculty, there has been an "intellectual malaise" in the Church nearly from the beginning that comes from confusing intellect and love. Because of this confusion, intellectual doubt is conflated with disbelief and souls may think that they have lost faith when in reality they are only investigating it. But there is something more, too. In this criticism there is a positive point hidden: if the Church shouldn't prescribe to the intellect, the Church *should*, on the contrary, propose its doctrines as objects for contemplative attention. As we have already seen, she declares that "the mysteries of the faith are not a proper object for the intelligence as a faculty permitting affirmation or denial. They are not of the order of truth, but above it" (LP 57; GTG 118), she says, adding that it is attention alone that has access to them. Far from forbidding the Church to say anything about such transcendent truths, she thinks that, upon recognizing the proper domain of faith, the Church really does have a duty to be a guardian of the sacred mysteries and doctrines. Moreover, for the faithful there is an obligation to pay attention to the mysteries and doctrines of the Church. Its definitions command "a permanent and unconditional attitude of respectful attention" (LP 60; GTG 119), which, in Weil's eyes, is no small thing. In addition, the Church can and ought to be able to "impose on the intelligence a certain discipline of the attention" (LP 61; GTG 120). It should teach us how to pay attention.

It is this proposal to have people pay attention instead of forcing intellectual adherence that Naud found most attractive in Weil. He wanted to develop it into a proposal of how doctrines should be treated. Following Weil, he thought that they cannot be forced on one's adherence, nor should the Church use them to claim infallible authority, but believers should be able to contemplate and love them and, in that way, have them affect their souls. The Church should certainly be serious about what it teaches, but in the way that it is serious it should also teach something about the nature of the objects of belief, which demand an adherence that is commensurate with them. The Church needs to give far more liberty to the intelligence than it has traditionally, and, Naud thinks, still relying on Weil, it needs to undertake a philosophical cleanup of its teaching and the way it has taught. I agree with him on many of them. Nevertheless, save making one specific recommendation,[5] I want to pursue a different line of thought that needs further fleshing out, namely, what the role of the intellect is in the life of faith. While Weil distinguishes attention and love from the discursive intellect, as well as emphasizing that attention is what the Church ought to concentrate on with respect to doctrine, what is now not so clear is why the intellect should be as free as she thinks it should be. It may well be a very good thing to point out that the Church should not demand intellectual adherence because faith has to do with attention and not systematic theology, but that does not leave one with any positive position on the intellect at all. It is not at all obvious what, if anything, the intellect now has to do with faith. As such, one is left scratching one's head in trying to justify the supposed need for the intellect to be free—or to be anything. If intellect and supernatural love are different, it is not clear where and how they intersect. If they do not, it would therefore seem that thinking philosophically or theologically would have nothing to do with the increase of faith.

Although this is to put the question as a dilemma, Weil's position on the issue really is not much of a mystery, although she does deem it a mystical position. While it requires that one distinguish the domain of supernatural love and that of the intellect, it does not necessitate putting them in opposition. Rather, she sees intellect as functioning *within* the larger worldview that is accessible only to attention. Intellect is nested within attention. In outline, her position is this: the mystics have always "accepted the Church's teaching, not as the truth, but as something behind which the truth can be found" (LP 39; GTG 108). This does not leave the intellect to the side, except perhaps momentarily. Rather, whatever is impressed on the attention descends and is incarnated in the intellect. Intellect thinks through in particulars and, as it is able, in what is sensed of the whole. This is why supernatural love is known not so much in what it proposes as in the way it disposes, for the supernatural is known through the way that the natural moves in response to it. The supernatural defines the logical and moral space in which the rest of the person moves. This, then, is faith as Weil defines it. Faith is not belief in an intellectual fact without evidence, nor is it what supernatural love discovers per se; rather, "the consented subordination of all the natural faculties of the soul to supernatural love is faith" (FLN 131). This position bears some similarities to Augustine's famous use of Isaiah 7:9: "Unless you believe you will not understand." By this Augustine meant not that faith replaced or overwhelmed intellect, but rather that in what it accepted of revelation, the intellect was set in a new, fecund direction.

However, further precision is needed in saying how intellect thinks through in particulars what we "read" (to use Weil's term—and here it is well worth remembering that Weil calls faith "a gift of reading").[6] How does this happen? According to Weil, the natural intellect does not and cannot reach into the realm of mystery. It can only think being and beings under the heading of necessity. She argues, "Only necessity is an object of knowledge. Nothing else can be grasped by thought. . . . Necessity is the thing with which human thought has contact" (FLN 143). Necessity, however, she claims can be thought at differing levels: as brute force, as a tissue of mathematical relations, and finally as something "persuaded by goodness," i.e., as what is created and obedient to a goodness that is beyond it. These "levels" are not closed worlds; indeed, because the first two ultimately depend upon a goodness that is beyond them and obey it, and speak of it, there is a mystery behind all that exists. "What is contradictory for natural reason is not so for supernatural reason, but the latter can only use the language of the former" (FLN 109), she says. Attention and love may open us in such a way as to let that mystery dawn. Intellect, for its part, will encounter it insofar as it comes up against contradictions within these readings, contradictions indicating that none of these readings is actually complete in itself. Thus the intellect, in seeking completion, is forced to move up in level. As Weil notes, "Contradiction is the lever of transcendence" (FLN 134). This upward movement is not the result of its own power because it reasons within a reading; it is desire, the desire that is found in welcoming attention that lets the higher level be revealed. At this higher level, then, the earlier contradictions are resolved on a higher plane. This process is repeated as the intellect encounters the transcendent mystery that lies behind all ways of conceiving necessity.

At this point, we need to be somewhat careful about what interests Weil most, for it is *not* that the intellect has reached a higher level and comprehends more and comprehends reality better, even if it does. She is interested in the spiritual relation found in the mind's giving of itself to a reality that it did not create. A highly intelligent mind can comprehend a lot on the level of the intellect and yet be spiritually impoverished. The village idiot can be spiritually superior to any number of intellectually talented people, she observes. The point is the spiritual one of giving consent and love to what is. By virtue of the very nature of the spiritual relation, this means for the intellect that its value is *not* in its systematic comprehension, which is always limited anyhow. If it reaches a conclusion, its spiritual strength is in bowing to the necessity of the conclusion as something not of its own making.[7] One does not *have* to bow in this way. However, when one assumes that the proposition fully defines the doctrine, one tends to turn mysteries into something that is oppressive and totalitarian. If, on the other hand, one is willing to bow, then mysteries are "turned into ko-ans by contemplation by the elect who disdain both rebellion and servility of mind" (FLN 109).

This emphasis on developing one's consent to reality is the basic point of the luminous essay "The Right Use of School Studies with a View to the Love of God." The point of school studies, she gently points out—the point of intellectual learning—is not competence, comprehension, and control; it is the development of attention, the ability to give oneself to a reality. The point of intellectual exercise is to develop a habit of readiness, openness, and availability to reality. Whether we succeed in comprehending the problem in front of us does not really matter; it is our respect for it on its own terms that is most salutary in the learning process when that process is taken as an advance in attention and spirituality. This is why school studies and intellectual work can be an image and a preparation for prayer and the love of God. It is not in their intellectual comprehensiveness.

We now finally see Weil's real answer to the question of why the intellect needs freedom. It is not because she subscribes to an "ethics of belief," or because she thinks the intellect is the highest faculty, or even because, like Mill, she believes in a sort of capitalism of ideas that demands a free marketplace so that the best ideas can emerge. The intellect must be free because it must be able to give itself to the necessity it sees, as it sees it. If it does not have this freedom, if it is forced (as the words *anathema sit* mean to force it by threat), two things may happen. First, it becomes easy to mistake what the real, the spiritual point of doctrines and mysteries is. One who does not realize that the love of God lies in attention may come to believe that it is chiefly an intellectual position, despite having no comprehension of what exactly it is. In this case, one continues to treat it as an intellectual position, which is to say as an ideology, and misses the spiritual opportunities of thought.[8] When one encounters contradictions, which always happens when any limited conception meets reality, the thought of surrender will not arise; the temptation to insist will, however. Weil asserts that "real genius is nothing else than the supernatural virtue of humility in the domain of thought" (LPW 119). The need for intellectual freedom is to encourage this kind of genius. Second, when the intellect is treated as something to be coerced, the person as a spiritual being and as a thinker is not respected. To be treated with respect is to be able to give one's assent freely, to be asked and not forced to give it. One can only assent within the limits of what one conceives. One will, of course, submit to necessity one way or another. But to treat others with respect is to let them see necessity for themselves and give themselves.[9] It is for this reason that the Church really is obligated to present the soul with mysteries for contemplation. To let others think that there is no mystery is to imprison their souls. But, for the same reason, one has to let thinkers come to intellectual obedience themselves, through love.

This solves one problem. But it also raises the very interesting question of what place philosophy and theology now have in a life oriented toward supernatural love and the knowledge of God. It is clear that rationalism and intellectualism are out, as is propositionalism, in things of faith. If those disciplines have any point, it clearly is *not* that of constructing an edifice to believe. Something else has to be the case.

Since Weil makes some rather explicit comments on the question in essays and notebooks written about the same time as the four texts we started with, we can assume that this was a question for her, too. She gives two suggestions for what the role of the intellect in a discipline might be. The first is the task of giving a "certain discipline of attention" for the intelligence. There can and ought to be some sort of *scientia* of how the soul can best discipline itself to think well and remain oriented toward supernatural light. But more important for conceiving the sort of philosophy or theology that Weil thinks is appropriate are the comments that open her London notebook. She writes,

> The proper method of philosophy consists in clearly conceiving the insoluble problems in all their insolubility and then in simply contemplating them, fixedly and tirelessly, year after year, without any hope, patiently waiting.
>
> By this standard, there are few philosophers. And one can hardly even say a few.
>
> There is no entry into the transcendent until the human faculties—intelligence, will, human love—have come up against a limit, and the human being waits at this threshold, which he can make no move to cross, without turning away and without knowing what he wants, in fixed, unwavering attention.
>
> It is a state of extreme humiliation.
>
> Genius is the supernatural virtue of humility in the domain of thought. That is demonstrable. (FLN 335)

One way to describe Weil's view of philosophy and theology, given these comments and others that we have noted, is that it is, indeed, a mystical one. More precisely, it has at its core an apophatic approach, one of what is called "negative theology" because it is aimed at ultimately unsaying positive, but essentially limited, conceptions of reality. This is apparent, for example, in her claim that "atheism can be a purification." She does not stress an approach that demands balance between positive and negative affirmations, at least with respect to the intellect, but in one who was not trained as a theologian and who was not a professional theologian, that is not surprising. In some senses, she therefore bears in contemporary thought certain similarities to the deconstructionists, who have seen philosophy's task as unsaying and unmasking totalizing affirmations that cannot live up to their promises of presence and totality and become oppressive. There may even be a limited similarity to certain of Derrida's later religious reflections about *différance*. For Derrida, for example, the constant difference between concept and thing that makes for the ever-recurring deferral of meaning has a mystical sense. In the hands of some theologians—John Caputo, for example—this constant unsaying is what fully recognizes and brings into play whatever underlies Being.

Weil's thought differs from the deconstructionists here: Somehow one is always left with the sense that for these philosophers the intellect is always left in charge, despite their claims to the contrary, which is to say the philosopher is the one who is in charge, no matter how ironical his or her own utterances. The intellect is always left; it is what is doing the deconstructing and the prophesying of a messiah. There is a certain odor of *pride*. There is little or no sense of giving one's assent to a reality outside oneself and little sense of a desire for good that drives one to do so. It is mainly a matter of not being deceived.[10] In Weil, however, it is the intellect itself—the philosopher—who is undone by reality so that reality may exist without illusion. The unsaying is precisely in order to hear a real word. When that happens, for Weil, all that remains is the pure desire for the good. Philosophy as decreation may indeed be for Weil intellectually a negative operation, insofar as the intellect cedes primacy of place to transcendent mystery; as a spiritual operation, an operation of supernatural love, however, it is actually overwhelmingly positive on two fronts. If it unsays anything, it is because something fuller comes to replace what we used to say. In this respect, perhaps what Weil is proposing does not have to change many positive works of philosophy at all; it simply changes the spirit in which they are done. Second, as an exercise that means to eliminate all that fences God off from the soul, this operation allows the soul to be transformed into God's own life. In this way Weil's view of philosophy does not demand that as an intellectual exercise philosophy should be self-destructive at all. It need not as a matter of thinking spend any time at all in deconstructing anything, except as a matter of pulling up the weeds that threaten to choke the real plant. It simply needs to expose itself rigorously to a reality that made it and encompasses it. And it may indeed praise it as best it can while it is doing that.

Obviously, a lot more needs to be said to flesh out how philosophy or theology in this vein should actually function. Let me leave this, however, with the possibility that it may not be an entirely new way of thinking about philosophy. In fact, Weil may be quite right in thinking that she simply rediscovered the ancient approach, pagan and Christian, to wisdom.[11] As Hadot famously argued, ancient philosophy was primarily a matter of healing for the soul and therefore was not simply a matter of developing intellectual positions or assertions but instead a way of life. Lying behind many ancient writings, such as Marcus Aurelius's *Meditations*, is not a philosophy as we understand it, but a set of spiritual exercises designed to move the soul ahead spiritually. And it is not at all unusual within later Christian philosophy to put love ahead of intellect or to enclose intellect within an act of love and a certain moral disposition, such as attention is. One sees it in Newman.[12] But above all, one sees it in Augustine.

CHAPTER FIVE

"I DREAMED I SAW ST. AUGUSTINE . . ."

It would, in the strictest sense, be a mistake to call Simone Weil an Augustinian. She quotes Augustine directly, and with occasional frequency, but her citations are mixed. On the one hand, she approvingly points to his saying "God is a good that is nothing other than good" as a positive example of Platonism (LPW 60); on the other, she not only cites his canonization as the ironic proof that the Church replaced genuine faith with "the doctrine of an idolatrous state" (SNL 145) but also criticizes him for making doctrine and ceremony the condition of salvation, not its grammar and symbol,[1] and finds his consignment of unbaptized infants to the nether regions particularly loathsome. On the whole, though, she does not seem to have delved very deeply into him. Augustine, for Weil, is chiefly to be cited—positively and negatively— as an authority of official Christianity and not somebody whom she herself read as a guiding intellectual and spiritual master, the way she read, say, Plato or John of the Cross.

Nevertheless, Weil does share at a very deep level something with Augustine—as she does with Pascal, whom she treats similarly—namely, a particular type of Christian Platonism and, most specifically, Augustine's "inward turn." This is at the heart of the sort of thinking that mysteries engage. It, of course, is a point on which Augustine is most frequently misunderstood and most criticized. For example, his search for the inner self in *Confessions* is often claimed to be the beginning of our unholy individualism and our obsession with the self and personality as the ultimate expression of ultimacy.[2] Weil had much to say about *that*. Moreover, the "inner self" is just as often criticized as an example of the wrongheadedness that lies at the heart of metaphysics, the need to posit an inner entity to explain the outer workings of the world, or a privileged place of vision in which luminosity guaranteed truth.

Augustine is easily and now regularly defended from these sorts of charges. His invention of the inner self is not individualism, nor a matter of inward gazing, but a discovery of an inner place where God, where otherness, is met.[3] It is not a private, lonely place at all, a place where one is isolated and insulated from the world; on the contrary, it is the space where our isolation from the world is actually overcome. To be stuck in the world of the senses is to live in the most private world of all—who else can feel what we do?—while the inner world is where we discover ourselves, as sought by and grounded in God, where God's own Word becomes our inner word, welcoming and, for once, open to all that God has wrought.[4] Here doctrine is not a replacement for the movement of the heart for God, but a teaching meant to form a character and to focus the wandering mind, as well as a discipline meant to order outer life precisely so that one can proceed inwardly, a movement from *scientia* to *sapientia*. It is, in Weil's terms, a *metaxu*, a bridge, an intermediary. Indeed, how else could one fairly read a work such as *De Doctrina Christiana*?

But if this is Augustine, if Augustine can be defended, then the real question that his authority poses is not whether he is guilty of being a bad influence, but whether he is right even when read accurately. If he is right, then his Christian Platonism, which is at the heart of his "inward turn," stands against and diagnoses our spiritual malaise and may well be an alternative to it. That by itself, however, may not make Augustinianism more welcome or understandable to the modern mind, which is individualist, isolated, and distanced, and even imperialistic and dogmatic, although it tends to be dogmatic about its own relativism. For what is Christian Platonism to us any longer? It may still simply be an alternative rooted in an outmoded metaphysics of the self and hence no real alternative. Here is where it is important to understand the Christian Platonism that Weil broadly shares with Augustine. It is the spiritual heart of a living tradition she thinks ought to be inherited from the past be pursued in the future, for it is not a philosophical doctrine but a way of life, and an alternative way of doing philosophy. She therefore sees in Christian Platonism something that may allow us to recover that tradition, including Augustine as a real authority, in a meaningful way. But Weil herself may be one who actually is able to distill and present that in a way that is even purer than Augustine.

What, then, is Christian Platonism? Within Christianity it has actually been two things. First, it has been frequently regarded as the mother of all heresies, chiefly those of the gnostic variety, as Hippolytus of Rome argued in the third century. This Platonism is a speculative doctrine that encourages and begets speculative doctrine, an attempt to say a final word. It is frequently at odds with orthodoxy. Second, however, it is a very different sort of tradition, one in which philosophy is assimilated to contemplation and contemplation is assimilated to prayer and the life of prayer. In this assimilation, John Cassian, for example, without any trace of irony or being metaphorical, could call the desert hermits Christian philosophers. In a similar vein, Evagrius of Pontus claimed, "If you are a theologian, you pray truly. If you truly pray you are a theologian."[5] In this Christian Platonism the foundational story of Platonism, namely, the Allegory of the Cave in *Republic,* book 7, is likened and assimilated to a foundational story of Christianity, the Exodus and Moses's ascent of Mount Sinai.[6] Here religious life and philosophical life are united, and united in such a way that philosophy and theology flow from and are rooted in the fullness of religious life.

To be sure, these two forms of Christian Platonism were not always distinct in either the ancient or medieval period. Evagrius himself is an excellent example of mixing the two, as he both assimilated Platonic contemplation to the life of prayer and managed to get himself into serious trouble for speculative excesses that were rooted in his Origenism. Origen, for that matter, is another example of their combination, and there are elements within Augustine that on occasion put him under a similar cloud. Weil criticizes him for precisely these things, namely, that he tries to say in doctrine a final word that is both a necessary and a sufficient condition for faith.

If, however, these forms of Platonism often overlapped within Christianity, in good part it was because thought and life were not regarded as distinct, as we often make them. That they were not, is, in fact, the most positive aspect of the second type and suggests its basic criticism of the first type, that is, it separated life and thought too easily and proceeded with religious life as if it were a matter of uncommitted thought and speculation alone. It was not only Christian Platonists who voiced this criticism; non-Christian Platonists did as well. For example, in arguing against the gnostics, after showing how silly their pseudo-Platonic speculations really were, Plotinus goes straight to the heart of the matter by pointing out that the real problem is that their Platonism was strictly a speculative doctrine that had nothing to do with the amendment of life, and that offered no *way* to the God who was so glibly spoken about. Plotinus complains, "They have never made any treatise about virtue . . . nor how the soul is tended, nor how it is purified. For it does no good at all to say 'Look to God,' unless one teaches how one is to look. In reality it is virtue which goes before us to the goal and, when it comes to exist in the soul along with wisdom, shows God; but God, if you talk about him without true virtue, is only a name."[7] Similarly, when criticizing the Manichaeans, Augustine echoes Plotinus's criticism of the gnostics when he confesses that his problem as a Manichaean was that he believed Manichaean intellectuality made him look more clever and sophisticated and thus actually prevented him from learning or improving in virtue. It made him smug and arrogant.[8] In a very real and uncontroversial sense, what the gnostics and Manichaeans lacked was any sense of an inner life, a life of self-reflection and consciousness of the self with respect to the demands of religious life, a sense of distance and closeness to God as the absolute good.

It is precisely *this* sort of inner element that Augustine found attractive in Platonism. Augustine recognized it in Socrates and Plato and saw it as akin to Christianity. For example, Augustine notes that Socrates saw that the causes of things are reducible to nothing else than the will of the one true and supreme God—and on this account he thought they could only be comprehended by a purified mind; and therefore that all diligence ought to be given to the purification of the life by good morals, in order that the mind, delivered from the depressing weight of lusts, might raise itself upward by its native vigor to eternal things, and might with purified understanding, contemplate that nature which is incorporeal and unchangeable light, where live the causes of created natures.[9]

Similarly, Augustine says, Plato followed Socrates on this score, emphasizing that the conduct of life and contemplation of truth were inseparable.[10] Thus Plato perfected philosophy "by combining both parts into one."

So it is important to bear in mind how the two forms of Christian Platonism are distinct. They are *not* two ends of the spectrum. One does not represent a more intellectual approach to Christian philosophy and theology and the other a more affective one, a mysticism of experience. To suggest that they are related this way would be to impose upon ancient Christianity a modern distinction, a very Cartesian or even Kantian one, that did not exist within its own period. At their hearts these two types of Platonism are opposed, for their difference is not between reason and faith or reason and affectivity. Rather, there is a distinction in how one reasons. One can speculate by unaided reason, without grace or virtue, or one can reason within the context of a moral and spiritual life that sees the moral and spiritual reformation that is an integral part of faith at the heart of understanding. In this sense, if desert monks with little learning can be appropriately called Christian philosophers, so, too, can people such as the Cappadocian fathers and Augustine, who not only wrote works that are recognizable as philosophy to us but also wrote more devotional works and worked out much of their own theology and philosophy in sermons. They themselves probably did not see a lot of difference between the two forms as ways of thinking. Surely there is more to be said about this distinction; nevertheless, it ought to be clear enough to give some sense of what Christian Platonism is and the role of the inner in it. It is the "inner" in this sense, I suggest, in which Weil is most interested in Platonism; it is what she thinks really is at stake in Platonism and why Platonism is so very important. It is also this sort of inner sense that she recovers of Platonism and reformulates, and it is what she shares with Augustine.

When in Marseille, Weil wrote a number of essays on the ancient Greeks for her confidant and would-be converter, Father Perrin. She did so to show him the universality of grace. She would have had no hope of convincing him of this unless she could somehow show that thinkers such as Plato really were Christian in some important sense. In the end, she seems to have convinced him, and he was no fool on these issues. It is in this light that one must read an essay such as "God in Plato" (LPW 45–96). In it, Weil is not so much trying to defend an old friend and tradition. In uncovering what is most important in Plato's thinking, she is trying to show what she thinks is most important in Christian thinking. The essay therefore goes to the deeper point about the nature of Christian thinking itself and the nature of philosophy in general. Plato's teaching—and Christianity's—is not speculative doctrine but a way of life and a way of thinking. Specifically, then, she wants to argue that if Platonism is not a doctrine but a mysticism, and is an intimation of Christianity, then, by parity of reasoning, Christianity itself is not a doctrine but a mysticism. But this mysticism is not a matter of gaining *an* experience; it is the development of a certain inner life that permeates and configures our knowledge.

At the outset, and throughout the essay, Weil argues that Plato is a mystic. His wisdom "is not a philosophy, a search for God by means of human reason. . . . [It] is nothing other than an orientation of the soul towards grace" (LPW 55). Weil here is obviously drawing a sort of Kantian distinction about philosophy, but prescinding from that, if we still are willing to call Plato a philosopher, she is then saying that he is a very different sort of philosopher than Kant had in mind. The knowledge that Plato was after was, from beginning to end, a spiritual knowing. But what exactly does this mean?

Weil argues that Plato's spirituality contains these things: 1) that we are children of heaven, children of God; 2) that our lives are lives of forgetting this, and the supernatural truth; 3) that the condition for salvation is thirst for this forgotten truth; and 4) that "if we sufficiently thirst for this water, and if we know that it is ours to drink it insofar as we are children of God, it will be granted to us" (LPW 47).

Let us first consider what she has in mind in calling present life a forgetting. Doing so will help determine what remembering amounts to. While Weil does not spend a great deal of time analyzing Platonic memory, her few comments are striking. Platonic memory is not, as a naive reading of the *Meno* might suggest, simply remembering some past fact gathered in a previous state of existence that we have now forgotten. Plato himself drops that sort of imagery after the *Meno*. Rather, if the thought has any meat, it is that the mind has a natural affinity to know, and that natural affinity lies at its very roots. The point is not so much one of where we have gained knowledge, then, but rather of the very personal nature of knowledge. It is also about *how* we gain that knowledge.

Weil observes what the phenomenon of memory is like in relation to "remembering" the supernatural truth. If there is some fact that we have possessed and then forgotten, we direct for a few moments our attention to an empty space. Suddenly the thought is there. Oddly, in this phenomenon, at the very instant before recognition, we did not know what it was we were searching for. If we did, we could have said what it was. But we could not. Yet, suddenly we can now say what it is. Two things are striking about this phenomenon. First, although we have forgotten, in directing our attention to an empty space we somehow want and desire to know, even though we can't exactly say what it is that we want to know. Memory comes from this sort of attention, and Weil is interested here in attention in her own highly developed sense. This is her inward turn. Second (although Weil herself does not draw this conclusion out), in remembering like this, when the thought does come back to us and we have a sense that it is familiar, it somehow belongs to us.

This is what it is like with the knowledge of God. To come upon it is like remembering. We first have to wait with attention for it to come to us. Second, even if it is startling and puts everything in a new light, there is a sense that it is at home with us and that in knowing God we are more at home than we have ever been. It is like "the smile on a beloved face" (WG 69). It gives a sense of self-possession and self-consciousness that we did not have when in a state of forgetting. The knowledge of God that we now remember is knowledge not of a new fact but a familiar one. It often comes to us not only as a knowledge of some thing but also as a matter of self-knowledge. So, even if this is a supernatural knowledge and comes about only by grace, as Weil adamantly insists, it is not the sort of knowledge that conquers our minds and wills; rather, it makes them more fully what they are. To know God is to know, as Nicholas of Cusa put it, an other that is not other (*aliud non-aliud*).

We begin to see where the suggestion that we are children of heaven might arise. It is not the result of giving human beings an a priori metaphysical status that elevates them and the importance of their projects above the rest of creation. It is, as Weil puts it, an "experimental truth." Indeed, it cannot be otherwise, since knowing God is inseparable from knowing one's own self. To have any true sense of God, one has within that very conception a sense that somehow we, and the creation, belong to God. Furthermore, since God is good and nothing but good, as Weil quotes Augustine, one cannot come to know God without moral and spiritual self-knowledge and reformation. Similarly, there is no genuine self-knowledge without God. Weil points out,

> 1. *There is not, there cannot be any other relation between a human and God except love. What is not love has no relation to God.*
>
>   2. The object belonging to love is God, and *everyone who loves anything other than God deceives oneself, and is in error, as if one were to run towards a stranger in the street as a result of mistaking him for a friend.*
>
> It follows that it is only insofar as the soul is oriented towards what it is necessary to love, that is to say, insofar as it loves God, that it is fit to love and know. It is impossible for a man to exercise fully his intelligence *without charity*, because there is no other source of light than God. (LPW 60–61)

Herein lies precisely the problem that Plotinus and Augustine saw with the gnostics and Manichaeans respectively, and the problem that Weil imputes to Aristotle: their search for God by reason alone is a distanced search, one that is not self-involving, a search wherein the thinker can stand apart from what is known. This, of course, is not simply an ancient problem; it is the obsession of the modern world from Descartes to Locke and onward. Its quest for neutral reason is not simply Stoic detachment in order to cultivate amor fati but ultimately involves a sense of foreignness and alienation. The inward gazing of the modern self is like watching a movie.[11]

This, then, gives form to the Platonic claim that we have forgotten. Even if the name of God remains within a culture or philosophy, once the sense of self-involvement disappears, once the sense of who we are in relation to God disappears, so, too, does any genuine knowledge of God. It is not knowledge of an Other; it is just other than the knowledge of God. How can be seen in Weil's linking of falsehood and unconsciousness (LPW 65) as the chief characteristics of the inhabitants of the cave. Because we are unconscious, what we think is false. Because knowledge involves the knower, real knowledge involves treating the world and standing in front of it in a very different sort of relation. Judging shadows and seeing in the light of the sun are very different sorts of activities. The difference is not simply a matter of right or wrong information; it is a different way of thinking.[12] Weil aptly suggests that the opinions of the Great Beast are not necessarily wrong. Since the beast's opinions are formed by chance, it is likely that they will be on occasion correct. Nevertheless, she continues, "even when its opinions *conform to the truth they are still essentially alien to the truth*" (LPW 56).

It is, however, equally important to understand just why Weil claims that "the precept 'Know thyself' is not practicable in the cave" (LPW 65). How and why we live in a state of unconsciousness and forgetfulness helps draw us closer to what she is ultimately getting at in the positive case.

The problem, she argues characteristically, is the social, which she never tires of claiming kills real thought. It makes us passive, for, in the social world, "We do not budge. Images pass before us and we live them" (LPW 65). Here Weil certainly has in mind the great degree to which our very sense of the self is shaped by the images we are given in social life. For example, young girls raised on *Marie Claire* come to think of themselves and their roles in life in a very particular way that leads them to adapt, usually uncritically, those same roles. Similarly, it is no surprise that boys raised on stories of Roman glory want to be warriors. Ironically, everybody thinks they are wholly autonomous in doing so. But of course they would, since autonomy is one of the most powerful of these images. As Augustine might have pointed out, when this comes to pass, they have come to live their lives entirely by the "outer man."

But if passivity is the face of the problem, paradoxically, that passivity results from human activity. The deep problem with the world of the cave is, she says, "that it is fabricated" (LPW 65), by which she means it is a world that we construct, that is not made by "the supreme Good" (LPW 65). We have written our own script. The problem is that in constructing a world for ourselves, a world in which we are protected from the outside and in which we set out our own space, we lose both the world and ourselves. It is precisely in asserting ourselves in trying to construct a human space that we lose ourselves and are passive. In good part this is due to the fact that the more successful we are in making this world *ours*, in making it self-contained, and making ourselves masters of it, the more it in turn makes us, as it is the sole source of our sense of self and value. Far from actually making us autonomous, free, and open, it isolates us from any larger world and from each other. Moreover, the degree to which we are successful in making the social world self-contained is the same degree to which we will lack any awareness of—that we will forget—a larger good.[13] So "we do not know that we are under punishment, that we dwell in falsity, that we are passive, nor, indeed, do we know that we are unconscious" (LPW 65). The effect of constructing a world, particularly when the construction is all-embracing, is to lose the sense that it is constructed. The only way out, of course, is some sense of otherness that can either break the walls of or somehow limn the artificial world. Without such an other, one might well think the world perfect. As Weil notes, affliction often plays this role: "Without affliction, we might think ourselves in paradise. Horrid possibility" (NB 294).[14] The Platonic ways of contradiction and contemplation of the beauty of the world a priori also give that sense of awakening us to the fact that the world we see is not the real one. Contradiction forces us to face the limited nature of the images by which we think, and then to resolve them on a higher plane. The contemplation of the beauty of the world a priori gives a promise of a greater good that beckons the soul on. Both incite an important dissatisfaction with the constructed world and direct desire to a something larger; by actually changing the soul's thought, both change the soul and can cause it to remember itself.

On one level, this process is one of deconstructing the unconscious, amnesiac self that has invested itself so passively in the images it has been given and in false senses of presence. Appropriately, Weil cites John of the Cross's "dark nights of the soul," nights that are not mere low spots in the spiritual journey, but moments of the deep disorientation that the self experiences as it loses its familiar polestars, first in giving up dependence on the senses for life and then when all other values, including good ones, disappear in the blinding vision of the sun. But, more importantly, this process is a matter of opening oneself to pay attention to the world and take it into oneself, a process of remembering in which we actually do "direct our attention for a few minutes towards an empty space." It is a process of coming to identify with the world as a whole, in which the world becomes our body and we feel each and every thing in it as our body. In commenting on Plato's *Symposium*, Weil notes, "Our vocation is unity. Our affliction is to be in a state of duality" (IC 110).

To summarize briefly: for Weil, the core of Plato's mystical thought, of Platonic philosophy, is attention. If it is at all appropriate to talk of any sort of inward turn in Weil, it is here, and attention is its substance. The contrary, the being lost in the outer, is our construction of the world.

Weil's reading of Platonism—and her own Platonism, which in its broad outlines sets her thinking squarely within the Platonic-Augustinian tradition of the inward turn that discovers itself in God—stresses the practice of philosophy as a learning to die and as a wisdom that is self-involving. Enough has undoubtedly been said to this point in previous chapters to make this much obvious. But what bears further investigation is how this is philosophy at all. Weil, of course, in "God in Plato," wants to call it mysticism and not philosophy, but this is more a bow to the way these terms tend to be used now. The issue is one of what philosophy is and ought to be, of what it means to love wisdom. Thus, it is especially worthwhile to look at what point Weil ultimately makes about philosophy, for, in writing about Plato the way she does, she is deliberately pushing for an alternative.

What this alternative is might be approached by a similar attempt made by German philosopher Josef Pieper several years ago. Pieper pointed out, in reference to Kant, how we tend to look at philosophy. For Kant, he argues, philosophy is exclusively discursive, not contemplative, and is therefore a form of work. Plato, Kant claims, is that "Father of all raving enthusiasm in Philosophy," while "Aristotle's philosophy is truly work."[15] While Kant's criticism may be aptly directed against a version of the Romantic vision, which it in fact was originally, it is also highly revealing of what we think philosophy positively is since Kant. Reason is exercised on things, and since it does not mirror nature but rather constructs the impress of the world into something thinkable, we are barred from any direct knowledge of God and ourselves, and the most reasonable world we can have is a constructed world, a world always mediated by our representations. It is always our world, but our world is not necessarily the world as it is. Kant has much more to say than this, and it would be puerile to make him into somebody who thought we make up the world according to whim and want. Nevertheless, the Kantian world still remains the cave, even if it is a very sophisticated cave.

Just as important to Kant is that philosophy is work, indeed, a "Herculean labor." Pieper, in commenting on Kant's saying, argues,

> In this laborious aspect, [Kant] saw a kind of legitimation of philosophy: philosophy is genuine, *insofar* as it is a "herculean labor." The fact that "intellective vision" didn't *cost anything* is what made it so suspicious to him. Kant expected no real gain in knowledge from intellectual vision, *because* it is the very nature of vision to be effortless.
>
> Would not such a viewpoint bring us to the conclusion, or at least close to the conclusion, that the *truth* of what is known is determined by the *effort* put into knowing it?[16]

This conclusion, of course, is thoroughly in keeping with Kant's own highly Pelagian theology.

Pieper's contrast highlights two very different ways of thinking philosophically—and theologically. It also sheds direct light on the commonly understood division between philosophy (and again theology in the modern world) and mysticism. Philosophy, on the one hand, is rational, that is, strictly discursive, public, propositional, and determined by method and universal canons of rationality. Or, at least, if it is not yet determined by such canons, it would like to uncover them, or it despairs about the fact that there are none that we know of. Mysticism, on the other hand, is affective and experiential, and generally defies formulation; it therefore is strictly private and hence not rational, nor a matter of knowing, although assessments of that are both positive and negative. Pieper, however, is suggesting that knowing *is* vision. Indeed, in order to know what is really worthwhile, one has to stop working, stop constructing, in order to look and listen.

Weil certainly knew her Kant and admired him. She particularly admired his moral philosophy, its stoicism that demanded utter altruism and the need to discard a heteronomous imagination. But, in the end, she uses those moral elements in a very different way; what she is driving at is ultimately far closer to Pieper. For example, if she is deeply interested in the spiritual value of labor, it is not because labor constructs a world but because it deconstructs one, because it can wear down the self-centered imagination and erase the screen that keeps us from the world. For Weil, the result that comes out of this altruism and effort of the will is a purgation, a requirement to face the void and our own nothingness. Only then can the light break in upon us—but it must break in upon us. So, the role of the will is a negative one of suppressing natural desires (as Kant would have believed) but also is undertaken so that a much deeper desire—a supernatural one—may be freed. The will's effort is an effort in the void.

Knowing—or, at least, the right kind of knowing—is then decidedly *not* a construction; it is vision. For that reason it is also always a matter of grace. It can only be given, and no amount of effort can achieve it. After all, Weil thinks, if it came from us it would be no better than us. It is something for which we have to wait. This waiting and openness is what Weil claims is the heart of Platonism. This is also at the heart of the Christian mystical tradition itself, the tradition in which contemplation is the acme of the Christian life, the telos towards which it tends.

This, however, is to put matters very sharply and probably somewhat misleadingly with respect to the problem Weil is driving at. Vision and construction are not sharp alternatives in that one age consistently thought one way and another age thought another. Rather, the problem as Weil saw it is a perpetual one. We *do* continually construct. Kant was right in seeing this, she thought, and his insight is underlined more boldly by thinkers after him who saw this construction as depending upon historical factors. The problem, then, is and always has been how to transcend the solipsism of this construction and let the world penetrate our minds. But even to put it that way for Weil would also be misleading if by talking about transcending this construction we were to talk about that transcending as another way of what the ancients and medievals called *scientia*, the knowledge of the empirical world, in order to replace it with knowledge of an inner world of essences. Rather, for Weil the question is not whether or not *scientia* is possible, or even how it is possible—construction or vision. The question rather is one of *sapientia*, wisdom, that inner quality that defines understanding and wisdom and sets it apart—at least for thinkers such as Plato and Augustine—from mere *scientia*. The question is then one of how the two are related. This is the deep issue for Weil. The key to Platonism lies here, and this is where her contribution lies.

For Weil, in the strictest sense, we never leave construction behind; even the philosopher who leaves the cave returns and, indeed, must return as a direct consequence of whatever vision of the good she has had. Upon returning, even she continues to deal in representations. Weil calls the *Timaeus* the book of one who has returned to the cave. Vision and understanding never leave the world. We continue to have a perspective and to read the world from it. As bodily creatures we handle the world through media—first through our bodies and the sense of pleasure and pain, and then later through symbols. We feel it through the end of a blind man's stick. But if we are always reading and always have a perspective (God alone does not read), for Weil there are nevertheless levels, and one can move up through them. One can, for example, move from the thoroughly egocentric world of pleasure and pain that reads the world from the highly individual perspective of one's one body to a world of symbols that is at least impartial and indifferent to our narrow desires.

From there, Weil thinks that we can move to a point where the world is our body, where we feel and think from a perspective that takes in as its own whatever goes on in the world, with consent and without resentment. We are not gods in doing so, but have a sense, a memory, that whatever God has ordained belongs to us intimately.

If we never stop reading, then wisdom is not an alternative to knowing, nor is it the vision of a private and otherwise hidden world, similar to but distanced from this one, a world of separable and separated essences. Rather, the issue of wisdom is about an underlying moral stance from which we read the world. It is, for example, to look at the world justly—as Augustine also argued—as it is, and not as we would like it to be. Wisdom is what we do with our knowledge, which is not itself a separate knowledge but the very configuration of our knowledge, although, to be sure, the facts that we pursue and come up with may look very different, given different moral levels. This was Weil's point in "At the Price of an Infinite Error: The Scientific Image, Ancient and Modern" (LPW 155–98). If there is a problem with construction, it is not that it represents the world, and such representation is not the true world but represents the world with an eye to using it in a certain way. The problem is not just our construction of the world but also that our construction of the self and the world is no longer the world as God intended it, but the world we have willed.[17] It is the outer expression of our inner being. But inner and outer here are not related as cause to effect, but instead are inseparably linked. Similarly, the knowledge of God is contrary in spirit to that of construction. As *sapientia* it infuses whatever *scientia* we might possess.

So, vision never leaves the world, nor is it meant to do so for Weil. As she points out, "To love God, to think on God, is nothing else than a certain way of thinking on the world" (NB 25). It needs stressing that the mysticism Weil sees at the heart of Platonism and of Christianity is not *an* experience. Neither can one just think oneself into wisdom. One needs an apprenticeship, one that for Weil involves a training of the body but succeeds only when we pay attention to what we are learning. When that happens, we experience the world differently, that is, we take the world in a new way. Mysticism takes in the world and does not rest in itself. Remember here Weil's most explicit definition of attention as consisting in "suspending thought, leaving it detached (*disponible*), empty and ready to be penetrated by the object" (WG 111). To be *disponible* is to be open, available, and ready for use. It is not a blankness but a desire that does not reach out to grab the world; it desires to be filled and used by the world.

Vision, then, as distinguished from construction, is something like a habitual practice or attitude of the soul. It is a sort of *lectio divina* in which self-will is silenced, wherein one is radically open to a world that strikes one—particularly as it does not cooperate with one's cherished individual projects—as alien and other, but that is also beautiful and beckoning. This openness has as its heart's desire the desire to know, to see things simply as they are and as God intended them. In order to know the beloved, it waits and does not press, and it waits even in absence and darkness. This is a moral stance and is itself born out of love and desire.

Here the Platonic/Weilian philosopher does not *intend* to construct a world, although construction may be coincidental and unavoidable. Philosophy is an education and an apprenticeship on the one hand and a willingness to teach on the other. But it is not and cannot be a doctrine, a final word. What defines it is precisely a love of wisdom, which, of course, is itself already a sort of wisdom itself.

This way of treating Platonism that we have just outlined is to look at the "inward turn" of Platonism, taken so clearly and definitively in Augustine, in a very different way than it often is. It is not a movement to an alternative, private world that is fascinated by and dwells on "inner experience." Nor does it involve gazing upon metaphysical objects. Rather, as Denys Turner has argued, within the tradition of Augustine, Dionysius, Bonaventure, Eckhart, John of the Cross and others—which is the tradition of Christian Platonism—that the distinction between "inner" and "outer" ultimately belongs to the one who remains in the "outer." The one who dwells in the inner has overcome the distinction. That one's "spiritual knowledge" is the way of looking at the world as a whole. This does not mean that the knowledge of God is nothing more than a way of looking at the world, but it does mean that it is linked to and inseparable from how we look at the world.

Clearly, Weil belongs to this tradition, which is not surprising since she was indebted to many of its chief figures, particularly John of the Cross. And insofar as she does belong to it, she ought to be read in such a way that she draws our attention to it—and helps us see what is really at stake in it. Once we realize that what Weil is talking about is at the heart of this tradition, we begin to recognize its seeds within thinkers such as Augustine. For example, one should begin to recognize in Augustine's own intellectual and spiritual growth a trajectory from his early, very intellectualistic project of designing an *ordo studiorum* that would propel the mind by thinking alone to the highest knowledge to a point in his later works, such as *Homilies on the Gospel of John,* where knowledge and righteousness are related far more intimately. There, for example, in an image strikingly similar to Weil's suggestion that "there is no fire in a cooked dish, but one knows that it has been on the fire" (FLN 145), Augustine claims, "By forsaking God the soul becomes unrighteous; by coming to Him, it becomes righteous. Does it not seem to you as it were something cold, which, when brought near the fire, grows warm; when removed from the fire grows cold? A something dark, which when brought near the light, grows bright; when removed from the light grows dark?" (19.11). Here the reformation of one's inner word, which comes from the indwelling of the Word, *is* the gifts of wisdom, godliness, righteousness, charity, and all active virtues. It is the ability to give the quality of justice to what one says and sees and says. It is not a flight from the outer to the inner.

Consider how this works in a treatise such as *De Trinitate*. In exploring the analogy between the human mind and the Trinity, Augustine is *not* trying to use the former as a way of conceiving the latter in order to write doctrine. Instead he is using doctrine to contemplate the perfect unity of the three persons of the Trinity in order to heal our inner fragmentation. In doing this he fully understands that he is at best presenting us with an image of the Trinity. Yet, in doing so, he believes, he is simply following Christ's own pattern. Christ, in his incarnate life and death, sets a pattern for the outer person, so that once the outer person is healed one may go inside and have an inner life. But to have an inner life—to be healed of our fragmentation—is then to overcome our alienation from God; it is the point at which understanding, will, and memory are united and work as they should.

If Weil is at all a help to recovering and rereading the tradition of Christian Platonism, it is well worth stressing that she is so because in the end she herself, in her own work, brought it to one of its highest points and focused on its key elements. She is as severe a critic of inner-self metaphysics as any postmodern metaphysician, with perhaps a sharper eye than most for the ways in which we do construct an inner self and even sharper tools for deconstructing it. She does not believe we enjoy presence fully here; that is, indeed, her descriptive task and her problem to contemplate. Her own journey from Descartes to John of the Cross is decidedly a move toward this deconstruction, and it is exemplary in this respect. But if she makes this move and voids our inner self of any comforting images, she is also an important example of what Christianity and especially Christian Platonism can say in response to other attempts at this deconstruction. For if, in, say, Derrida, all we are ever left with is virtual persons, in Weil "there is at the bottom of every human heart something that goes on expecting, from infancy to the grave, that good and not evil will be done to us, despite the experience of crimes committed, suffered, and observed. This above all else is what is sacred in every human being" (LPW 105). This "something" is not a some *thing*, however; it is the human itself. Knowing this and respecting it is the heart of wisdom. She thinks it is also at the heart of Christianity and its transformation of the human being. Time and time again, she insists that the radical *disponibilité* of attention is the very image of the Word's Incarnation and Passion, as we have seen in chapter 4. In its desire for perfect good and in self-kenosis, attention receives its form (as one can particularly see in *The Implicit Forms of the Love of God*) as well as its contemplative and moral sustenance and, finally, its completion. The seeds of this analogy of participation are in Augustine, and indeed, it is something she shares with him and the Augustinian tradition. But it is also hers to draw out consistently and explicitly in the contemporary world.

CHAPTER SIX

SPIRITUAL APPRENTICESHIP

To take Weil's inward turn, to have an inner life, is not dreamy inward gazing, nor passivity, nor even the search for a hidden true self. It is a life of transformation. To ascend from the cave is to be educated, and to be educated means more than just learning things. It is an education of desire that reorients human lives. Or, to put it in explicitly religious terms, one might think about John Calvin's idea of "effectual calling." Calvin taught that God calls men and women to a life of communion with God and our brothers and sisters. But to make that happen, God always gives to those called a way of life that would turn them into the people who would fulfill their calling. Effectual calling involves our daily lives. It often involves our jobs. It certainly involves spiritual discipline. There is in this, as Charles Taylor has noted, an affirmation of the importance of ordinary life. But as the world has become secularized and a sense of mystery lost, this affirmation has been turned into shallow notions of "following one's passion" on the way to a discovery of the true self.

Weil, of course, didn't know anything about Calvin. But like him, and the whole of Augustinian Christianity, in a way that is rare in our time, she recognized that in order to reach what we are destined for, we need transformation, a transformation that goes to the center of our being. We need an education in life. She called it, simply, an apprenticeship. In a world that thinks we are fulfilled by discovering what *we* would like to do most, that even believes we are owed an interesting life, without considering how that puts us with God and humanity, any call for us to be apprenticed to the good is a challenge. We need to come to grips with what Weil thinks spiritual apprenticeship is about.

In order to understand the issue at stake, I want to begin by briefly considering a book about education, namely *Back to the Rough Ground: Practical Judgment and the Lure of Technique,* by Irish philosopher of education Joseph Dunne. In it, Dunne provides an insightful, important study of Aristotelian *phronesis*, that is, practical wisdom. This exercise in ancient philosophy is, in the end, a critique of modern assumptions about reason. We have long labored under a concept of reason that Dunne describes as "technical rationality"; such rationality aspires to a standpoint of disinterested detachment, control, and universal explanatory power. His point, then, in examining practical judgment and technical rationality, is that elements of *phronesis*, which is personal and participatory, were never entirely absent, even in Aristotelian *technē*, although they are now absent in our understanding of *technē*. The notion of reason *we* have is a modern invention. It is challenged by Aristotle as well as various post-Enlightenment thinkers, such as John Henry Newman, Hannah Arendt, R. G. Collingwood, and Hans-Georg Gadamer. Quoting Wittgenstein, Dunne suggests that we need to recognize that reason is not a matter of walking on a frictionless surface. Indeed, walking is impossible on such a surface; rather, in order to walk—and reason—we must get back to the rough ground.[1]

Dunne is hardly the first to question the assumptions of modern rationality. But the story he tells about why he, a philosopher of education by profession, thinks they need to be challenged highlights some peculiarly troubling aspects of modern rationality. There is in modern educational theory, he notes, an assumption about the relation between teaching and learning, and, by implication, between knowledge and action, that suggests that teaching and learning can be reduced to a set of empirical objectives and a set of universal techniques for realizing them. This assumption has numerous problems. It treats educational content as an "objectified *tertium quid*" that puts no personal demands on either party in the pedagogical relationship. Moreover,

> As a form of action . . . teaching is no longer seen as embedded in particular contexts or within cultural, linguistic, religious, or political traditions which may be at work in all kinds of tacit and nuanced ways in teachers and pupils as persons. Or, rather, it is suggested that everything essential in teaching can be disembedded from such contexts and traditions, as well as from the urgencies and contingencies of the classroom, and made transparent in a neutral model which, by isolating in precise terms the goals of the activity, provides the teachers with guidelines for controlling efficiency and straightforward criteria for evaluating success. It was in reflecting on all this that the appositeness of the words of Wittgenstein which provide the title for this book first struck me: one might teach by this model on ice but hardly in the rough ground of the classroom.[2]

Finally, the logic of such an endeavor is inescapably instrumentalist, and, with respect to its "objectives," atomistic. For both teaching and learning, then, the aggregate issues of character and mind are ignored, if not dismissed out of hand. Thus, a study of *phronesis* is appropriate. *Phronesis* and the sort of personal thinking for which it stands—the push and pull of situation and thinker, for *phronesis* is learned within a "conversation"—take into account precisely these things. Its study can therefore be a valuable way back to the rough ground so that we can walk as persons with character, the quality of our minds determined by understanding and not simply content.

Dunne raises crucial issues about reason in general and especially the personal and interpersonal nature of learning. These issues are particularly important for thinking about the nature of *spiritual* learning, which, at least in theistic traditions, is personal and interpersonal. Spiritual development—the transformation of the soul into the manifest image of God—is gained in the rough ground. This is important to understand in an age where spiritual formation is very often described as something without friction. This is precisely where Weil's concern with the concept of apprenticeship needs to be thought out.

Weil makes frequent references to apprenticeship throughout her writings. She does not develop the notion per se in any careful, explicit, and detailed way, such as a focused essay. Rather, apprenticeship usually serves as a striking metaphor meant to illustrate the upshot of some other set of concerns that Weil is working through—the concept of "reading," particularly; the relation of the self to the universe and God as what underlies the concept of reading; her idea of the *metaxu*, or intermediaries. But therein lies its importance, for in its conclusive obviousness to these meditations, or in the range of conceptual possibilities to which it points, it brings home some of the larger issues at which she is driving. Apprenticeship helps to show in a very concrete way how these concerns are integrally related and especially how they come to bear on what it means, according to Weil, to learn and to know something, and to be transformed. Of course, Weil's ultimate concern when using the notion of apprenticeship is almost always spiritual, and although it is my chief concern to use apprenticeship here to say something about spiritual learning and knowing, it should be noted that the idea is more general. And, insofar as it is, it also indicates the extensiveness of spiritual learning and knowing in what initially may appear to be far more quotidian and secular forms of education and knowledge.

It will help at first to explore briefly what is involved in apprenticeship as an educational notion in general. Clarifying the metaphor should give us some larger sense of the issues Weil is pointing us to—and away from.

Apprenticeship is thoroughly an educational concept, for it involves, from beginning to end, learning a craft. It is a very distinctive way of learning, for one is trained by actually doing the art. The apprentice is fitted to the art through a continual habitual practice, first at a rudimentary level and then, by degrees, by incorporating into this practice the more complex tasks that the finished art demands. Although the notion can be easily extended to practices such as learning how to read or how to play the piano, its original home is in learning the crafts of artisans.

The training involved in an apprenticeship, especially when the crafts of artisans are kept in mind, always involves a bodily component. What is learned in an apprenticeship cannot be learned from a lecture. The craft cannot simply be told to someone or learned simply by thinking it. How to think it at all depends upon the craft first entering the body; as the body conforms its movements to the art, the mind in turn learns how to think and imagine the craft. At the end of an apprenticeship, of course, the mind can turn its attention to a problem within the craft and solve it as a technical matter. But knowing how to solve it and what it would even mean to solve it—what it even means to imagine the problem—depends first upon having been shaped by the craft through bodily action.

If, however, this sort of knowledge cannot be learned by a lecture or through just reading a book or online, then teachers and masters of the craft are not dispensable, nor, indeed, is a whole tradition of teachers and masters. To learn the craft is to embody the knowledge and relationships of the teacher, relationships that entered their bodies and were passed on by them. To lose teachers is to lose the tradition and the craft itself, even if treatises on the craft remain.[3] Working closely with a master is also important, for learning by apprenticeship is to learn by illustration. To gain the habit is to imitate until it is, well, habitual. For this reason the knowledge gained by an apprenticeship is different than the kind gained by intellectual bootstrapping. Bootstrapping is to build up knowledge by one's own efforts from the ground one already stands on. Although this kind of knowledge is often aided by a teacher, say, one who lectures, it can conceivably be gotten without a teacher. The story is told of the young Pascal that when his father took away his mathematics book, he nevertheless went on to prove the first thirty or so propositions of Euclid entirely on his own. The knowledge of apprenticeship is not gained by this sort of lonely endeavor.[4]

Yet, if a teacher or master is indispensable to an apprenticeship, it cannot quite be said that the knowledge the apprentice gains is poured into him or her by the teacher, either. Because it is the sort of knowledge in which body and mind are conformed to the craft, unless the apprentice pays attention to the craft, no amount of outside help or illustration is likely to do much. So knowledge of a craft is a personal and intimate sort of relation between the artisan and a craft. It cannot simply be a matter of impersonal or objective information; it has to be personally and subjectively appropriated. The self has to be shaped to the craft; this shaping cannot come about without the self as self-involved. Socrates, Augustine, and Wittgenstein thought that all knowledge involves a shaping of the self, and thus they also thought that nobody could actually teach anybody anything; teachers are something more like midwives. An apprenticeship is not an exercise in behaviorism, even though obedience is required.

Some of the significance of apprenticeship as an educational technique or metaphor should now start to become clear. There is good reason to think that it does not simply signal *a* way of educating, indifferently chosen among other techniques; it may well be the model for a very wide range of learning and knowing, and when it is replaced by something else, that range may be completely lost to human learning. Why this is so may be seen by looking at two important views of Wittgenstein, namely, what it means to follow a rule and the grammar of the concept of belief.

In addressing what it means to follow a rule, Wittgenstein sought to undo a bewitching picture of how language functions, particularly as a matter of naming what facts are out there. Words on this view are simply tags we lay on external objects. However, using words simply as tags, Wittgenstein recognized, does not amount to understanding. Rather, if we understand something, we know how to use the word or concept; its effectiveness depends on its use and application. These uses and applications have rules distinctive to the concept. For example, while we might pick out a car on the street and say appropriately that it is blue, it would make no sense whatsoever to say that I have a headache and that it is blue. Different concepts have different rules for use and application. Recognizing this leads us to ask what it means to follow a rule. But following a rule is not a separate rule, or separable from the doing. We could of course try to give a formula for following a rule or rules. But, as Wittgenstein argues, the rule cannot be given in a formula, for we would also have to ask about how to apply the formula itself, ad infinitum.

Wittgenstein goes on to say that knowing how to apply a rule or use a concept depends upon others being able to follow the same rule, and our following it depends upon having learned it. It depends upon a shared life-world. So, understanding depends upon a context and a community. To understand means having learned within a community to use words and concepts. Understanding is not a direct, unmediated contact between the external world and our minds. It is a functional activity, and it has a great deal to do with our bodily reactions, too.

This has direct bearing on what it means to believe something. From the time of the *Tractatus* on, Wittgenstein was concerned to get rid of the dominant idea in epistemology that belief is a relation between an object—say, a mind or a soul—and an external fact. Believing is not a process or a state of aligning one's inner mental being with an outer fact, and to talk about what it means to believe is not a matter of referring to and analyzing this relation. If one says, "I believe there is a chair in this room," one is saying no more than one would if one were to say, simply, "There is a chair in this room." "I believe" adds nothing to the assertion, and it is misguided to search out the subject of the believing to analyze the proposition. This does not mean, for Wittgenstein, that all that we do when we talk is assert external facts. It is unquestioned for him that somebody is doing the talking. But this is not a ground for the assertion. Rather, Wittgenstein thinks that in any expressed belief there are two aspects: the sayer and what is said. In order to understand what is being said, we take both into consideration. The way I talk about something, for instance, the conflict in Palestine, says something about me, even though I am only trotting out the facts. Who I am and how I talk about the facts can also be enlightening as to what the facts are. And recognition of certain kinds of facts may well require certain personal sensibilities. Both these things are part and parcel of what we say all the time. What we say is the way we have disposed ourselves to the world and the way the world is opened up to us. The relation is as much internal, if not more, as external. But it is also important to note here that our ability to understand these different aspects of what is said, and the ability to say them ourselves in the way we do say them, involves an ability to shift our attention to the different aspects, and this depends upon having certain sensibilities. These sensibilities for Wittgenstein are not innate (although they may include certain "natural" bodily reactions) but come from being shaped in certain ways ourselves through the way we have interacted with the world, especially the human world.[5]

All this highlights precisely why apprenticeship is such an important educational method. If belief is not simply an adjustment of our inner minds to hard, external facts, a mirror image in the mind of external facts, then the greater part of education *cannot* be a matter of simply presenting the facts, for knowing them is not mirroring them. It requires making certain shifts oneself. Education, then, cannot be presenting theory that one chooses to apply. Theory and application, if one even wants to talk that way, are deeply intertwined, and what we know and believe is the result of having been brought into a way of life that we share with others. What we know is always, or almost always, a matter of apprenticeship, for it is a matter of adjusting ourselves to the world through our social being. It is a matter of being taught, but it is also a matter of what we have chosen to pay attention to, of where we have made the effort to make the necessary changes in attention to be able to take in the various shifting aspects of what lies before us.

With these general remarks about apprenticeship in mind, we can now turn to Weil's use of the term, beginning with its association with the concept of reading.

In Weil's earliest notebook entries on apprenticeship she introduces the concept this way: There are, it seems, two sorts of relations between the body and the soul. One is direct, such as when I want to shift a pen. I simply do so. The other is indirect, such as when I think a melody. In order to play it, I have to use an instrument, such as a piano; my fingers have to strike the keys. Unlike the first sort of action, which is unmediated, the second requires an apprenticeship in order to be pulled off. Science, she thinks, is based on the first sort of relation and aesthetics on the second. All action mixes the two. God, she adds, is conceived under both aspects (OC 6.2, 154).

In later entries and in "Essay on Reading" (LPW 21–27), which seems to be the culmination of the work done in all the notebook entries, the phenomenon of indirect action is considered again, but with a shift in concern. Here she is concerned not so much with the direct or indirect ways of putting a desire or thought *into* action as she is with the fact that there are direct and indirect ways of seeing what is in the world. What seems to fascinate her is the phenomenon she calls "reading." At the level of direct sensation, reading is nothing more than seeing black marks on a page. Yet, at the same time, for someone who knows how to read, those marks really do seem to put one in contact with the world of meaning. They even produce sensations, including very strong ones, as if and as directly as if one was present to the thing itself. For example, a mother reading a letter reporting that her son has been killed feels directly and immediately, and without having to reflect on things or to will the sensation, a strong sense of pain. Through a medium, the world imposes something on us. It imposes something *real* on us—the mother's reaction would hardly be any different if she watched her son fall on the field of battle, and yet she has this knowledge through a medium.

The idea of this indirect/direct grasp of the world upon us, and our grasp on the world, fascinates Weil. Reading is like a blind man's stick, for, on the one hand, we can't see what it is that we are dealing with, and yet, on the other hand, we are really dealing with it and we know what it is with which we are dealing. Moreover, certain things, she thinks—for example, aesthetic matters—if they are known to us at all, are only known by this indirect means. Here reading expands its meaning for Weil and becomes a metaphor for a whole range of activities and ways of knowing, especially moral and aesthetic knowing. Although Weil frequently dismisses the imagination as the source of illusions, if it is understood in the fuller sense of reading, it can have positive connotations even for her; while it in one way misrepresents the universe, it is also the way, and often the only way, that certain aspects of the universe and certain truths can come to our attention at all.

Reading is not innate, at least beyond the level of sensation of pleasure and pain; we have to be shaped in order to read. Weil thinks we are shaped to read in two different ways. One way is force. Our imagination, the way we read the universe, is often the result of force, natural and otherwise. At the simplest level, this may be a result of quite normal sensations, the impress of the world upon us as biological beings. But contingent social forces that function at the same time can also cause us to read the world in more complex ways. For example, whether we see the universe as a happy or a bitter place depends on what force has done to us. If the Romans see in a foreign king led in chains in a victory procession the ubiquity of Roman might and the smiling of Providence on Aeneas's descendants, the losers see something quite different.

War, Weil thinks, is particularly effective in imposing a certain sort of reading on us.

The other way by which we can come to read is education, but most particularly by an education that is an apprenticeship. We do not learn to read in the way Weil finds interesting by simply being told about other ways of looking at things. Some kind of force or physical adjustment is still needed to introduce some level of reality. She observes, "Use of force to check a dream, not to impose another one on top of it" (NB 40). To read as Weil thinks we should demands an apprenticeship; it is a learning, by a bodily adjustment, to displace direct, sensational bodily contact with the world with an indirect one. It *is* at its roots like a blind man's stick. Or, perhaps better put, it is to put aside the readings imposed on us by direct bodily contact alone, by force alone, and to expand our vision. But we can't simply *choose* to read in a certain way; reading in Weil's sense is more than just a "way of looking at things." We have to adapt ourselves to an instrument to change how and what we read. Rather than reading the world through the direct relationship between the mind and the organs of perception, a reading that is forever subject to being dominated by brute force, we replace the original organ of perception with something like the blind man's stick. *It* becomes the organ of perception, and new readings become possible. The physical world is not forgotten; it is read differently, though. "We do not choose our sensations. But we do choose (subject to an apprenticeship) what we feel through their medium" (NB 22).

For this to happen, she claims, an apprenticeship is necessary, an apprenticeship that fits us to the use of some tool other than our own bodies for sensing the world. "To change the physical relationship between oneself and the world (is 'physical' the right word?), in the same way as, through apprenticeship, the workman changes the physical relationship between himself and the tool. . . . The relationship between the body and the tool changes during apprenticeship. We must change the relationship between our body and the world" (NB 21). Thus an apprenticeship in reading changes the relation between the mind and the body that senses the world, transferring it to something that is not our body—a stick, the piano keys, the words on a page. That is the only way,

Weil thinks, that we can change the readings that brute force imposes upon us, and by which we can move beyond the hedonism that purely bodily sensations immerse us in. Ultimately, Weil thinks we are to make the universe itself our body and to sense the world through the world.

We are getting closer to the nature of spiritual apprenticeship.
If an apprenticeship has a negative function of suppressing fantasy, its chief function is nevertheless the positive one of acting as a lever to higher readings. Specifically, Weil has in mind that, subject to an apprenticeship, we can move first from the level of pure sensation to reading the world as necessity—the "mathematical ensemble of the laws of variation"—and finally to reading necessity itself as obedient to the good, wherein we read our obligations to the world and those around us. This last reading is what it means to make the universe our body. At the level of sensation we read the world as only pleasure and pain, which is also to say *our* pleasure and pain. This is an utterly egocentric world. This is also a reading susceptible to the way external forces help or hinder us at the level of sensation. By an apprenticeship to mathematics and letters, we learn to read the world as necessity in this way and not simply as brute force.[6] But to make the universe our body is to read it as obedient to God, for just as our bodies obey our wishes directly, so, too, do we now feel what happens as an obedient mechanism. What happens in it—its beauty, the suffering of others—we feel as our own and as what God has willed. We simply have a particular perspective on it. What we do experience, what we do read, is through this medium. As such, we then read others as also having a particular perspective on the same whole. To make the whole of the world our body is to consent to its existence and to consent, and even wish for, all perspectives under which it is viewed. As Weil notes in *The Need for Roots*, "It is one and the same thing, which with respect to God is eternal Wisdom; with respect to the universe, perfect obedience; with respect to our love, beauty; with respect to our flesh, brute force" (NR 295).

But how does one learn to read like this? What sort of apprenticeship is it that can do this? It is, in the first place, an apprenticeship in suffering, both the suffering inherent in accepting as one's body the same world that hurts one's particular body and the suffering of giving up a perspective. Herein Weil thinks lies the value of work, for work can change our relation to the universe in both these ways.

Suffering by itself is not ennobling, nor does it automatically cause us to learn. What is crucial to learning through an apprenticeship is *attention*. She argues, "The development of the attention ought to be the sole object of education. The same in the case of apprenticeship" (NB 251). One does not learn to read the world through the end of a stick until one has put one's soul into the stick, as it were. One similarly does not read the world as obedience simply by having it press down on you very hard. One also has to love. It is at that point that a transference takes place from attention to the sensations of pain and pleasure to attention to the world as a whole. Still, our love and desire is not real, until it is incarnated. So,

> Love of God is pure when joy and suffering *equally* inspire gratitude. The handshake of a friend on meeting after a long absence. I do not even notice whether it gives pleasure or pain to my sense of touch; just as a blind man feels objects directly at the end of his stick, so I feel the presence of my friend directly. The same applies to life's circumstances, whatever they may be, and God. This implies that we must never seek consolation for pain. For felicity is beyond the realm of consolation and pain, outside it. We apprehend it through a sense of another kind, just as the perception of objects at the end of a stick or an instrument is of another kind to that of touch in the strict sense of the word. This other sense is formed by a shifting of the attention through an apprenticeship in which the entire soul and body participate. (NB 236)[7]

Through this process in which the attention is developed, the experience of suffering changes; through it Aeschylus's phrase *tō pathō mathos*—"through suffering comes learning"—has meaning. At the level of sensation, pain and suffering are evil because they thwart us. We take things personally. At the level of necessity we do not see our individual wants and desires as being at the center of the world. We take things impersonally. At the level of obedience and obligation, we see whatever comes to us as somehow playing a role in the whole, a whole that is good. We see each particular and the whole itself as gifts of goodness, and we touch the giver through them. We love the world and do not want to change "my place, my importance in the world, limited by my body and by the existence of other souls, my equals" (NB 38). Here are "time and space sinking into the sensibility" (NB 222). At this point, having associated our own self with the good of the universe,[8] we read our obligations to the world and to others as naturally and as directly as we feel hunger when our stomachs are empty. One could, of course, still say that we take what happens personally; clearly the sense of who I am as a person has changed, though.

But this development of the attention is then precisely the point of apprenticeship, of genuine learning. To learn in this way is to develop the attention, to teach it to be "detached, available (*disponible*), and ready to be penetrated by the object" (WG 111). This is the only way to know certain truths. But knowledge in this sense is not simply knowledge of what is the case; it also involves self-knowledge at the deepest level, for it is a formation of the self. To know is not simply to *reflect* the external world, to establish a relation between the internal mind and an external fact; it is to have developed as personal capacities the abilities to feel what is going on in the world and respond to it as directly as one's hand obeys the wish to lift it or withdraws from something that is hot. It is the ability to shift appropriately and concretely to the world as it is. But it is also an ability that we possess only by having shifted our relation to the world.

This gives a rather fast-paced sketch of Weil's thinking about the nature of learning by apprenticeship. Its value is chiefly in a sense of where Weil wants to go with the notion of reading, as well as a broad sense of how one gets there and even what it means to get there or be there. But, left in broad outline like this, while surely a heady thing, it is also surely *too* heady; there is something *too* broad about it. For example, there is a legitimate insight and a matter of genuine philosophical interest in the concept of reading. It is interesting to think about the indirect way we grasp the world and how symbols (for such are our aesthetic and moral sticks) are not simply fancy ways of talking about the world, but essential to knowing certain truths about it. It is also interesting to think about how we learn to read, and Weil certainly makes a contribution here. We learn through a combination of bodily practice and personal attention to and association with practices. Like Wittgenstein, Weil clearly recognizes that knowing is not a flawless mirror of hard external facts and that learning and knowing are a matter of internal shifting to accommodate oneself to what is being talked about. But once she starts extending this to the point of talking about making the universe itself one's body, she also seems to have left the legitimate bounds of concepts such as apprenticeship and what it means to learn concepts by an apprenticeship. Whereas, for example, Wittgenstein sees a very human context for this—it is ensconced within the biological, social, and cultural realms of humanity, and as such depends upon a teacher—Weil seems eager to escape that realm. In many of the examples she uses of an apprenticeship, at least in her earliest examples in the notebooks, she seems to avoid this interpersonal element. Her examples of apprenticeship are all natural: pain, suffering, beauty. Even labor is chiefly talked about as a relation between a person and the natural world. The context for learning how to use a tool is largely missing. So, particularly when she talks about making the universe my body, she seems to have stepped outside the realm of symbol and interpersonal dealings. She seems to have forgotten all the intermediaries.

But she has not forgotten all the intermediaries. She warns, quoting Plato, that one dare not forget them. In order then to make some fuller sense of what she is thinking about, we need to look briefly at her theory of the *metaxu,* the intermediaries.[9] For while the goal of learning is making the universe one's body, much as on the Cross it became Christ's body insofar as he accepted the full force of necessity as the Father's will and loved it, that is the *telos,* not the process—although the two are related. It is in the realm of the *metaxu* that all this takes place. Or, because the *metaxu* are the way of getting to this goal, what it means to reach it is linked to the nature of the *metaxu* themselves, since it can only be reached by an apprenticeship.

As Weil describes them, the *metaxu* are bridges to and from transcendence, the mediators between God and us that lead us to God. They are inscribed by God in the nature of the universe itself so that we might reach our spiritual destiny. How are we to understand this? One way, of course, would be to regard the *metaxu* as symbols, or metaphors to the degree that metaphors, in the root sense of the word *metaphor* ("to transfer"), are ways that meaning is carried across from one thing to another. But what exactly does this transference amount to?

In Weil's initial discussion of the *metaxu* (NB 20), they are introduced within the context of a broader discussion of the notion of reading and are loosely associated within that context with education and apprenticeship. They are, in fact, that which apprentices us. As such, they are not things to be read, which is very often the way that we mistakenly take symbols. Rather, they are either that *by which* we read or which *teach* us to read. They apprentice us. They are not what is to be contemplated; *through* them, Weil thinks, we can pay attention to what is not at all apparent. Thus, faith, for example, she calls a "gift of reading." Faith sees the world as God's; it does not just see it as if it were God's. The *metaxu* are more like concepts and less the object of concepts. So, while we have to pay attention in order to learn, it isn't to the *metaxu*, the symbols or metaphors, that we pay attention, but to the world through them. They are, as in the case of pain and death, things that wrench (NB 22). Or, in the case of work, which is for Weil a prime example of a *metaxu*, work has the effect it does not because we *think* about work itself, but because in working we change our relation to the physical universe. This is surely the difference between the son who tells his father he will go out and do the job, but doesn't, and the son who says he won't, but ultimately does. To be sure, we can talk *about* any *metaxu* as an object, but whether or not our talk is true depends upon being able to use it, which is to say how through it we grasp something of the world. Work is a concept that we know somebody has when we see them working, not because we see them voting for the Left (a point Weil thought many intellectuals were confused about).

Weil does have a tendency to lay her case heavily on natural examples. There are reasons for this. She is after the sort of readings she thinks give us access to real moral, spiritual, and aesthetic aspects of the world, readings we could not have unless we made real and not fantastic contact with the world. She does think there is a truth and that the glimmerings we have of it in our limited intuitions are real. She says that the *metaxu* can't be invented; they have to be found inscribed in the nature of things. It is only by opening ourselves up to the world, by apprenticing ourselves to it, painful as that may be, that we will see the world as it is. It is also the only way she thinks that we will ever escape the fantasy in which fatuous modern symbol-making immerses us. She is also suspicious of the social world, particularly in her early and middle writings. A fondness for Rousseau causes a lot of suspicion about what we are handed socially. But, in the end, she does believe that the personal, social, and cultural world of humanity is where and how we learn meaning.

Even the social can serve as a *metaxu*, a defining idea of her last works in social and political philosophy. Especially in those works, cities, cultures, and human institutions serve to train the attention. Indeed, as she says in one fragment from the London period, "Culture is the formation of attention" (SWW 119). But in this case, culture is not that formation of attention by our contemplation of how cultured we are or might be; it is the habits of being instilled in us by our very human interactions that are important. Even if our obligations are permanent and belong to another realm, obligations are themselves a way of reading the world, and we come to recognize them only through an apprenticeship of seeking the permission of others in very concrete contexts. We don't first see our transcendent obligations as if they were a theory of human morality and then seek appropriate application. We learn the transcendent nature of our obligations, our moral identity with other beings of a spiritual nature, through the particular practices of actually respecting them. The degree to which cultures shape us and focus our attention in these ways is the degree to which the culture acts as a *metaxu*. To be cultured morally is not to have a theory, but to read automatically, and immediately, the needs of others. Before the world is our body, our culture is our body. Our spiritual apprenticeship very much depends upon the human teachers who form the sensibilities we need to read the values that are part of the warp and woof of the world.

It will be helpful to give an illustration of the sort of process that Weil seems to have in mind. It does not fit all the above points exactly but is nevertheless helpful.

In the essay "The Theory of the Sacraments," Weil points out that human "nature is so arranged that a desire of the soul, unless it passes through the flesh by means of actions, movements, and the postures that naturally correspond to it, hasn't any reality for the soul" (SWW 100). Without the body being involved, such desires are mere phantoms. This presents a problem, Weil thinks. On the one hand, by an exercise of the will we can discipline ourselves so that we don't fall into evil. On the other hand, we can't increase the amount of the good in the soul because our self-imposed discipline rises no higher than our present understanding of goodness. So, to be made better we have to *receive* the good. But herein lies another problem. We need to desire the perfect good, but that by definition exceeds the nature of the "things here below" with which the body deals.

Nevertheless, Weil continues, if something is indispensable for salvation, while it may seem naturally impossible, "it is certain that there really exists a supernatural possibility" (SWW 100). God will provide such a possibility. In religious practices, this is in the sacraments where God, by covenant, makes a piece of bread signify the person of Christ. Through the sacrament, then, by bodily partaking of it, our souls can receive God's real presence, God's perfect goodness.

To our point is how Weil thinks this comes about. There are two conditions (beyond actually approaching and partaking). First, we have to desire nothing but "the unique, pure, perfect, total, absolute good which is inconceivable for us" (SWW 102). Second, we have to believe "in a certain identity between the piece of bread and God" (SWW 103), a belief that is not intellectual, but imaginative, involving both our sensibility and flesh.

But why is this effective? It sounds like auto-suggestion. First, as Weil incisively observes, any desire for the good is itself a good. We are better if we desire good than if we don't. But such a desire is a mere phantom in the soul unless we act on it. So, if we approach God's presence in the sacrament with the desire for pure good, by really approaching, and not just dreaming about it, we have incarnated that desire. We have made good a reality in our lives.

The argument is perhaps not entirely convincing at first. Weil goes on to suggest how we are made better by this, although she largely does so in a negative way. A man who sees the goodness of being brave in battle is dealing in fantasy if he never joins the army. But if he does join, he will become brave by any number of small steps, marching toward battle and actually facing death, and the soul will have to overcome very real and indeed sensible fear. When it does overcome that fear, it really is brave. Similarly, to approach the sacrament with a desire for good and a belief that the perfect good is here is to deal with the fear of one's own mediocrity. To still approach with the belief that good is better than mediocrity is to overcome, at least in small steps, our mediocrity, to be dissatisfied with it. It is to be made better.

Weil largely develops her case by talking about the burning away of evil and mediocrity. She has her own reasons for doing so, particularly since on her account the good that we are finally to see cannot be seen until all limited goods have been erased from our imaginations. We need to pay attention, however, to the positive points about the sacraments as a *metaxu* and what light they shed on the nature of the *metaxu* in general. The sacraments function as *metaxu* by their ability to apprentice us, that is to say, by changing us and by changing our ability to read the world. They develop certain sensibilities in us and abilities to shift our attention. If the sacrament is a symbol, the sacrament's effectiveness as such is not in *pointing* to a higher realm or providing a merely intellectual key to understanding the world, but rather in effectively first focusing *our* attention and then giving us the opportunity to incarnate the good and let it shape us. It does this through our approaching it bodily and thereby changing the nature of our participation in the world.[10] Because of the way a sacrament apprentices us, *we* read and grasp the world differently, knowing a truth about it that we would not be able to know otherwise. But that truth is not just about the world; it involves the thinker in the world in a deeply personal way. The love of the beauty of the world, love of neighbor, and friendship for Weil are similarly *metaxu* because they cause us to read the world differently. They are not supernatural objects embedded like diamonds in a mine in the natural world, a world otherwise of mud; they are the means of the world itself and the means of God's own covenanted grace, by which we can come to see what truth is in the world. Just as two prisoners can communicate through the wall that separates them, so spirit speaks to spirit through the natural order, for the natural order welcomes the supernatural and is filled by it.

Augustine once complained of students who, when he pointed to the stars, looked at his finger instead. In much of our thinking about symbols and in our religious use of them we have been like his students. But if Weil is right, symbols have their use in being like letters on a page. They are that by which we read the universe, and without them we miss what is really important about the universe. To read them as marks on the page misses the point.

So, what, then, does this finally say about the nature of spiritual learning? Let us take the question from the nature of the supernatural. The supernatural is not an object, even an object of contemplation, at least not at first. Its nature as we know it lies in the transformation of our knowing. It is a transforming presence, but presence also by absence. This does not mean that it can never be something that we contemplate. Newman suggested that our knowledge of God comes through conscience; our knowledge of God is a sense of the personal demand of the good upon us. Conscience is played out in actual moral choices as we identify with them. Their exercise is what allows us to see the good that plays upon our conscience more and more clearly. In time, as that is developed, we may well come to see the face behind the demand, a face that he thought paganism kept trying to invent and Christianity found revealed. But seeing the face only comes through the development of conscience itself. As the psalmist said, "In your light do we see light" (36:9).

If that is the nature of the supernatural itself—to engage and to transform—then the way that we learn the supernatural *cannot* be anything but an apprenticeship, a transformation of our reading habits, and a matter of a certain kind of self-knowledge—one where we identify our very selves with Christ's body and the body of the world, not solely with the sensations of our own bodies. To read the higher truths about the world, no part of the world can be foreign to us. Spiritual learning is done in the rough ground, increasing our participation in the world.

CHAPTER SEVEN

A SACRAMENTAL UNDERSTANDING OF THE WORLD

What kind of world is it that allows, supports, and even demands human action in such a way that the supernatural penetrates human life? If, as Sartre thought, we are purpose-seeking beings in a world that is itself purposeless, then we are "accidents vomited up by nature." Our goals—our transformation—are then up to us, and we should not expect the world to cooperate or even to suggest goals. Or, if the world is by nature flat and nothing is expected of us, even by us, then perhaps we need to tailor our aspirations. But if there is something about the world that lets something higher and deeper into human life, then some account of what that means needs to be given.

Giving such an account is not a matter of providing an undergirding metaphysics. It is not a matter of building a case for commitment out of uncommitment and neutral facts. It is to give an account of how we are pressed to make a response that can be lived—that should be lived—to a world that has mystery and depth.

In a post-metaphysical intellectual environment, we have become skeptical about a lot of claims that metaphysics used to make about God and the world. "God" and "the World" are human constructs, it is said, and the most that we can do is to set ourselves to do the best job we can in the construct. But to approach things this way is really to get the wrong end of the stick. Yes, we do construct reality. But there is more to thinking and the life of the spirit than that, or just recognizing and unmasking it. As the late American philosopher Hilary Putnam, in a confessional moment, put it, "Values may be created by human beings and cultures, but I see them as made in response to demands that we do not create. It is reality that determines whether our responses are adequate or not."[1]

The world that we necessarily deal with in our learning needs to be talked about in this vein. How are the spiritual demands we feel pressed upon us related to larger reality? How does light shine in the darkness? What kind of logos is there that permeates the world—the human world, the natural world, and the world of exchange between God and humanity? Which is to say, what kind of coherence is there to these worlds that we live in? Is there any ultimate cohering connection between the way of sorrow and the way of joy, the way of faith, the way of knowledge, the way of beauty? In short, in a world of gravity, does grace penetrate and have the final say? To see this is also to allow a connection between the spiritual concerns that Weil raises and her social and political ones, which we will treat in the next section.

A helpful way of framing the account Weil gives and its significance is first to look at one of the most important chapters in twentieth-century theology. This is the story of the attempt to break down the supposedly impermeable barrier between the world of nature and the world of grace, a barrier that had been assumed since the dawning of the modern period in the sixteenth century. This task was exemplified in the work of Henri de Lubac, who aggressively challenged the idea that there was anything like "pure nature" that could be considered apart from the "supernatural" and with its own distinct ends for humanity. De Lubac fully understood where the concept had come from; by stressing the notion of a pure nature, modern theology sought to protect the gratuity of the supernatural.[2] The intent was laudable enough. However, the concept of a pure nature tended to divorce natural life from a supernatural end, an end given to humanity in its very creation, or so earlier thinkers such as Aquinas and Augustine had taught. The newer concept of pure nature, however, gave human beings a natural end *and* a supernatural one. Rather than strengthening the concept of grace, though, it undermined it. The idea of pure nature tended to make the divine superfluous while strengthening the natural and making it autonomous. The supernatural appeared as an add-on to the natural and even a sort of continuation of it. The supernatural thus became domesticated and naturalized, a mere adjectival quality laid on basic nature; basic nature became the measuring rod for most everything. So, de Lubac argued, safeguarding the gratuitousness of the supernatural actually led to secularism. Others have since argued that the formation of the concept of a pure nature also constituted an important moment in establishing the imperialism of modern science on, ironically, theological grounds.[3]

Through several critical studies of the ancient fathers, especially Augustine, de Lubac sought to show that such a strong division between the natural and supernatural did not exist for early Christianity, nor was it to be found in the ancient Greeks; it does not appear in the Eastern church and appears only late in Western theology. For the ancients, creation was made for a supernatural end. God made humanity for himself, and creation and history were to bring humanity back into God's life. Thus, while the supernatural *is* a free gift, de Lubac wanted to insist that creation always bears in its deepest parts a relation to the God who is its alpha and omega. Similar efforts that were deeply appreciative of de Lubac's work were later made by Hans Urs von Balthasar, whose development of a theological aesthetic saw the world as an interplay "of manifestation and concealment" wherein "the radiance of God's glory penetrate[s] the darkness of the world."[4] For Balthasar, the created world is a sort of sacrament because it reveals God, although it is other than God. Life lived in the created world is never separate or distinct from life in God.

Having a sense of this project can help one understand Weil's thinking, especially concepts such as necessity, reading, and her inventive notion of the *metaxu*, which all converge in her profoundly illuminating and challenging essay "The Implicit Forms of the Love of God" (WG 137–215). This essay gives an account of how grace penetrates the world of nature, of human affairs, and of how there can be an exchange between God and human beings. Weil died before the publication of de Lubac's and Balthasar's most important works and so, obviously, what she says is not the result of their influence. Yet, what she wrote not only parallels what these thinkers were doing—and at an early date—but also adds an important dimension to the question of why it is important to reject the notion of pure nature and to see at least an integral relation between receiving nature and donated grace. As we have already noted, Weil was not in the strict sense a theologian; she was a philosopher with deep religious sensibilities and experience, with a decidedly theological and Christological center to her later work, as we have seen in chapter 3. As such, I suggest that her contribution consists in giving some sense of the deep epistemological dimensions of what it means to say that there is no pure nature and that human life is created for fellowship with God. To put it in the strongest terms, Weil shows us what it means to think through the idea that something(s) in natural life can be regarded as a sacrament(s), and how that affects how we see natural life and its relation to life in God. It means, for example, that in looking at nature, we are forced to recognize a dimension of depth to it and that it is surrounded and enveloped in the divine mystery. Ultimately, of course, viewing the world this way has a great effect in areas beyond theology or philosophy, as it makes a great difference to how we think about ethics and social and political philosophy, as well as how science and technology are related to those fields, topics Weil herself took up in her last writings.

In "The Implicit Forms of the Love of God," Weil describes three forms of love that she says are implicit loves of God (she considers a possible fourth, friendship, at the end of the essay). What she means by "implicit" is that in some distinctive sense, God is really present in these loves, although God is present only secretly. God's hiddenness lies in the fact that in these loves, the soul that loves does not see God directly. It is not yet ready to see and love God directly and without the mediation of its natural milieu. As implicit loves, these loves are, she says, preparatory to a full, direct, and explicit love of God, where finally God as God is known and loved by the soul and is no longer loved through a natural form. Yet, Weil goes on to stress, these preparatory loves "do not disappear when the love of God in the full sense of the word wells up in the soul; they become infinitely stronger and all loves taken together make only a single love" (WG 138). Significantly, she adds that because these loves are preparatory, and because God is present but veiled, "each of the forms that such love may take has the virtue of a sacrament" (WG 138), which is to say, they are given by God to draw the soul into God's life.

The three loves that Weil considers as sacramental in this way are the love of neighbor, the love of the beauty of the world, and the love of religious practices. As a group, they represent the ways that we may, by love, be related to all that is, as they involve our relations to 1) other human beings; 2) the created, natural world as a whole; and 3) God as known to us under the form of religion. As Weil discusses them, each of these implicit loves is already at a very high spiritual level. They are not simply the penultimate steps of a smooth continuity between other forms of love that we might bear to others or to the world and the beatific vision. Rather, there is already something different about them, something that the purely natural cannot give. The difference between these loves and any others is not one simply of intensity, but of quality. Or, in sacramental terms, the difference is that each of these loves, as a real but veiled form of the love of God, constitutes something like a transignification or even transubstantiation of our other forms of love, even as the explicit love of God ultimately transforms the implicit loves themselves. God's presence, and the need to talk about these loves in some sense as "supernatural," constitutes for Weil a real difference between them and others forms of love. This difference is precisely what the permeation of the natural by the supernatural amounts to.

What exactly, then, is that difference? What marks are there that allow us to say that God is somehow secretly but distinctively present in these forms of love? What makes them *sacramental*? The answer comes in two parts.

In the first, for Weil, in each and every one of these loves, the form of the love is patterned on God's self-emptying sacrifice for the life of others in the Cross of Christ. This kenosis is the mark of the divine for Weil, and it constitutes a pattern that she consistently and *insistently* uses to discern the divine. It is not simply a sign or a pointer, however; it is the life of the divine within one. It is a matter of participation in the divine life. For example, in speaking of the love of neighbor, which she sees exemplified in Christ's thanking those who gave meat to the hungry and thus to Christ himself, she says simply, "How can one give meat to Christ, if one is not raised at least for a moment to the state spoken of by Saint Paul, when he no longer lives in himself but Christ lives in him?" (WG 139).

This divine kenosis that makes each of the implicit loves a form of the love of God can easily be seen in each one as Weil describes it. With respect to the love of neighbor, Weil intends a love that is directed not to our friends but to those who are distinctively *other*. Most specifically it is directed to those who are afflicted, who have no power or ability to make us deal with them and who have nothing to offer us. Real love toward them is thus never motivated by strictly natural factors. As Weil points out, whenever human beings have to settle something and neither is in a position to dominate the other, they have to come to an understanding, and "justice is consulted, for justice alone has the power to make two wills coincide" (WG 142). However, when dealing with the afflicted, that is, those who have no power to command and who are moved around at will by others, there is no need to consult such justice. To accomplish what we want, we need not obtain the consent of the afflicted nor do we even have to consult them. The afflicted are invisible to those with power. When someone actually pays attention to them, even though nothing makes one do so, and when one treats them as equals, there is, Weil thinks, something more than nature operating. She asserts, "The supernatural virtue of justice consists of behaving exactly as though there were equality when one is the stronger in an unequal relationship" (WG 143). She adds, "It is not surprising that a man who has bread should give a piece to someone who is starving. What is surprising is that he should be capable of doing so with so different a gesture from that with which we buy an object" (WG 147).

This sort of attention is even creative, for where there was in the afflicted no person left inside a breathing body, this willingness to treat the afflicted as an equal gives that person the possibility of entering into the human world of give and take and mutual consent once again. Thus, just as God created the world out of nothing—and Weil thinks God did this by an act of renouncing being everything so that beings might live—the love of neighbor can bring a person into life from being nothing. This creative act of paying attention is divine in Weil's eyes because it bears the marks of bringing something out of nothing, marks that were established in the beginning of the world and in the Cross. God renounced the right to command, and a world began. Christ renounced his divinity and gave life to the afflicted. If one makes a similar sacrifice for others, one can bring life to them. From this true life is gained, both for us and for our neighbors, as we participate in the love of God himself.

As an implicit form of the love of God, the love of neighbor is essentially a way of sacrifice and suffering. It involves accepting as one's own the suffering and affliction of others in all their pain, distress, and destroyed aspirations. It seeks not redemption for the self but only the redemption of others. It accepts their hopelessness, and yet it is, in the end, God's own life in the one who loves like this.

The second form of the implicit love of God is not a way of sorrow at all. Appreciating the beauty of the natural world is a way of joy and growth. Yet, it, too, involves a sacrifice. When we love the beauty of the world for itself and not for the pleasure it gives us, although this love is a source of joy, we only love this way, she says, because we are able to sacrifice the perspective that tells us that we are at the center of the universe. We, of course, do not rule over the universe in the same way that we might rule over one who is afflicted, and so we do not renounce any real power in this sort of love. But we do tend to act and think most of the time as if the universe ought to provide especially for us. We don't love the beauty of the world as a whole and as it was created; we love it for the pleasure it gives us. We find beautiful what aids us and ugly what thwarts us. The beauty we normally see is nothing more than our pleasure and pain. To give up our narrow perspective and see and accept the world as it is, beyond pleasure and pain, and to find it beautiful in itself, is actually very hard to do. It certainly involves a sacrifice; it requires an important elevation. Just as the one who truly loves a neighbor by setting aside self-interest is morally elevated by self-emptying, so one elevates one's perspective here by setting aside self-advantage, even though this does bring joy.

Weil contends that if this sacrifice is made, while in one sense it is not creative insofar as it doesn't bring into existence a world that didn't exist before, still, it allows a world whose existence we formerly refused to acknowledge to have a place in our souls, a place where we had not let it exist before. Ultimately, Weil thinks, this is not an abstract move on anyone's part, as it means accepting and loving a world that, while beautiful, is capable of destroying us. It can be creative, also, since reading the world this way inspires the best art and science.

The third form of the implicit love of God is the love of religious practices. While the name of "God" is explicitly brought into play in this love, Weil still calls it an implicit love because "it does not involve direct immediate contact with God" (WG 181). As in the other forms of implicit love, God here is present as mediated in a form of life that is still inside this world. But God is really present, and the mark of God's presence is again in the elevation of the natural.

Weil says that the "whole virtue of religious practices" can be conceived from the Buddhist tradition of the constant recitation of the name of God. However, what she has in mind is seen not only in the Buddhist practice of calling upon the name of God but also in the very way that she describes the Christian sacrament of the Eucharist. We will therefore treat both.

The virtue of the practice of calling on the name of the Lord is found, for Weil, in what she describes as attention. Elsewhere, she calls attention the heart of prayer. It, like the other forms of the love of God, involves a sacrifice of perspective and a renunciation of straightforward power. Why? Because attention consists in emptying the controlled content of our thought and making our minds available to the other. It suspends the outward projections of the ego; it leaves one open to be permeated by and available to the reality of another. Attention of this sort is the kind of self-emptying Weil has in mind when talking about both the love of neighbor and the love of the beauty of the world. In the case of religion it also carries the sense of being a response to being addressed.

Weil talks about religion, including the Christian sacraments, as a matter of *convention*, a word that, translated as an English cognate, carries misleading connotations of nominalism and the arbitrary. What clearly is in her mind, though, is something far more like what we would call in English an agreement (e.g., the Geneva Conventions) or even, as is biblically appropriate, a covenant. Why would we think this is what she means? Because, Weil contends, while the name of God is not written in nature, and therefore, when using the name "God," we are not reading it from nature, in this "conventional" name God has nevertheless revealed himself. God has given us a name for us to call God.[5] To pay attention to the name, to trust its elevating power, gives faith as Augustine described it, consisting of three things: believing that there is a God; believing God (taking God at God's word); and doing so because one believes in God, that is, because one trusts and loves God. Weil's sense of calling on the name of the Lord is paying attention to the name by which God mediates himself to human beings; it is believing that the name, which is *given* and not discovered, has the power of God. And that, ultimately, is as Augustine would have it, trusting and loving the God who revealed it in human language.

There is already a sacramental sense in this notion of calling on the name of the Lord; the name conveys both presence and veiledness. But what is most important in talking about a sacramental sense here is seen even more clearly in the way that Weil goes on to talk about the Christian sacraments. In "Theory of the Sacraments," written not long after "Implicit Forms," Weil spells out several ideas that are only hinted at in the earlier essay. She argues that in the sacraments proper there is above all a covenant (*convention*) involved—God has instituted the sacrament and commanded its commemoration, and humans are to respond to the institution—with the promise that God will be found in this sacrament. While certainly a key to the sacrament's virtue is in our attention paid to it, it is also quite clear for Weil that our attention *receives* the goodness promised and does not confer it. The grace of the covenant changes what we partake of; as she makes clear, the divine institution is a "divine signifying that supervenes over nature" (SWW 101). The institution results in a transignification of the bread and wine. To the one who pays attention to what God has given, namely, his presence, the bread and the wine, natural in every other part, have, because of God's promised presence, ultimately the capacity of being transformed themselves and of being transforming for the one who has faith. Nothing here is changed by credulity, nor can it be changed this way, even by well-meaning credulity. "The good only comes to us from outside, but it penetrates us only as the good to which we consent. . . . A bit of matter hasn't the power to transform us. But if we believe that it has that ability by God's willing it so, and that for this reason we should eat it, we really accomplish an act of welcome towards the wished-for transformation, and by this fact transformation descends upon the soul from the heights of heaven" (SWW 102).

So, what constitutes an implicit form of the love of God for Weil is the secret presence of God veiled in the natural. There is little ambiguity about what makes this veiled presence a matter of *God's* presence. At the heart of each and every love lies the divine kenosis that was revealed in Christ's cross. Throughout her writings, Weil uses this kenosis in an analogous way to cover what is involved in the intersection of nature and supernature and in the permeation of the natural by the supernatural. What exactly does this mean for Weil?

Let us recall here Weil's talk about the *metaxu*, which we heard in chapter 6. The term—Greek for "in between"—signals a claim that grace permeates the created world and thereby makes the created world something that does not stand *against* the supernatural world but can be enfolded into it, and that indeed hints at and promises the supernatural from which it comes. What we know of the supernatural is for the most part always as it is present, but also hidden in the natural. This also means that the natural is never just natural. At the heart of the world, our world, is a divine mystery, and also a way to the divine.

Weil says that the *metaxu* are "bridges" to and from God. In a helpful analogy, she suggests that they play a role similar to that of a geometric mean, for they put into relation things that are otherwise incommensurate. She was so struck by this analogy, in fact, that she claimed that, for the ancient Greeks, geometry itself played a religious role; it was itself a sort of *metaxu* because it was not just about numbers, but also a search for divine mediation. It both symbolized the relation between the fullness of God and the emptiness of human life and was itself, as a practice, a way by which one crossed from human emptiness to divine fullness.

For Weil, all sorts of things serve as *metaxu*: human cities, human loves, the beauty of individual things, the beauty of the world, and the science and art inspired by that beauty. She thought good thinking would show just how we are surrounded by these things that can elevate us. She suggests, "We should turn everything into an intermediary leading toward God (everything—occupations, events, public functions, etc.). This does not mean adding God on to everything (it is then the imaginary form of God). But each thing must be wrought upon to bring about a change so it may be made apparent to the light" (NB 328). The Greeks thought this way, she believed; but we have forgotten how to do this and have instead taken these bridges to be dwelling places, forgetting that they are meant to carry us beyond and to change our level of love and understanding. So technology, for example, is no longer the sort of science that increases love of the beauty of the world, but rather something that fixes our gaze only on the immediately useful.

The *metaxu* are present as a matter of grace and cannot be, nor need to be, invented. They are signs that God wants us to love him and to draw us into God's life since, although God may be hidden to human eyes, what is evident to us has the ability to draw us upward. That is by divine design. "Thanks to God's wisdom, who has printed on this world the mark of the good, in the form of beauty, one can love the Good through the things of this world.... Dense matter is attentive to God's persuasion.... Through love, matter receives the imprint of the divine Wisdom and becomes beautiful" (FLN 139).

But what makes something a *metaxu,* a thing that acts as a lever to elevate us, is not simply its use as a sign or a pointer to what is "beyond," any more than a sacrament is simply a sign or pointer. Its primary purpose is not to point away from itself. Nor does it operate *on* us, *ex opere operato.* Rather, it elevates us and lets us move ahead by awakening desire and love. More accurately, it awakens a new way of desiring and loving. It helps transform us by transforming the ways we think and will. In good part, this transformation, as we can see in the implicit loves, is a transformation of the way that we think about and act toward the object. We come to see in it what we had not read in it before. We see that there is more to matter, and to our neighbor, than we had ever previously imagined.

Understanding the effectiveness of a *metaxu* cannot be done by trying to grasp a pure objective nature that exists outside its relation to us, open to a neutral observer's sight, any more than one can grasp a sacrament's effectiveness without understanding its relation to the one who participates in it or to that one's faith. No *metaxu* simply operates on us as an external object; it is to be engaged, for intermediaries apprentice us. They train us in a way of being and in a way of reading, moving us from an older, clumsier, and inadequate way of life and reading to one that is more elevated. This even includes how we come to see any given *metaxu* itself. We especially come to see that in the role it plays in our lives it is not just for us, for what it does for us is change our relations with the rest of the world. It lifts us in all ways. In this respect, the virtues of the *metaxu* are never strictly intellectual, but, as with sacraments, they always involve a material element. A good deal of any apprenticeship is the training of the body so that the mind may learn the concepts of the craft.

The transformation is qualitative, and the mediation implied is between concepts of the object that we read that are not all on a level. We do not simply learn more empirical information about, say, our neighbors when we love them as ourselves, or about institutions when we realize that a city is a *metaxu*; we see them differently. The transformation is a transformation in the level of the concepts we employ in the way that we think about and deal with the object in question. They can and ought to be read in all these ways; to understand them well is to do so. But to do so requires a corresponding change in us. The implicit forms of the love of God are certainly prime examples of *metaxu* in this respect. They are changed loves that, in the way we love, bring us closer to God and bring God's presence to us and to the world. A *metaxu*'s virtue lies in relation to our transformation, which is a transformation of how we read the world, as, for example, when we no longer see it as a world of cold, brute fact that provides pain or pleasure, but rather as a world that moves in obedience to the impulse of divine love. Thus, Weil suggests,

> Change of level. Not more love, but another kind of love; not more knowledge, but another kind of knowledge, etc. . . . By apprehending with attention both the level and the limit we can burst open a ceiling. . . . The presentation of several forms in the same object lifts the spectator (the reader) above form. By such means one obtains the without-form which is above form; for there is always the danger of falling below form. That

which is below is like that which is above—in a reverse sense. Each state is a *metaxu* towards a state similar to the one below the first, only transposed. (NB 62–64)

There are two conclusions to which I would like to draw our attention after looking at Weil's thinking about the implicit forms of the love of God and their connection to her broader thinking about the *metaxu*. The first is a reiteration of the central claim made in chapter 2, namely, that at the heart of the world lies a sense of mystery. Here we now understand that this means that there is no "pure nature" that can be fully understood without a relation to the divine. This is important because when this sense of mystery is lacking, the world becomes *flat*; mastery and technique dominate such a world. This is a world where the beautiful is irrelevant to understanding and where disinterested investigation easily exists side by side with self-interest. This is our contemporary world, the flattened world that Taylor has talked about. Weil challenges us see that there is depth—to our neighbor, to the world as a whole, and even to religious practices.

To talk about a sense of mystery to the world, though, is not just to talk *about* the world. Weil had no interest in sacralizing the world in a pseudo-objective way. One unfortunate result of recognizing that the world can be understood in a sacramental sense is that many of those who find this an enlightening claim tend to trivialize the notion of the sacramental. All sorts of things are now called sacraments. Too often, that effort has been little more than what Weil called "adding God on to everything," an invoking of an imaginary form of God. In most of the cases where sacramentality is invoked, one might appropriately apply the criticism once made by one thought to have been Solomon of those "who were unable from the goods that are seen to know the one who exists . . . through delight in the beauty of these things, people assumed them to be gods" (The Wisdom of Solomon 13:1, 3).

Weil's important insight, however, is that mystery is seen and known only in its engaging us, of introducing us to a different way of life and a different way of thinking.[6] If we see that we owe our neighbor respect and believe that we always need to consult our neighbor's will, even if that person has no power and is afflicted, then in that case we are not just reporting on a fact *about* our neighbor, something that could be known without altering ourselves to be open, and it is *then* that the love of neighbor is sacramental. For, as the supernatural is understood to permeate the natural, we only understand that it does insofar as we have taken a radically different stance to the world. To see that the divine lies at the root of the natural is to live and think in a very different way, and to think and live in that way is a matter of incarnating, in our bodily life, the supernatural.

PART II

Social and Political Thought

CHAPTER EIGHT

BEYOND THE PERSONAL
Weil's Critique of Maritain

It is a commonplace among social theorists to note that every political theory, implicitly or explicitly, involves a theory of what human beings are. Aristotle in his *Politics* asserted that humans are social animals; they naturally live in communities. Politics, as well as the ethics that subtend that politics, must take this seriously at every point. Locke largely reversed that earlier view. For him, human beings naturally live alone, or in small family groups, and only join together for protection and advantage, giving up in the social only as much of their autonomous natural freedom and choice as is necessary. Civil society needs to protect their individual wants and needs. Rousseau saw humans as being not protected but undone by their present groupings; he looked for a new way of being social, one that would form human beings differently, but he did so while also looking to a story of nature for direction.

Weil was no different. Her social and political philosophy, especially in its most remarkable writings from the last year of her life in London, also relies on a certain understanding of what human beings are and what their destiny is. She does not develop an explicit theory, but, at this time, she has a breakthrough in understanding social and political life, and it has to do with how she sees human beings. On the one hand, this comes about from a depth that she sees in them, something that requires a broader and deeper treatment of the relation of the human being to society than what Locke envisions. On the other hand, this is not just an objective requirement but a subjective one as well. The response has to be one of depth on the part of the one who is responding. It cannot simply be procedural. And this is just as much for the sake of the one responding as it is for the good of the one to whom one responds.

This breakthrough comes in the essay "What Is Sacred in Every Human Life?" ("La Personne et le Sacré"). Likely the first of her essays in London, and the basis for a perspective that runs through all the others, it takes a very different view of the human being than is found in the liberal democratic theory that dominated political discussions of her time and that dominates so much in ours. Especially striking is her rejection of rights as the moral basis of our interactions; she replaces it with the notion of obligation. This is the great beginning of *The Need for Roots*. That, however, is not just a philosophical move. It is the result of a profound shift in perspective that is, in good part, the result of her experience. That experience is a result of the way her thinking changed from her early years to her later ones. In this particular case, though, a very specific challenge causes this change in perspective, and it was the cause for writing "What Is Sacred in Every Human Being?"

The essay has long puzzled readers. In it, she explicitly criticizes the philosophical doctrine known as personalism, but for a long time it was not clear whom she had in mind in doing so. At first, it was thought to be Emmanuel Mounier, the best-known French personalist, who had developed a philosophy of personalism. However, it isn't possible to pin specifics of her critique on Mounier. In some ways, it doesn't matter. Her own thinking is clear enough, for what she is against, or at least its broad outlines, is fairly clear, no matter who the personalist in question was. Yet, further research shows that there is a tale behind the essay that helps us understand her argument much more clearly. It is usually the case that when we understand what the question is, we understand better what the answer means; when we understand the rejected alternative, we better understand the depth of the proposal. This is all the truer in this case because, as it turns out, her target is neither Mounier nor an imagined abstraction. The target was the personalism of Jacques Maritain, at the time one of the spiritual guiding lights of the Free French and certainly one of the preeminent Christian thinkers of the twentieth century. Maritain worked hard and conscientiously to deserve his reputation. But, Weil points out, he may well have let any number of factors into his thinking that diluted the strength of his witness. That is the negative case. In telling the tale, however, we are interested not in Maritain but in understanding Weil's alternative, for it is what she thinks is sacred in every human life.

When Weil arrived in New York in early July 1942 with her parents, she had one plan of action fixed firmly in her mind. That was to return to the occupied portion of France—indeed, to parachute into it. Sometime earlier, she had conceived a plan to parachute nurses into the front lines to take care of the wounded in the heat of battle. There were, of course, grave risks in such a venture, but taking them was at the heart of the plan. Weil believed that in such a war, the Allies could show what they were fighting for by risking themselves in an effort of brave, self-sacrificing compassion.

It would be nearly impossible to overestimate the importance of this mission to Weil. Its moral significance had captured her conscience, and she was desperate to do something for the war effort. Living in the comfort of New York, she felt like a deserter, and were she to be isolated from France much longer, she wrote, it would break her heart.[1] She wrote numerous letters to anybody who might listen to her plan and help in its implementation or get somebody in authority to listen. The recipients of these letters included Admiral William D. Leahy, the Unites States ambassador to Vichy France, and probably President Franklin D. Roosevelt himself. When ultimately she did reach England, only to be stuck (she thought) writing reports for the Free French and having her plan declared as mad by Charles de Gaulle, she resigned her post with the Free French and fell into a despair that ended only with her death from tuberculosis in August 1943.

In an effort to enlist his help, Weil wrote to Maritain shortly after her arrival in New York, figuring that he might not only be sympathetic but also have some influence. Maritain was out of town but replied on August 4 with a letter. Although the correspondence has yet to be published, Simone Pétrement, who saw it, described his reply as friendly, praising Weil's purpose as lofty and noble and implying, although he did not know if her plan was practicable, that he would try to help her meet with appropriate authorities. He also advised her to meet with Alexander Koyré and to discuss with Father Couturier certain questions about her "spiritual position" that she had mentioned.[2] It was, of course, out of her meetings with Couturier that the well-known and controversial "Letter to a Priest" emerged.

Aside from any implied promise to help, this should have been the end of the exchange. It clearly was for Maritain. But it wasn't for Weil. He stayed on her mind. We find Maritain twice mentioned explicitly in *The Need for Roots*. The first is when, in discussing the soul's need for truth, Weil quotes his claim that all the greatest thinkers of antiquity accepted slavery, despite, she notes, the very clear evidence of Aristotle, who says that there were people who did not. Since readers of Maritain might well not have the wherewithal to do the research themselves and would have to take his word on the matter, he has offended against the need for truth and ought to be hailed in front of a tribunal, which could censure him (NR 38).[3] (This is somewhat less silly than it sounds because it is simply a "for instance" of a larger and very serious point about the responsibility of writers in a society and about truth telling in the political realm.) In the second instance, at the end of *The Need for Roots*, she directly quotes him as writing that "the notion of right is even deeper than that of moral obligation, for God has a sovereign right over his creatures and he has no moral obligation to them" (NR 277–78).[4] This thought absolutely appalled her, and she cites it as an example of what she deemed "the Roman conception of God," that is, a God who is like the emperor exercising sovereignty over subjects as slaves. This is a very important point, as we shall see. Clearly, its expression also indicates a less-than-exalted opinion of Maritain. This is confirmed elsewhere, for, as will become clear, Maritain is also Weil's target in "What Is Sacred in Every Human Being?"[5] He is, then, one of the originators of personalism who is "warmly wrapped in social consideration," one of those "writers for whom it is part of their profession to have or hope to acquire a name and reputation" (LPW 17).

Why the antagonism? If it is personal, it may be because Maritain ultimately did not do anything to help after his original warm letter. It may well be the case that the warm tone of the letter and its kindness when he did not help were taken by Weil as condescension, the sort of encouraging politeness one receives from great people but that ultimately is designed to get rid of a petitioner. One feels a sense of expectation, but when disappointed, one feels played for a fool. Maritain may not have meant this, but Weil, who was very sensitive about these sorts of things and had a lot of experience with them while scouting for support for her project, might very well have thought he did.

That does not at all capture what Weil writes, though. There is a lot more, and it lies at a genuine and far deeper philosophical level. It goes beyond their exchange of letters and reveals her own distinctive challenge to how the human being should be understood and respected. It concerns the very idea of depth in human life.

Weil finally reached London in November 1942 and joined the Free French. She was given the task of examining the developing projects of the Resistance committees for the reorganization of France after the war. Her identity card stated her title as *rédactrice*; she wrote reports, an appropriate job given her talents. She was, though, bitterly disappointed at not being sent to France on a dangerous mission and grew even more so as she received no serious hearing for her project. Yet, despite this, it is because of this assignment that we have many of her most important works. Her time in London was incredibly productive time. Far from simply churning out the easily forgettable reports of a bureaucrat, she wrote, in a period of little more than six months, numerous essays on the spiritual and political renewal of France—which have come to us as the book *The Need for Roots*—as well as other essays on politics, religion, and ancient philosophy.[6] Her thought in these works is at its most mature and most integrated. Indeed, she herself, in a letter to her parents at the time, suggests that her thought had taken such a turn that it had become more and more compact, more indivisible, as it grew (SL 196).

"What Is Sacred in Every Human Being?" was written at this time and provides something like a center to Weil's thinking. As a shift in perspective and a turning point in her social thought, it clears the decks of numerous ideas so easily assumed in thinking about the human being and human communities. It also clearly distinguishes Weil's own views, introducing many of the great themes of the London writings, such as her notion of the "impersonal" and her argument that obligations absolutely have precedence over rights. It is above all an extremely original essay, and it has a timeless quality, as do many of her writings.

Yet, despite this timeless quality, it is also a highly contextual essay. One part of that context is, of course, the concern over just what France should look like after the war, of how it would conceive and organize its laws, social concerns, and politics. In short, she was very concerned about how justice would be conceived, especially given all the competing voices. That much has always been recognizable and recognized. The other part of the context is Maritain's little book *The Rights of Man and Natural Law*, which for Weil was perhaps the chief competing voice, as it was read by the same people for whom she wrote.

There can be no doubt that Weil had read *The Rights of Man*, which was published in French in New York in 1942, and that she could even put a copy in front of her. The passage she quoted in *The Need for Roots* attributing a "Roman conception of God" to Maritain is from this book;[7] it is also the source for Maritain's contestable claim about how the ancients viewed slavery.[8] While "What Is Sacred in Every Human Being?" never explicitly names Maritain and has no direct quote from him, there are numerous clear indicators that it is a direct response to *The Rights of Man*, which she thought had turned the heads of the Free French leaders. The most incontrovertible example is a point that can only be taken from Maritain's discussion of natural law in that book. There he calls the natural law an "unwritten law" and proceeds to cite Antigone as an example of it.[9] Weil notes, in a way that leaves no doubt as to what she is referring to, that "it is by a singular confusion that one could assimilate the unwritten law of Antigone to natural rights" (LPW 114). Since this point is not an aside or a mere "for instance" but an essential one about the status of rights in the Greeks, part of an extended argument about rights and their linkage to the concept of "person" and "personality," an essential theme of the essay and of Maritain's book, it is immediately clear that this essay is a response to *The Rights of Man*. The connection becomes even clearer when one sees Weil clearly attacking a number of Maritain's points about rights and the concepts of "person" and "personality" in *The Rights of Man*. Simone Fraisse, who was the first to notice the connection, points out, "We find in this book an elegy on the person, with which he associates the terms that Simone Weil refused to recognize in it: sacredness, respect, expansion of the personality, rights."[10] I would add to this list Weil's discussions of the relation of the person to the collectivity and her equally subtle but insistent differences from Maritain on the issue of human labor.[11]

So, this is a direct response to Maritain. But what sort of response is it? While thorough in covering many of Maritain's points, it is not exactly a systematic critique or point-by-point refutation. Nor is it, despite everything else, entirely unsympathetic to Maritain's project. On any number of items of concern that both canvass, they might well agree, for example, on the deep problems of individualism and totalitarianism and the need to establish the human being as ontologically related to God. For this reason, a point-by-point refutation would miss the mark because it is the philosophical approach to these problems that she is worried about. Indeed, to read it as a point-by-point refutation would suggest that Weil had let prejudice color her reading of Maritain and that she had in fact utterly misread him. Her attacks on the concepts of "person" and "personality" are attacks on concepts of the empirical, social ego, and that is clearly *not* what Maritain thinks he is trying to get his readers to consider and what he is trying to avoid by rooting the concept of person in a relation to God and calling it sacred. She understands this and does not make him a strawman.

The response is more subtle and more pressing. Its nature is indicated in the sixth sentence of Weil's essay. In her opening lines, she makes a common-sense appeal to a distinction between a sentence such as "You do not interest me," which is genuinely cruel and offensive, and "Your personality does not interest me," which, she notes, could be used in an affectionate conversation between friends. One might imagine, for example, in the latter case, two friends pursuing a philosophical argument and one musing about how amenable a position is to him personally. The other can without offense suggest that that is irrelevant to discovering its truth, which is what really interests both. Given this distinction, she then comments, "This proves that there is something wrong in the vocabulary in the stream of modern thought called 'personalist.' And in this domain, whenever there is a grave error of vocabulary it is hard to avoid grave errors in thought" (LPW 104). The accusation, therefore, is initially not so much that Maritain has gotten hold of the wrong sort of problem or that he has failed to define his terms accurately, but that in using the term *personne* he has failed to get a hold on the *mot juste*.

That is not a trivial or merely rhetorical point, and certainly not such for Weil, whose own concern for calling things by their right names was categorically imperative. The most charitable interpretation of her objection, then, is that no matter how carefully defined *personne* might be—and Maritain certainly tried to define it carefully—this would simply be *recherché*, and its subtle distinctions would be lost, given the normal freight that the word carries. Weil is absolutely right on this. What is usually heard and celebrated when one says that the person is sacred is *not* that "one can find alone his complete fulfillment"[12] in the absolute of God, which is what Maritain thinks he means. What is heard is that the confused mass of desires that constitutes our social egos and aspirations, what we normally call the person or our personality, is sacred. When that happens, the sacred is created in our image. Given Maritain's intellectual influence among the Free French, and because his point has a certain initial plausibility, Weil was particularly concerned to warn them about its failure to reach to the proper depths.[13]

That is the most charitable interpretation. However, while Maritain may have been less misled by his use of the term *personne* than his audience, Weil believed nevertheless that he, too, was misled, and seriously so. He makes exactly the sort of mistake she fears will be made when one uses the term *personne* for what is sacred in a human being. The problem is Maritain's easy connection of *personne* to the notion of rights, which Weil thinks belongs to the realm of "words of the middle region" (LPW 128), the realm of ordinary institutions. Rights are a matter of commerce and property, she claims, and are defined by *jus utendi et abutendi*. That, of course, makes them quite fit to deal with issues of personality and the social ego. But when Maritain then suggests that rights have priority over obligations because God has rights over creatures and not obligations to them, she thinks something has gone very wrong indeed. Not only has the law belonging to property and commerce been applied rather unequivocally to the divine with no apophatic sense that would qualify the claim, the whole sense of the proposition runs counter to the more genuine Christian understanding of God, the one Maritain thinks he is defending. God acts out of his goodness and love to creatures, she thinks, going out from himself to meet their needs. Obligations, as she understands them, are not laid on one—and they are not laid on God. Maritain, however, seems to think they are, and that is why he refuses them on God's behalf. They are, Weil thinks, not something laid on one but a response of goodness to need, a matter of heart. To talk about rights preceding obligations in the case of God is then to utterly misdescribe the nature of God's goodness and love as portrayed in the Gospel. As she puts it elsewhere, "God loves, not as I love, but as an emerald is green" (OC 6.4, 171). To say God has obligations to us, or that we have obligations to others, is, for Weil, simply to say that God loves us, or that we are to love others, unconditionally.

The disagreement between Weil and Maritain can now be seen to enjoin a legitimate and important philosophical debate.[14] What it meant to Weil will become increasingly evident over the course of the following chapters, especially the next one. At this point, however, something more needs to be said about Weil's deepest objections to personalism, her original alternative in suggesting that what is truly sacred in the human being is the impersonal, and why she was so insistent on liberating the minds of her colleagues from Maritain's claims.

Weil has two important reasons for rejecting personalism. One is her considered view of what constitutes personality. Rather than seeing it, as Maritain explicitly did, as the highest and deepest dimension of our being, that wherein our freedom is most clearly expressed and needs most respect, in arguments similar to Marx's earlier and then Foucault's in a later generation, she held that personality and its value are constituted by what she called "social matter."[15] The person and the value we put on persons are historically contingent and manufactured by the play of social forces. So, more often than not, when we focus on the person and personality we tend to miss what is of genuine and lasting value in human aspiration. Moreover, since personality is born out of social struggle, there is always an element of contention involved in personality and its expansion. As she points out quite observantly, rights, which are linked to the concept of the person, are always asserted in a tone of contention, and even inhibit movements of genuine charity. In this case, it should be added, what Maritain has done is adopted common secular thinking about the person, especially in his exaltation of rights and personality, and sacralized it. Which, ultimately, flattens the sacred.

Her second reason for rejecting personalism is that it doesn't protect and value humanity to the ultimate degree that it thinks it does, no matter how many rights are defined and how clearly. Even when one's rights are scrupulously guarded, Weil thought, one's deepest inner cries are not necessarily heard or responded to. Those lie behind easily defined words, and until one can hear the inarticulate word behind the words, one has not heard the human or what is sacred about the human at all. Weil bases this claim in her own watching of court cases where, according to procedural justice, everything is done fairly but somehow those who lack articulateness have a profound sense that good has not triumphed, that they have not been heard, and even that they have been humiliated by the flow of fine words (LPW 122–23).

Given this critique of personality, Weil's counterassertion that what really is sacred in a human being is the *impersonal* gains some plausibility and shows her own originality. For although the very word *impersonal* perhaps chills us as unfriendly and abstract, a good part of Weil's point is that to isolate personality from the human being's striving for good and to consider it alone is itself the very height of abstraction. When she then recommends "impersonalism," she is therefore not trying to cut humans out of the world but rather trying to make room for them. She does so by refusing to take the aspects of human striving for good that are essentially bound up with contingent historical circumstances to be the whole of humans. The human expectation for good is more than what counts as personality, and we are obliged to respect humans even when they show no signs of being persons. This doesn't just mean when they are boring; it is above all when they are afflicted. As she points out in another essay, in the parable of the Good Samaritan, the man set upon by thieves and lying by the side of the road had become nothing more important than a stone; it is no wonder that the priest and the Levite walked by him. Yet the Samaritan, his natural enemy, somehow didn't let that limit him, nor did he let his Samaritan-ishness or the man's Jewishness limit him. So impersonality is meant to stand behind a stronger moral claim than can be generated from the notions of personality and rights.

The impersonal is for Weil absolutely prior to any individual aspects of the human. That may wound our vanity, for we like to think what we have made of ourselves is really important. But, in the end, the impersonal may alone be that which calls for and sustains infinite love and concern—and what allows us to transcend our own personal aspirations in order to care for another. Consider a point made by Stanley Cavell in discussing Wittgenstein's dismissal of private languages: people often object to that dismissal because they think that by taking away the privacy of, say, the way they want to talk about pain sensations, something important about our inner life is also taken away. He goes on to say,

> In a way this is true. I think one moral of the *Investigations* as a whole can be drawn as follows: The fact, and the state, of your (inner) life cannot take its importance from anything special in it. However far you have gone with it, you will find that what is common is there before you are. The state of your life may be, and may be all that is, worth your infinite interest. But then that can only exist along with a complete disinterest toward it. The soul is impersonal.[16]

Both Weil and Cavell are saying that if we are wholly and infinitely committed to making space for human souls in the world, it cannot be because of their interesting—or our interested—features. The commitment must reach further than that. It must transcend the world of the personal and be impersonal. For that is where the soul of the true lover and beloved dwells. It is not Maritain's point at all, I think. But I do think that he was in some way responsible for Weil coming to it.

CHAPTER NINE

THE LANGUAGE OF THE INNER LIFE

Weil's criticism of Maritain was very much a matter of his having borrowed the secular language of rights and sacralized it. At the heart of this criticism was a belief on her part that there is, indeed, a sacred, and that it is not covered by the language of rights. In fact, "rights" fundamentally misrepresents the sacred. This does not mean that she thinks that rights are pointless. They have a certain place; this is when and where power exists on both sides of an encounter. The power may be one's own, or it may be that of the state. But the place that rights have is not ubiquitous, and it is not deep, for the powerless do not live in that place of shared power. As a result, rights are not sufficient for talking about what is sacred in human beings. In a pointed example, she observes, "A peasant, whom a buyer in the market puts undue pressure on to get him to sell his eggs cheaply, can very well answer: 'I have the right to keep my eggs if no one offers me a good enough price.' But a young girl who is in the midst of being forced into a brothel will not speak of her rights. In such a situation, the words would seem ridiculously not up to the situation" (LPW 115). In the latter case, something else is needed.

For Weil, Maritain has flattened the sacred, despite his intention to bring it into play in human social life. But this also means, positively, that, for Weil, there is a hierarchy of values. This is played out especially at the end of "What is Sacred in Every Human Being?" where she makes the startling claim that "there are words that, if one makes good use of them, have in themselves the virtue of illumining and raising us towards the good" (LPW 127). "God and truth are such words," she says. "So, too, are justice, love, and good" (LPW 127). These words are to be contrasted with words of the "middle realm," which include "rights, democracy, person" (LPW 128). This is not the only place where she invokes the idea of a hierarchy of value and does so with respect to the *language* of value. She makes a related distinction in words in *Waiting for God* when she suggests the "language of the market place is not that of the nuptial chamber" (WG 79).

To claim a hierarchy in value is not unusual. Values and hierarchies go hand in hand. Simply to say that an ethical choice should be made one way rather than another invokes some kind of hierarchy; one always chooses for the greater good, not the lesser. Even a philosopher such as Jeremy Bentham, who had a single-principle ethics that he thought could decide all value decisions, had to assume that as a principle of decision it is useful chiefly as a way of deciding between what is more valuable and what is less valuable. This is the case even if in employing it he flattens values qualitatively, "making poetry as good as pushpin." But Weil is decidedly not talking about the relative *quantitative* values of outcomes. She is saying 1) that we need to choose among qualitatively different kinds of values; 2) that different kinds of values compete for space in our moral lives, often the same space; and 3) different kinds of values require different kinds of talk, and understanding a value requires speaking of it in the way proper to it. Specifically, we talk with words of the middle range openly and in the marketplace; they are meant for that sort of place and have their proper usage there. Words that we use to talk of what is most valuable to the human being, matters of depth, however, she thinks are words of intimacy, words that are not spoken openly. Why? There are things we do not say out loud because to do so would betray what they are meant to do, or because they are so deeply personal that talking about them out loud in the marketplace would be akin to pornography—or, in the case of love, it *is* pornography—as what is intimate becomes a market item. As Rilke insightfully suggests, "But the best things that happen, after all, are the ones which hide their deeper reason with both hands, whether out of modesty or because they don't want to be betrayed."[1] So, confusing the two sorts of language can lead to all sorts of mischief, including a debasement of our *understanding* of value. It affects us and our ability to flourish as human beings.

This claim is important just as it is striking, and we need to come to grips with it if we are going to understand Weil's later political and social thinking and how it is related to her philosophical and religious thinking, which certainly in her last years involved, as we have seen in the first section of this book, an "inner turn." So, I would like to accomplish two things in this chapter. First, I would like to establish that we do, in fact, recognize this kind of distinction and it is important. I will argue this by looking at Harvard political philosopher Michael Sandel's *What Money Can't Buy: The Moral Limits of Markets*.[2] Sandel argues that, despite the leveling arguments of many economists, there are things that should not be given a price. In some cases this is because of fairness, but more importantly, there are cases where doing so would *corrupt* what we are trying to put a price on. His argument underlines Weil's argument, which claims that there really are different kinds of values, those of the marketplace and those of the middle realm concerning the public, open air, and then inner ones that need caring for in a much different way. Inner values are debased by talking about them as we talk about other values, which is another way of saying that they have been flattened. It also helps put Weil's argument with Maritain in much more contemporary terms. Second, I would like to say something about how these values of intimacy that require much more modest language are not to be confused with the private, and hence nonpolitical, which is what liberal theory wants to do. Instead, they are involved in what it means to have an inner life, and our inner lives are the shape of our moral commitments—even in the public square. Having an inner life means reflection, certainly, but it above all means a personal commitment to God, human beings, justice, and so on that gives them their true value in our lives.[3] These commitments are not beside the point when entering the public square. They are actually reflected in how we approach any conversation about social goods. Any other approach changes the very nature of the values we want to think about. All of this is at the heart of the vision that Weil articulates in her later political and social writings.

Sandel notes that in an earlier generation, the field of economics dealt with things such as markets, prices, money, and the like. Currently, however, economics has far greater pretensions. It has made itself out to be a science of human behavior, even *the* science of human behavior. As a result, "to a remarkable degree, the last few decades have witnessed the remaking of social relations in the image of market relations."[4] This is more than a matter of how some academics choose to view and analyze human behavior. These people have a lot of influence; unlike philosophers, economists have a great deal of influence over how and what public policy gets made. This has meant that the use of market relations has now remodeled human relations. Health, education, public safety, national security, criminal justice, environmental protection, and any number of other social goods are now allocated by using markets. Important examples can be seen in how often social motivation is now thought to be best done by monetary and market incentives.

Sandel argues that this change is troubling on two levels. In the first place, when all goods are "bought and sold, having money makes all the difference in the world."[5] The problem here is one of fairness, since there is an issue of inequality. Some people have a lot of money, while others have less and therefore less access to marketed social goods. But there is a second and even more damning criticism: "Putting a price on the good things in life can corrupt them. That's because markets don't only allocate goods; they also express and promote certain attitudes toward the good being exchanged."[6] Even though economists argue that markets don't affect the goods exchanged, this simply seems untrue, and "sometimes, market values crowd out nonmarket values worth caring about."[7]

Since Sandel provides many, many examples to support his argument, it is worth noting at least one of them. In the case of one nursery school, unsurprisingly, a number of parents picked up their children late, causing the school staff to work longer hours and making them unpaid babysitters. In order to curb the problem, the school began fining parents for picking their children up late. But the policy had the opposite effect to the one intended. The number of late pick-ups actually increased. Why? Originally, the parents seemed to have felt some sort of moral obligation to pick up their children on time and many felt bad about being late. However, once it was a service they could pay for, they simply chose to pay for it. The moral incentive to get there on time, based on a certain respect for the children's teachers, was no longer operative.[8] So, in this case, it can be fairly claimed that market incentives had the effect of crowding out nonmarket, moral incentives. Sandel multiplies at length the real-life examples of cases where monetary incentives have crowded out moral incentives. These include paying kids for good grades, bribes to lose weight, selling the right to immigrate, purchasing the right to speed or to have access to less crowded traffic lanes, trading pollution credits, and paying to kill endangered species. In all these various types of cases, money has been used to solve a problem that moral incentives have traditionally been invoked to solve. But as it turns out, in almost all, if not all, of these instances, the monetary solution tends to be less effective and often does not lead to fairness. There are two sorts of problems here. In some cases there is a problem with fairness: only the better off have access to the good, or they use it up first. In many others, there is a clear erosion of the moral incentives that all people had used to control their behavior, without the increase in utility that economists expected.

It is the second problem, the corruption of moral incentives, that I am concerned with here. It is a problem that does not have to do with utility or fairness; rather, it suggests that *there are certain goods that need to be respected in themselves.* Treating them as marketable goods diminishes them and may, in time, erase them as motivating factors in human behavior. Sandel gives a list of examples that can be easily recognized: friendship, apologies, compliments, honors. Once money becomes a factor in any of these things, it loses its worth. In fact, these things lose their being. A bought friendship or apology is not a friendship or a real apology. His point—and this is the one that I want to take away here—is not to argue that any particular good belongs on the list, but simply that it seems obvious to most of us that there really is a distinction between what money can buy and what it can't buy without damaging the social fabric. The economists who think that the markets are neutral and nothing more than a more efficient way of distributing goods are simply wrong. Even if we found fair ways of distributing such goods, "even in a society without unjust differences of power and wealth, there would still be things that money should not buy. This is because markets are not mere mechanisms; they embody certain values. And sometimes, market values crowd out nonmarket norms worth caring about."[9]

The conclusion to draw from this is that there are different kinds of goods and economic and moral goods can be quite distinct. With each in its place, they are not necessarily opposed to each other. They may both be important. However, if, as Sandel argues, market values crowd out and replace certain kinds of moral values, then we do have evidence that there are qualitatively different kinds of values. There is also good reason to think that moral values are more important to human flourishing—that without them, market values alone will diminish the quality of human life. While there is a complicated and real relation between physical well-being and moral well-being, still, it certainly seems possible to have a good life with the moral virtues of human cooperation, love, and respect and without all the efficiency that markets are thought to bring. After all, people were happy and good before the advent of current economic theory. However, the reverse is not true. Markets unbridled take something important away from human life. Virtue does not.

Sandel is hardly the first critic of utilitarianism, even in its current economic theory costume. The most valuable service he provides, therefore, is not in simply saying that economic utilitarianism is wrong, but rather in saying that using the language of markets in places where we have previously used the language of moral and civic responsibility is corrupting.

In this he approaches Weil's position in "What Is Sacred in Every Human Being?" and helps to illumine its social relevance. She, too, is worried about a confusion in levels. She is also worried that a confusion in language will lead to a debasement, or already shows a debasement, in thought.[10] That similarity, I think, helps us understand more clearly what Weil is getting at in this essay and where the deeper issue is as she criticizes Maritain for his personalism. She thought that Maritain, in making the notions of the "person" and "personality" the grounds for his moral and social thought, had traded a hard-to-define sacred concept for one that seems to be easily defined and that is defined in terms of market relations. But in that essay, she also goes a level deeper than Sandel is trying for. This is not a criticism of Sandel; what I want to point out is that, in a discussion that depends upon distinguishing different moral levels, for Weil there are more levels still to be noted. These involve further considerations and complications. For example, in his concern for the corruption of the language of morals by its replacement with the language of the markets, Sandel is chiefly worried about the civil society and social values. Replacing, as we have done, the hard and intractable discussions of what constitutes the common good and our place in it with the efficiencies of the market is damaging to us. We need these discussions; we need to have them because "this is how we learn to negotiate and abide our differences, and how we come to care for the common good."[11] We cannot assume a common denominator in the valuations of the market, nor can we believe that the market is simply a mirror of our moral choices. So far, so good. Where Weil, however, goes a step further is in this: Sandel deals with an important and obvious opposition—market values and human values.[12] Weil, however, wants to see some important distinctions in the wide range of what counts as human values. Specifically, she worries about how the language of the common good itself might be capable of corrupting an even deeper need of the human being for good than the common life provides or, more importantly, one that the common life itself depends upon.

Her concern is that thought will be subjected, perhaps in some very subtle ways, to the collective. So, important as a discussion of what is truly valuable in the collective may be, if there is no real source of insight beyond what is already known and believed in the collective, then the discussion may well just repeat all the platitudes and dynamics that are already in play. For example, once the markets have corrupted discourse, how can we expect to have a discussion that, at the outset, isn't tainted by their influence? Where is the source of insight that will turn things around to come from? Furthermore, something must have been at play that allowed the corruption in the first place. What is therefore needed is a recognition that social morality may well be subject to all the dynamics that Plato thought it is when he described collectivities as "the Great Beast."[13]

Subsequently, Weil is concerned with how, if we do not recognize this deeper need of the human being, we may end up betraying it and trading it in for something that is better than brute force or naked capitalism but that, nevertheless, fails in real justice to the human being. In doing so, she is not trying to denigrate the common good or common life. Terms of the middle level are better than those of a base level. They have a place—an important one—in human life. But she is trying to understand those terms sub specie aeternitatis. As such, she wants to see them in a more ultimate relation to the souls that the common good serves *so that they are not understood in its terms, but so that the common good is understood in terms of the souls that constitute it.* That is a major point to be considered in any discussion of justice or the common good. It is not one usually considered in contemporary social thought.

Weil is concerned that the human being will become subject to the collectivity, which is to say, to necessity and not the good. She was concerned about it from her earliest writings. Upon inspection, however, this concern is not a species of individualism. What she is concerned about is that the collectivity, even in its finest expressions, is not sacred and does not understand the sacred, which is a need of every human being. Collectivities can only deal in the general. The problem, therefore, is that terms that make sense within collectivities get used to express the sacred, which can only properly be used in a very different way. The substitution may be very subtle, and the terms may look a lot like each other. But to accept it is ultimately to forget the deeper needs of the human being and accept something as salvation that is not capable of giving it. It is easy to recognize this in difficult times; it is very easy to ignore it in times of prosperity. Prosperity can be insidious.

This substitution was Maritain's mistake, and it is continually repeated. When Weil wrote "What Is Sacred in Every Human Being?," she probably could have agreed with Maritain on certain social issues, including issues of labor, at least within certain grudging limits. In depressed times, she certainly would not have objected to laborers making a living wage, as Maritain insists they have a right to. What she objected to was his attempt to make his case on the notion that what is sacred in every human being is personality, for the concept of personality, as he explicates it, is tied to the notion of rights, and the notion of rights is ultimately a social concept that never goes deep enough in treating souls justly. If it is, then giving the workers what they need for the expansion of their personalities hardly gives them what they need most, even if they are not aware of what it is they do need. Her objection runs this way:

> When someone speaks to [workers] of their lot, generally one chooses to speak to them about salaries. They, under the fatigue of being weighed down and for whom every effort of attention is painful, welcome with relief the easy clarity of numbers.
>
> They thus forget that the object that they are bargaining about—the one they complain that someone is forcing them to hand over cheaply, the one someone is refusing them a just price for—is nothing other than their soul.
>
> Imagine that the devil is in the process of buying the soul of some poor afflicted being, and that someone, taking pity on the one afflicted, were to intervene in the debate and say to the devil: "It is really shameful for you to offer only this price; the thing is worth at least twice that." (LPW 112–13)

So, while Maritain may have ended up with the right results on certain issues, he started in the wrong place. Why should that matter? It happens all the time in ethical debates. Frequently, our disagreement in principles means little in comparison to our agreement in action. Or so it would seem at first. Yet, what we assume when we begin can affect what we think we have accomplished at the end and how we take our accomplishments. So it is in this case. Weil thinks that, if he ends up in the right place once in a while, he only does so on particulars. Getting there is the result of a sleight of hand. Maritain hands out descriptions of the personality as sacred that bolster his insistence that the workers have a right to a certain wage, for without it they would be stifled. The eternal in them would be stifled. So, it would be good if they got that wage. But is that really why those in power should give them that wage?

What if they weren't going to creatively express themselves? Isn't there really something much more basic at stake here? So, even if Maritain ends up in the right place on this issue, the way to it comes by making a social concept do service as a sacred concept, much as Sandel thinks that market concepts are being made to do service as moral concepts. Perhaps what Maritain is doing is simply hyperbole. It might be in a lesser thinker, but in one who is putting forth a serious argument—and this is how the Free French took him—it is the argument and its terms, not the recommendation, that often as not will have the lasting effect. In that case, what is said and remembered ultimately debases the sacred, despite the lip service paid to it.

That has consequences. For example, Weil, who is sensitive to the powerless who have no words, believes that this sort of consideration, this concentration on the rights needed to develop personality, keeps us from hearing them. Personality is bound up with the public use of language. So, in this case, if they are given their rights in a court of fair, procedural justice, what more can be said? What more could be suspected of them? Yet, after all the words of justice are spoken, often they believe they have not been heard or acknowledged. The deep issue Weil wants to stress is that if we really do have a moral commitment to the human being, then, if that is a sacred commitment and not a contractual one, the commitment is limitless. Personality and rights, she claims, extend no further than the realm of the social; they demand no more of us than social responsibility. Moreover, Weil believed, personality and rights are social and are historically contextual. They are not universal or eternal, or, at least, the only way to show anything like a universal right is to paint it very thin.[14] So, even while the liberal celebration of the person has a lot going for it, ultimately, if one rests on it, it will crowd out a different, deeper sort of moral commitment to human beings. It will crowd out any deep first-person commitment, one that liberal values themselves may need. It will allow us to excuse ourselves when we are pressed too hard.

Why is this so? Because ultimately the notion of person that is being used and promoted is the person observed. This includes by self-reflection, ourselves. And the person observed is the social being, and the observing being done is through social categories. That simply is not enough, as far as Weil is concerned. It does not let us show sufficient concern for or commitment to the afflicted, and it makes us sell ourselves short.

Weil wisely realizes that with regard to anything that is genuinely sacred, we cannot just substitute another concept. She says that words such as *God*, *truth*, and *justice* are inconceivable. Another concept isn't what is needed. Giving one would inevitably be slipping in the back door what we just ushered out the front. What we do need to do is to use such words differently than we use other words. Not only do they have a different grammar, but that grammar is reflected in the *humility* we need to use them. That is not easy, and she says, it is a trial to use them properly. But that difference in how we use them can also give away a real difference in value.

How should one use such words? They are not magical incantations. One gets a sense of how to use them by recognizing that, as Weil suggests, these are words that are matters of intimacy and need the language of the nuptial chamber. But what does that mean? It means that in using them we recognize the deep, inescapably personal involvement *we* have with what we are talking about when we do use them. This involvement is not simply sentiment, which is its ersatz and even its poison. Nor is it a matter of speech that we are embarrassed to be caught using in public. It is that in our relation to God, to our neighbor, to justice, there is something profound and personal demanded of *us*. This is the language of conscience and the language of love and commitment. It gets bastardized when it is traded in the political realm—which is why we should be ashamed to speak it too loudly. That happens even when we trade it for the finest words of the political realm. This sort of language deepens, however, by being brought into play as we act in the world and act responsibly and without personal reservation.

All this might well suggest that *God*, *justice*, *love*, and so on have no particular role to play in discussions of politics or social goods, that this intimacy cordons them off in the realm of the private. That is the standard liberal objection, which insists on public reason and not love or commitment to settle public issues. But this is not the case at all. Far from it. For in using such words as they should be used, we end up being deeply committed in a distinctive way in the social realm.

Let me put this in Sandel's terms. In resisting the language of the marketplace, he hopes that we come to realize that we need to have a hard discussion that negotiates our differences and goods. I think he is right, although *negotiates* is probably not the right word, given the rest of his argument. I think Weil could have said he is right. Her last writings in London for the Free French challenged a French government that would come to power when the Nazis were driven out to rethink the moral bases of social and national life. But in order to have that sort of discussion—and this may well be why we are not having it in the public square now—whoever is in it has to be committed to something beyond market negotiations, beyond a "deal," which is what standard liberal conceptions of justice tend to come down to, and which is why they are so susceptible to being cast in market terms. Lockean liberalism leaves the choice of what goods are good up to the individual, and the individual is left unsituated in making that choice. For a long time, perhaps, we might *believe* that we are unsituated while remaining unaware of how deeply that choice really is indebted to all sorts of institutions and relations that shape us and put us in touch with God and neighbor in meaningful ways, that give us a sense of obligation and responsibility and care. As Tocqueville put it in 1836, there are in American institutions "countervailing forces" that offset the strong individualism of Americans. Such institutions are religious, communal, and legal. Tocqueville cites churches and the obligation to serve on juries as two examples.[15] But at some point, the influence of those countervailing forces can be eroded. At that point, each institution that shapes our moral being is no longer a bridge that puts us in touch with deeper being and can be turned into something that is a part of the market. We then become *truly* unsituated. A people no longer aware of anything deeper may not notice the difference, or even the irony as they have serious discussions about the common good. For example, anybody who has ever listened to American Christian leaders on either the right or left talk about how to increase church membership will know that the exchange of an intimate value for a market value is now largely assumed and unchallenged. Those discussions are almost entirely market-flavored discussions.

As Weil wrote in her last months on what she thought would be required for a new France—one that would once again sustain souls, one where social life would be something to believe in—she argued that there are elements that need to be cultivated in order to have that discussion, a discussion that is ongoing. Above all, and this is her chief point in "What Is Sacred in Every Human Being?," is a deep personal obligation to the other that is not limited and will therefore always commit one to that social conversation. That commitment is not just a matter of being a participant. It also, and necessarily, means listening to others and taking them seriously, not just presenting one's own case for negotiation or being a player in the game of powers. For that reason, the language of the inner self is not a private language but a language of personal commitment and moral responsibility. It may be used and developed out of sight of the agora, and it may not use the terms of the market. But for the person who knows how to use it, its depth is realized in the way that one acts and talks, not only in the nuptial chamber but also in the agora. It is the first-person moral language that takes us beyond the third-person distance of moral systems and commits us to others in conversation and to those who cannot speak.

This, however, is not a one-way street. It is not the case that an individual must have this commitment before entering into a sufficiently deep conversation about social goods. The conversation itself in a healthy community, one where people are aware of all that gives human life its goodness, can and should awaken in its people the sense that we do have an obligation to others and that there are behind all social phenomena issues of personal commitment. Weil makes this point in *The Need for Roots*. Collectivities and societies are not ultimate. They are meant to serve the souls who live in them. But they, like cornfields, feed those souls. What does that mean? Well, it would certainly seem to mean that the social conversation of a good society ought to be what awakens and trains the souls of those who live in it to something that is greater than the collectivity itself. The discussions that go on in social and political realms should not be driven only by the results they might achieve; they should also teach the people who are in them. These discussions, and the documents that enshrine previous discussions, such as constitutions, are how a people educates itself. But that will not happen, if, in the course of such discussion, no one talks about the sacred properly, if no one goes into one's own chamber and speaks silently from the heart, and then comes out transformed. It will not do this if we do not know how to talk about values and how to talk with meaning. It will not do this if we talk about everything in the same way. We need to use words of value according to the value they express, and we need to talk about them in proper ways. If we do not, we run the risk of altering the conversation for the worse.

CHAPTER TEN

"THOU HAST GIVEN ME ROOM"
Weil's Retheologization of the Political

Simone Weil insists that there are several different levels in our lives, and it is clear that the sacred is part of our lives. What else comes out of her thinking in the seminal "What Is Sacred in Every Human Being?" is that the sacred is important to the social and political. But that should be expected, given that she thinks *everything* needs to be turned into an intermediary leading toward God. If so, then those areas of our lives in which so much of our time is spent, and that are so determinative of our thinking—communities and nations—are such intermediaries. If the world is such that these things can be turned into intermediaries, then there is a connection for her between religious and social thought.

Yet something more needs to be said. Clearly, many of her late political ideas are rooted in her religious vision. But, by itself, this does not make her a political or social philosopher. Attention surely blooms in righteousness. It does so for both prophets and social critics. But to be a social or political philosopher, one also needs to be a thinker who understands how power and justice are related, for better or worse, in front of us now, as well as how they can and ought to be related possibly for the realization of human good. The prophet Micah told ancient Judah to love justice and walk humbly with God. So did Augustine tell his congregation. But Micah never wrote anything like *The City of God*.

So, what makes Weil a contributor to social and political philosophy? How does she add a third dimension to flattened social thinking, beyond the prophetic? One way of characterizing her thought is to say that she "retheologizes" the political, moving away from the liberal idea that it involves a neutral space delineated from the private. For Weil, politics as well as so much else needs to be thought sub specie aeternitatis; like Plato, she thinks politics is the art "whose business it is to care for souls."[1]

That much may have been anticipated. But how her thinking can be considered genuinely *political*—for it is not by some of her readers—needs to be carefully spelled out. Weil can be a heady and exciting figure. Her own actions are inspiring to many. She is readily invoked as support for many ideals of justice and also for particular policies of our day. But far more rare, though, is an understanding of how she runs contrary to many commonly accepted ideals of the tribe and how, even as she is invoked in support of a cause, she challenges how that cause is to be thought about. T. S. Eliot was not wrong when he said that she is far more "a lover of order and hierarchy than most of those who call themselves Conservative, and more truly a lover of the people than most of those who call themselves Socialist" (NR viii). She was not, for him, to be classified.

This gives this chapter two tasks: first, to explore briefly what it means for the political to be retheologized, that is, what it means for the space in which we dwell, but particularly the public space, to be thought of as moral and religious space in some sense, one that is related to, not divorced from, the more intimate spaces of love and faith. Second, I want to say something about how we might read that retheologization in such a way that Weil can, given her theological vision, still be thought a genuine political thinker, albeit with a revised version of what *political* means, and not simply, as some have suggested, a mystic who has made some idealistic and completely unrealistic suggestions about politics.

Let us begin not with Weil herself but with a brief consideration of how we think about the spaces in which we dwell. We think about them in some very different ways, each of which has its own logic. We can consider just a few to demonstrate.

Despite occasional provocative forays by people who actually understand something of Einstein, much of our talk involving space, I suspect, is what we might call "Newtonian." That is to say, when we talk about space, either terrestrial or so-called outer space, we are assuming something like a universal Euclidean grid where the place of each thing can be mapped out in relation to every other thing, showing where it borders other things. This space is blank, waiting to be filled in, ever present, ever eternal. But no matter that it is blank, it is *there*; indeed, it defines "thereness." That is what is most important; it exists independently of us. It is universal, too. That everybody has the same map is the point. Our task, then, is seemingly to find out what is there and how to get from one place to another. This might also be called the "in-space" picture, for it pictures us in a universal, neutral space.

Much of the talk about a "public space" carries the flavor of Newtonian space. This is the first point we need to make. When we talk about the agora or the public square, we talk about it as if it were a place, a place we must leave the privacy of our homes (in most senses) to enter. To the degree that something like this picture operates in our minds, political philosophy is largely a matter of talking about how to enter this space and how to occupy it. The space itself is rarely in question, as is its universal and neutral nature. We need to leave behind, at least in theory, our personal and private commitments. Liberal politics operates with just such a picture. The preeminent theorist of justice, John Rawls, is a good example of it, particularly in his *Theory of Justice*. But even his later work, when he responded to criticisms that he had written off any number of important commitments, such as religion, that people have when making just decisions, shows it. In that later work, where he tried to wipe away largely theoretical commitments about what constitutes a person in favor of what he called a more genuinely political view, one where individual, personal commitments have to be considered, is the best example. This political space demands a justice that is framed to its "main political, social and economic institutions as a unified scheme of social cooperation; that . . . is presented independently of any wider comprehensive religious or philosophical doctrine."[2] To enter into this space, one has to leave behind such private doctrines.

The in-space picture is one way of talking about public space, and insofar as it causes us to make a crucial distinction between the public and the private, between the political and the nonpolitical, it is terrifically helpful. But it can also be very misleading as to the nature of that distinction. Not only does it confuse the private and the intimate, making intimate values just private, beside-the-public-main-point choices, it fails to see that the logic and grammar of those spaces can be different. Consider a comment Wittgenstein makes in another context about words that aren't *in* a space but are themselves a space: "That is to say, not something bordering on something else (from which it could be limited off). . . . And so, something language cannot legitimately set in relief."[3] The importance of this notion, what is sometimes called "logical space," is great, for armed with it, we are compelled to recognize the incommensurate nature of certain concepts, to recognize when we are operating with a picture and what kind it is, and to take seriously the life-world in which a concept is rooted. In short, as Wittgenstein hoped, as a way of doing philosophy, "it leaves everything as it is."[4]

The appropriateness of Wittgenstein's distinction in this context is this. Often in talking about public space, particularly when guided by the in-space picture, we forget that it is an important task of political philosophy to describe the conditions that actually create the space that gets called public or political. For example, to the degree that we picture public space in something like a Newtonian way, we have a tendency to slide away from paying attention to the sorts of problems that make the space of politics and begin to assume that such space is universal and neutral and that all our political talk takes place within such space. This is true even in an age in which theorists strive to be ever vigilant of differences and colonializations. One assumes, for example, that the difference between the public and private is a distinction within the political; it may well, instead, define it as it currently stands. To the degree it does, it behooves us to think about what actually constitutes the space in which we dwell.

The fact is that it is not "just there." Nor, at least according to the ancients, is it in fact neutral, a place where philosophical and religious commitments are to be set aside. Indeed, for the ancients, the political space was precisely where these commitments arose, where alone we could find meaning. The home, the private, was the place of the unimportant.

Consider then some ancient references to the spaces in which we live, all of which are created precisely by ethical and religious assumptions. Heidegger, for example, suggests that for the ancient Greeks, "*ethos* means abode, dwelling place. The word names the open region in which man dwells. The open region of his abode allows what pertains to man's essence, and what in thus arriving resides in nearness to him to appear."[5] This is to say, the space in which humans dwell is less a place we enter and go from; it is the home, where we find ourselves and Being finds us. (Heidegger thought we had lost such a dwelling place, that we had become homeless and rootless.) Or consider the fourth psalm, which says, "Thou hast given me room when I was in distress." That surely means something like this: that we, when pressed upon by others, frequently demand that we be given room to operate, that we be given space, that we be "cut some slack." Those are important requests, for we are active beings, and to be active, to live, we need space, we need room. To be distressed is to be closed in upon, to be shut up, to be confined. To be given room is to be able to act, to be free to be ourselves, to have a self at all. Thus, it is no small thing to remember, as the psalmist does, that "Thou hast given me room when I was in distress." One has been sheltered, not just granted mere privacy; one has been given the freedom and power to act within human space.

Similarly, Jesus tells his disciples that in his father's house there are many rooms (*monai*), using a word that means not just a room, a stopping place, but which, by virtue of its root in the verb *menein*, has a sense of abiding with, of dwelling with. Thus the kingdom of God is a space, a room that is not a place but an abiding with God, created by Christ.

The point I want to make is this: The space in which we dwell, public or private, is not simply there, is not simply something we move around in. Nor is it conceptually accessible from all vantage points. It is something that can also be talked about as constituted by certain assumptions on our part.

It is then important to recognize that over the course of Western history these assumptions have shifted. Spaces have been created and lost as a result. One that is especially important to recognize as having been created is the very idea of the secular as we presently understand it. It isn't necessary or inevitable. According to British theologian John Milbank, the public space we now assume—the secular—which used to be the interregnum prior to the kingdom of God, was created in the modern period by staking out the realm of "factum as an area of human autonomy . . . and dominium a matter of absolute sovereignty and absolute ownership."[6] Its present existence had to be created, and that was done, he notes, ironically, by bringing certain parts of the theological vocabulary into prominence. That history is important to recognize because it forces us to realize that the "secular" and "natural" *do* depend upon us and our history. Neither is any more the *index et judex sui et falsi* than anything else.

Thus, what actually constitutes public space should be a vital part of discussions in political philosophy; it is not at all obviously the secular or the natural. We need to think about that sort of discussion in talking about Weil's conception of the political. In retheologizing the political, Weil is no dreamy-eyed utopian but someone who in her latest and most controversial political writings was challenging the prominence of the concepts that had created the present sense of political space and seeking to replace them with others.

Weil, of course, is not the only thinker of the twentieth century who sought to reexamine many of the assumptions that define our political space. Leo Strauss and Hannah Arendt easily come to mind as others who have critiqued contemporary politics, particularly liberalism, and who, like Weil, looked to the ancients for guidance. They both found virtuous activity in the public space as the ancients talked about it to be the fulfillment of natural life. Both Arendt and Strauss, though, drew a sharp line between political *philosophy* and religion, the area of mysticism and revelation. Weil did not draw such a line. Indeed, key to her rethinking of the public space is casting doubt on the Enlightenment assumption that there can be a religiously neutral space. Said otherwise, Weil sought to retheologize political philosophy, to see it much as Augustine and Aquinas did, sub specie aeternitatis.

Because she did, doubts are now regularly raised about the degree to which Weil is genuinely a political thinker at all. The way in which these doubts have been raised is extremely interesting, for it is usually assumed that there is a basic incompatibility between being a religious thinker and a political one. Thus we have seen, for example, debates about whether there were, in fact, "two Simone Weils"—the religious Weil and the social activist Weil. Other thinkers, such as Mary G. Dietz, who was one of the first to do so, have noticed the integration of Weil's political and religious concepts and suggest that the fact that there aren't two Weils means that Weil really isn't a political thinker at all.[7] She ignored chief aspects of the political, such as the fact that it does not assume any normative sense of the good and certainly does not depend on theological ideas. That, of course, is true if one assumes that the philosophical underpinnings of modern liberal democracies are normative. If they are not, however, then one might well draw a very different conclusion. One might even get a perspective on liberal democracies that is too often missing.

For such critics, this does not mean that Weil does not have important moral suggestions to make as a voice within the political, suggestions that are both brilliant and troubling. Weil's critique of rights in favor of emphasizing obligations is one of them. But, it is always noted, such ideas are combined with suggestions that seem outright loony (*folle*), failing to capture the real sense of the political. The idea that one would jail an author such as Jacques Maritain for sinning against the sacredness of truth by failing to discover a citation in Aristotle would seem to be a case in point. At most, therefore, Weil is a social critic, but that does not make her a political thinker.

What would make her a political thinker? At first, it would seem to involve showing how her theological categories actually do allow a genuine public space that is political and not something reduced to religious activity. But things are a little more complicated than that, for part of the point of challenging the assumptions that have hitherto defined public space is to suggest that public space is not a given, but is created by the configuration of certain other assumptions, of certain values that light our communal paths. In this case, it is important both to show that Weil does not reduce, say, voting, to a liturgical act and also to try to understand how voting and the administration of civil justice cannot be understood apart from a larger context of a justice that is sacred, or that has something to do with or is identical to love.

Augustine's *The City of God* would be a good parallel to consider. In that work, Augustine seeks not to deny the City of Man and the activities that give it actuality, but rather to put both within a larger context, the providence of God. He does not seek to deny that the virtues of the City of Man are virtues, for he is not blind to what embodiment means to human communities. Although he calls them splendid pagan vices, they have worth in some human sense, which is why they are splendid. He does, however, put those activities and virtues in the context of the virtues of the City of God. In doing so, much is thereby left alone and the ancient polis is in important ways preserved. But it is also inevitable that insofar as life in the polis—in Rome—is now no longer seen as the fulfillment of human activity, new institutions, rationales, and ways of interacting would come into being. They certainly did in the emerging Christian medieval world. But that is to say that what constitutes the space in which we dwell and what ought to go on within it has just changed. The Ciceronian virtue of the Roman citizen, *honestum*, a sort of pride, is transformed by *agapē* into something else.

There is much in Weil's later writings, particularly those penned in London, that allows her to be read in the light of this Augustinian parallel. While, unlike Augustine, Weil was not interested in providing a theology of history, she, like him, wrote under the influence of a vision that set the space of human activity firmly within the context of an overarching divine purpose and goodness. Or, to put it within her own Platonic terms, one that could make necessity a mediator of good. Most generally, that is the effect of her theory of the *metaxu*, which allowed nonultimate human activities, including political ones, to be related to a supernatural destiny. It is important to note that a theory of mediation allows for *levels* of value—or that the recognition of levels of value calls for some kind of mediation between levels. The relation does not have to be direct; the higher and the lower can hint at each other. More specifically, how this vision plays out can be seen in a very particular theory of culture with which she seemed to be operating in her last writings. According to it, each culture is a historical working out of a response to a divine revelation, a revelation she thought present in all cultures focused on the mysterious link between necessity and goodness, wherein the former is seen as obedient to the latter. This idea will be dealt with in the next chapter.

One of the key features to thinking about human activity and the space in which it takes place in this way is an understanding that it is an attempt to think through how to respond to necessity, not how to eradicate it. Weil in those writings is *not* trying to eradicate the values of what she calls "the middle realm," values such as rights or values that rights are meant to protect, that is, the very things that presently constitute the topical matter of discussions in political philosophy.[8] She is not trying to avoid gravity and necessity, either socially or theologically. What she is trying to do is to think about them in a larger context, one she called "supernatural justice." Within such a context, it would simply be question begging to argue that inevitable changes in certain practices that we might hold politically very dear—e.g., certain ways of self-expression—constitute an antipolitical stance. Perhaps getting settled on that larger context is such a difficult task that political philosophers find it more fruitful to ignore it. If agreement were required, then there might be no beginning at all. Still, it is a question that cannot be ignored, nor can a thinker who attempts to think it through be excluded from the discussion. She might be the only one to provide anything fresh and truly challenging.

That may well mean that she does provide a challenge and not a program. In that case, the changes in certain political practices Weil offered, which oftentimes sound bizarre, need to be understood less as correctives to an existing approach to social and political life and more as tentative conclusions to be drawn from reconceiving the very context of that life together. In this sense, she is in no wise offering piecemeal suggestions, but proposes instead one of the more radical and thoroughgoing revisions of how we understand the space in which we dwell that we have seen in this century.

Thus the long and short of Weil's political philosophy is that it can be called a "retheologization" of the space in which we dwell. Put otherwise, it is an attempt to think about the natural life of humankind in supernatural terms while keeping in mind that this relation is often mediated and veiled. While much worthwhile can be said about the nature or consequences of this revision of our understanding of the space in which we dwell, and will be the substance of later chapters, I here limit the discussion to saying something further about why Weil's "supernaturalism" is not antipolitical; why, her mystical encounters notwithstanding, it demands political resolution; and, finally, what it means for Weil to say that politics and political space needs to be understood in the light of the supernatural. This needs to be done because we need to see just how the natural retains significance for her. In order to do so, I would like to return to Peter Winch's discussion of the supernatural, noted earlier, and to some emendations that Diogenes Allen and I made to it.

In the by now well-known conclusion to his *Simone Weil: "The Just Balance,"* Winch claims the point of Weil's use of language about the supernatural, such as the place "beyond space and time . . . where our Father dwells," to be a way of expressing the connections between various attitudes, interests, strivings, and aspirations, which are all a part of our "natural history." It is only *because* they are part of our natural history that we have any chance of making sense of the notion of the "supernatural."[9]

The criticism that was frequently leveled against Winch's claim when it first appeared is that it looked like he had reduced Weil's understanding of the "supernatural" to a mere perspective on nature, or, more strongly, had, by a sleight of hand, turned her into what might be called a naturalist. Winch's point was more subtle and further reaching. The intent of it can be seen in a remark he made some pages earlier on Weil's claim that "earthly things are the criterion of spiritual things." He thought this to be the principle on which we are to interpret Weil's reflections: "Her insistence that 'earthly things are *the criterion* of spiritual things' shows that we are not being offered a 'metaphysics of the spiritual,' but a certain way of thinking about the earthly."[10]

Tolstoy gives an illustration of what this might mean in what he says about the central character in the last sentence of his novel *Resurrection*: "And, indeed, from that night a new life began for Nekluhdoff; not so much because he had risen into a new stage of existence, but because all that had happened to him till then assumed for him an altogether new meaning."[11]

I think Winch meant that, for Weil, the concept of the supernatural cannot ultimately be divorced from the worldly context in which it operates. Indeed, he seemed to want to go so far as to suggest that concepts such as the supernatural cannot be understood apart from the space in which they operate. One might suggest that they cannot be understood, for example, apart from the Christian life in which they are used, although Winch did not use that language. (And, to be sure, Weil expands what the limits of that life are understood to be.) That much is positive. There is also an important warning in what Winch writes. The supernatural cannot simply be dropped onto the scene as a deus ex machina. Defenses of the supernatural are utterly misguided when they try to defend faith by trying to prove that the god lowered onto the scene is not really a statue dangling from ropes but something different because it is from "somewhere else," even though it looks and acts like a statue, despite all the bowing and scraping in front of it. Invocations of God are, too.

Surely, one of the reasons that Winch was critiqued in the way that he was, was because of his phrase "natural history." In a time when the concept of the natural trumps that of the supernatural and has naturalized and secularized most religious concepts, making them operate in foreign logical spaces, readers of Weil who admire her for her uncompromising supernaturalism might well be suspicious of such a phrase. The suspicion is understandable but seems to involve an unfortunate confusion. Winch's intent may well have been exactly the opposite of what he was accused of: rather than naturalizing the supernatural, he was trying to get us to look at the unique space in which the supernatural operates and to *not* regard it simply as a gussied-up version of concepts that come from somewhere else. Metaphysics in Winch's eyes was a problem precisely because it ripped concepts out of their own proper space.

Because we believed this to be true of Winch's claim, Allen and I introduced the idea of a "supernatural history" as a complement to his "natural history." If Winch is right and the supernatural cannot be understood apart from our natural history, we suggested, then, conversely, our natural history cannot be understood apart from our supernatural history.[12] Our point was to draw out the conclusion that one of the crucial connections the concept of the supernatural makes between our various strivings, aspirations, and so forth is a matter of seeing history and nature themselves in a very different light.[13] If the concept of the supernatural is a matter of connecting our various thoughts and aspirations in a unique light, then we presumed that would involve seeing history and nature themselves in a different light. History and nature seen in this light *cannot* be the same space as that which, say, Hobbes and Locke made of them.

We need to go one step further here. The point of this redescription cannot be left just as a matter of seeing nature and history in a different light. To connect events in this way, and not in the older, secular naturalistic way, also should have the effect of creating a space in which we did not operate before, one that brings with it the recognition of the possibility of a whole range of activities that needs to come into being.

It is not likely that such space can be defined theoretically ahead of time. It is more likely that the space comes from the activity. Or, perhaps even more accurately, the activity that fills the space and the ways of seeing that allow it are inextricably intertwined. That is part of Milbank's point that certain theological assumptions allowed for the creation of the secular world as we understand it.

What should be concluded, then, is that Weil's concept of the supernatural does have political meat on its spiritual bones, although it means to create, deliberately, a different sort of politics. It does so by seeking to make available certain spaces in which we can dwell that did not exist before. It involves what we have called a retheologization of the public space. But we need to understand very carefully what that involves. It does not involve judging present political activity by divine standards. If we did that, given present political reality, fire and brimstone might be the only appropriate response. Nor is it a matter of reforming efforts. Admirable as they may be, too often they do not change or deeply challenge the way we put together our aspirations. Rather, retheologizing the public space of politics involves a reconfiguring of the whole space in which we dwell and a reconception of how we move from one place to another within it. It involves a completely new set of activities and a different way of connecting many of our old ones.

Some of that work of suggesting what those activities are or might be is the substance of the following chapters. Many of Weil's own suggestions in *The Need for Roots* and any number of the essays in *Écrits de Londres* were tentative explorations of just such a reconfiguration, explorations of what certain activities that are part of our "natural history" might look understood in the light of a "supernatural history." They were not an attempt to legislate human affairs directly by divine law or an attempt to *deduce* natural law from divine.

Weil did not think we could step outside necessity. She knew full well that a world rooted in the supernatural would still have criminals, the need to work, political disagreement, and ignorance. The thought that criminals, the need to work, and political ignorance and disagreement could be eradicated was not her idea but, she thought, a foolishness common both to capitalism and communism—two chief determiners of political space in her day—that suggests we can escape necessity. Still, how we look at our problems can be very different if we understand that we have eternal obligations and that humans have an eternal destiny. Justice is then not simply procedural, but involves hearing the silent word behind the outer words of the criminal, labor becomes a consent to necessity and not an attempt to find dominion, political debate becomes a concerted effort to hear a voice of truth and not an attempt to be a player and to negotiate, and education becomes a matter of understanding true greatness and finding our roots in the universe.

CHAPTER ELEVEN

THE NEED FOR ORDER AND THE NEED FOR ROOTS
To Being through History

By now it should be clear that one of the central features of Weil's thinking is that it is not just about the eternal, but how the eternal and the temporal are related. She distinguishes different levels of value and relates them, as we have seen in the essay "What Is Sacred in Every Human Being?" It is also a deep concern of *The Need for Roots*, her last work and the only one that could be considered a book. Written for the Free French, as were most of Weil's essays in London, it was intended to help prepare for a new French government upon the expulsion of the Germans. It was an opportunity to begin afresh, an extremely rare occurrence in the life of any nation, and an opportunity to reconsider not only forms but basic principles. *The Need for Roots* rises to the challenge. Its beginning is a bold critique of the notion of rights, which has been the basis of social justice and politics since 1789, not only in France but in much of the world. Weil wants to replace it with the notion of obligations: what we owe others instead of what we are owed. But that is not all she argues. She thinks through what the value of a nation is for the souls that live in it. Her striking conclusion is that it serves certain needs of the soul, which, if not met, cause the soul to wither and die. While these are not eternal needs but earthly ones, if they are not met—and they can only be met by a society—the soul might very well never come to understand what its eternal destiny is. While the nation itself cannot meet these eternal needs, it can serve as an intermediary that trains and shapes people for something greater. It can in its concreteness point to something higher than itself.

Weil gives in the opening section of *The Need for Roots* a tentative list of these "needs of the soul." In "Draft for a Statement of Human Obligations" she intentionally lists them "in pairs of opposites which balance and complete each other" (SE 224). When, shortly after, she pens *The Need for Roots*, she keeps some ordered pairs, but splits the need for freedom of opinion and the need for truth. She also adds the need for order, which like the need for roots is not balanced and completed by something else. She does not suggest that these two balance each other. Moreover, they are given a unique status that is underlined by what she says of them: "the first of the soul's needs, the one which touches most nearly on its eternal destiny, is order" (NR 10). Then she says, "To be rooted is perhaps the most important and least recognized need of the human soul" (NR 43).

These statements indicate the special status of these two needs in Weil's later political thinking. However, she appears to do more than claim special status for each of these needs; each is claimed to be primary. Is she contradicting herself? Is this hyperbole or simply the evidence of an unfinished manuscript? Or are these two needs somehow connected?

They are connected. Understanding how offers profound insight into Weil's project, for once again it is a matter of how the eternal and the temporal, necessity and the good, should be related. On the one hand, in asking us to think about the importance of a need for rootedness, she asks us to reverse a tendency of social being in our time, uprootedness. By itself that is an original proposal. But it also says something about Weil's thinking in this crucial last period of her life. It indicates the importance of the historical to her, something that has not always been recognized to be a concern of hers. She was always a thinker who emphasized timelessness. Now she begins to think historically, too. Yet, in recognizing the importance of the historical, she has not ceased looking to the eternal, and the need for order is central to this concern. So, the question of these needs' relation is in the end a question of how our historical situatedness and our eternal destiny are related. The answer has a significance that goes far beyond what France might have done in 1945, as now, in most of the North Atlantic nations, any sense of coherence between the soul's eternal needs and its daily material and social life is rapidly being lost. Even the question itself is being lost. If it is, careful attention to what she offered in 1943 may illumine what is now needed to save our social being.

In order to understand this relation, then, we begin by looking at what Weil means when she says that the soul has a need for order. She is relatively straightforward on the matter. The sort of social order she has in mind is, in the first place, "a texture of social relationships such that no one is compelled to violate imperative obligations in order to carry out other ones" (NR 10). Given her original insistence on the primacy of obligations, it is easy to see why this sort of order is important. Its absence would mean that the number of instances where our obligations are incompatible with each other would become intolerable. In short, one ought to do what in fact cannot be done in this society. That threatens one's spiritual being. If a man is not "able to offer any resistance thereto, [he is] made to suffer in his love of good" (NR 10).

This can be spelled out further. The need for order is a second-order need, as Weil herself recognizes. It only makes sense to talk about it after one has discovered other, more immediate needs that are to be ordered. As such, Weil distinguishes it from the needs that are "properly so-called." "To be able to conceive it," she says, "we must know what the other needs are" (NR 12). Nevertheless, it has primary importance for two related reasons.

The first reason is moral. As Weil notes, without social order, obligations come into conflict with each other, making it impossible to fulfill all of them despite being obligated to do so. The upshot? Very simply, because one is talking about obligations—that is, first-person commitments—one cannot be forced to fail in several obligations without severely damaging one's very sense of self as a moral person. Morally, much of who we are is by virtue of our actions toward others; when we cannot weave a coherent narrative about ourselves that puts our various obligations and actions together, we disintegrate as moral persons. It is in this sense that the need for order can be primary, not only in a theoretical but also in a very practical way, for if one cannot see oneself as a moral actor, one's love of good *is* made to suffer. A person, for example, may understand that it is important to be generous or to be truthful. A society that does not encourage and reward generosity, or in which lies are the substance of public discourse, and which actually encourages and rewards selfishness and seeking self-advantage without truth, is a society that will frustrate one's attempts to be good. It is also going to *teach* people to be selfish. The point is simple enough, and as any society becomes more and more individualistic, the examples of the conflicts will explode in number.

Why this is so can be seen by the second reason underlying the primacy of the need for order. Although in the first instance what Weil sees order to be is relatively straightforward and concrete, social order is not just a "texture of social relationships." It has a greater value as well, a symbolic or participatory one. Weil sees social order as analogous to the order of the universe, and as pointing to it. Few political thinkers of our time say anything like this—nor would many of them even want to. Weil, however, like Plato before her, sees the polis as both a microcosm of the larger universe and a macrocosm for the smaller individual soul to emulate. We will have a chance to think about this resurrection of Plato below. At this point, the value of this symbolic status of social order is that it provides an example to the individual soul of how competing needs and goods can be balanced within a larger whole, of the need to think of a larger whole, and that leads us to realize that social being is a bridge for participating in the eternal. It gives access to thinking about the world as a whole and its beauty. That access to the world's beauty is particularly valuable because it allows one to envision a whole and good life with some hope of actually living it. Weil poignantly observes, "If we keep ever present in our minds the idea of a veritable human order, if we think of it as something to which a total sacrifice is due should the need arise, we shall be in a similar position to that of a man traveling, without a guide, through the night, but continually thinking of the direction he wishes to follow. Such a traveler's way is lit by a great hope" (NR 11).[1]

This, in sketch, is what Weil conceives that in which the primacy of the need for order to consist. It is a very exalted sort of view. But, considered from a more mundane political perspective, one is led to ask what this emphasis on order entails. A comment by David McLellan may help illuminate the question. A political philosopher and accomplished Weil scholar, McLellan, in talking about Weil's shift of emphasis from her early Marxist critique and highly individualist "Reflections Concerning the Causes of Liberty and Social Oppression" of 1934 to the concerns of the *Need for Roots* of 1943, says,

> She is still profoundly interested in politics—indeed *The Need for Roots* contains more than *Oppression and Liberty* on the detail of how political power should be exercised. But she is now concerned to place this politics in the context of a new culture. She is still concerned with an order that will not fall victim to totalitarianism, still as opposed to any centralised state power, still advocating a strong liberty of choice with as few laws as possible, and still utopian in the sense of proposing measures whose realisation she did not think possible.[2]

What is significant in this observation is its connection between the notion of order and utopian thinking. McLellan is a sensitive reader of Weil and does not, I think, confuse the deeper sort of order that Weil talks about as a need of the soul with the very specific political order that constitutes the obvious outward characteristics of a regime. Nevertheless, the two are not unrelated. They certainly are not in Weil. While her notion of order does not come down to details of how political power should be exercised, it is certainly in service of a spiritual order that she makes the very specific sort of recommendations that she does. The suppression of political parties is an example, because they act like the Great Beast in pressuring their adherents, forcing them to lie or stop thinking. That may sound very fine and good. The problem, though, is that once one begins to talk about a need for order, even at the very exalted and pure levels that Weil wants to talk about it, one very quickly finds oneself talking about the sordid details of political life. At that point, spiritual values—the values of Being we might call them—are invoked to lend their authority to contingent political values. In short, the need to satisfy the need for an eternal order becomes the need to impose not simply an order, but *the* proper order. Seeking Being, one seemingly cannot avoid describing the order that best reveals it. That is utopian. It can also be dangerous.

While there are important uses for utopian thinking, it can be troublesome in the negative sense that Karl Popper used the term, for it can give society a closed and static quality. Even in its antitotalitarian bent, it can itself become totalitarian. Clearly, this is not what Weil intended to do by any means. Still, the suspicion remains and serves to explain certain reactions to her later political thought. It certainly explains, I think, McLellan's own description of Weil's later political thought as conservative.[3]

This is why the need for order, as Weil sees it, may not easily fit alongside the need for roots, particularly when both are put in a primary position. If the need for order suggests a need to instantiate the order of Being itself, or to link social order to the order of the universe, the idea of rootedness would appear to run in the opposite direction; rather than supporting any suggestion that there is a single order to be instantiated, it suggests that our particular and distinctive histories are what are most important. For example, Weil writes in her most important definition of rootedness,

> A human being has roots by virtue of his real, active and natural participation in the life of a community, which preserves in living shape certain treasures of the past and certain particular expectations of the future. This participation is a natural one, in the sense that it is brought about by place, conditions of birth, profession, and social surroundings. . . . It is necessary for one to draw well-nigh the whole of his moral, intellectual, and spiritual life by way of the environment of which he forms a natural part. (NR 43)

The suggestion that Weil's understanding of one's "roots" as something particular, distinctive, and nonuniversal receives support from the very way that she goes on to describe uprootedness and the suggestions that she gives for the growing of roots. She spends, for example, little time on the general aspects of rootedness and uprootedness, giving only a brief general description of what roots are (i.e., the one above). She also adds in a general vein that nations lose them for pretty much the same reasons, that is, money and military conquest. But, after that, the major portion of her case consists in detailing how France became uprooted. It did so by the loss of so many of its specific traditions, especially regional ones. Her essays on colonialism complain that traditions that might nourish the French when imported into another context do little for Algerians or Vietnamese. So, too, did France become uprooted when regional roots were erased in favor of a demand for national loyalty. Likewise, she suggests that the problem with both liberalism and Marxism is that they both think that they can provide a universal order anywhere, anytime. Weil gives clear indications that she does not think that they can. That is uprooting.

This should allow us now to form an initial understanding of the sort of problem that is at stake. Whereas an emphasis on order, particularly an order that is somehow supposed to reflect Being itself, tends to the universal and unchangeable, the notion of rootedness implies an emphasis on the historical, the distinctive, and the inevitably changing.

Weil makes this tension a creative one by suggesting something like this: In talking about rootedness, she stresses how we are morally nourished by means of our roots. It is through them that we have contact with what is beyond us. Specifically, it is by having living spiritual traditions that play out in daily life that we are connected to something larger than us in a way that really does touch our lives. (I will say more about this in the next chapter.) We are starved spiritually when we lose roots, we lose Being, and we lose the ability to think deeply about moral and spiritual things. Having roots, therefore, gives us the moral nourishment, the moral formation, that we need to conceive order properly and draw upon the eternal. Uprooted people do not understand good order. At least, that is what Weil wants to argue. How that sort of solution actually works, how it is possible that the need for order is actually satisfied through finding a distinctive history that we can own, needs further explanation.

Consider, for a moment, some issues raised by McLellan's claim that Weil was, in some sense, utopian. They will give us clues about a problem about order that only the concept of rootedness can solve.

Weil certainly was not a utopian because *The Need for Roots* is a literary description of a utopia, that which is the best place and yet, at the same time, no place at all. But, of course, that is not the only sort of utopian thinking that there is. One definition of utopias suggests a positive and enlightening function for them: "Utopias perform two important functions in political thinking: first, they explicitly criticize existing political and social arrangements from a radical rather than a reformist perspective; and, second, they offer new ideals and illustrate how these might be realized in a different society."[4]

By this definition, Weil could qualify as utopian. *The Need for Roots* is not a reformist document. It does not pretend simply to *correct* problems in French political thinking; it tries to *reconceptualize* them and put them on an entirely different footing. This begins with the suggestion that obligations are prior to rights, "*pace* the men of 1789," and then runs through her suggestions about how to reconceive the relations between science and morality. As McLellan notes, she also is proposing measures whose realization even she could not have thought were really possible; in that sense, too, she is utopian. That is no special mark against her. If critique is the goal, if providing a sort of measuring stick for thinking is the object, then utopianism is not a mere flight of fancy but an important philosophical enterprise. Utopianism, in this way, "is a unique method of reflecting on politics and society, which seeks the perfect, best, or happiest form of society, untrammelled by commitments to existing institutions."[5]

It is at this point, though, when we attempt to discover such an "untrammelled" method, that a problem must be raised. It is *not* the problem of impracticality, of how actually to institute these radical recommendations. This is understood from the outset. The problem is a conceptual one. Or, at least, Weil sees it as a conceptual one. It can be seen this way. In discussing Weil's early essay "Reflections Concerning the Causes of Liberty and Social Oppression," Peter Winch suggests that the problem that the project of that essay runs up against is its excessive individualism. Winch's complaint is that Weil at this point in her thinking seemed to want to talk about individuals as if they came out of nowhere and as if the problem of social and political philosophy were a matter of constructing a state for them to dwell in.[6] The conceptual problem raised by this attempt is that such a project does not make a great deal of sense. We know nothing of human beings who are so unrelated to each other in this way; what we do know are beings who have histories, which admittedly are more or less flexible, but without which they do not appear.

This sort of problem seems to beset most utopian thinking. To be "untrammelled by commitments to existing institutions" *can* be a failure to appreciate the very problems one wants to critique. Rarely is bad order in a society a problem of having the wrong order in general; the problem of bad order is usually one of having *this* order because it forces one to violate *these* moral expectations that we, as a matter of who we are as *these people*, have. Recommendations to improve the order of social obligations can fail to make sense if they do not take into account the history of the people who are expected to live within it.

Michael Walzer, in his *Spheres of Justice*, stresses just this point. In developing a "theory of goods," Walzer gives a number of criteria for an adequate theory of social goods, some of which are helpful to us with respect to our problem. He notes that "men and women take on concrete identities because of the way they conceive and create, and then possess and employ social goods." But what these goods are is not unambiguous, for "there is no single set of primary and basic goods conceivable across all moral and material worlds." Each of these goods carries some kind of social meaning, and "social meanings are historical in character; and so distributions, and just and unjust distributions, change over time."[7] The value of goods, even material goods, is so tied to our history that they have little meaning or value outside it. The proper or just order of distributing these goods or organizing anything within a society that is similarly bound up with a culture's history therefore only makes sense within that history.

The problem, then, of utopian thinking, even as radical critique, is how to critique the existing order without failing to understand and appreciate the very people whose lives one hopes to help. Unfortunately, the history of political thought is littered with carcasses of those whose lives had to be helped by the imposition of the "right" order. And, far too often, those who would help are precisely those who are untrammelled by any commitment to the institutions that actually go into making the people they would help. However, as we move into an era of nationalisms and identity politics, we also have to be aware that of the problems we have to face, "order" is not the only one. Some kind of balance, some sense of level that is not just a cheap verbal compromise, is needed.

To put the problem of order as conceptual and not simply practical lets us see fairly quickly the importance of the soul's need for roots, according to Weil, and how it can be helpful for treating problems of order. When Weil, for example, says that "it is necessary for one to draw well-nigh the whole of his moral, intellectual, and spiritual life by way of the environment of which he forms a natural part," she is not making a simple observation about how human beings just happen to operate in the world. She is saying something far more profound, namely, that one is not thinking very clearly about human beings unless one realizes that what human beings hold valuable is bound up with their social and historical existence. The whole importance of the soul's need for roots is because of this, and it is this feature that makes the need for roots the key to discovering a social order that can give meaning to existence. For it is through the values and solutions of one's own roots, and not through abstract schemata, that one does anything about order. An observation about Weil's project will be helpful to establishing and clarifying this point.

When Weil begins discussing the problem of how roots may be grown again in France, after a long history of destroying spiritual values through the growth of the modern nation-state and the defeat of that state by the Nazis, she sets the problem as one of trying to breathe genuine inspiration into France (NR 198). That is a problem, she says, of education, but especially an education that "concerns itself with the motives for effective action" (NR 190). The result, if the Free French are to be successful, will consist "in being able to mold the spirit of the country" (NR 199). This is a problem of order, of trying to find the right order for postwar France. But it is not a matter of imposing a preconceived order on the country. It is not even a matter of finding some order in the past and reinstituting it. It is a matter of finding a good order implicit in the minds and hearts of the people. Through techniques of listening and understanding the history of the people[8] one can find the words that "are likely to find an echo in the hearts of Frenchmen, because they correspond to something that is already there" (NR 199).

To underline the point, one may observe that as Weil, in the remaining third of the book, makes specific recommendations about how to grow roots, she does not try especially hard to be inventive. Instead, she concentrates on finding, written on French and Western hearts by virtue of their history, an order that is natural to the people with that history that will let human lives flourish and find their good. She is not trying to invent an order or to reason the nation into one. She is trying to find something deeper that may still remain in people's lives. It is in this way, then, that the need for roots is the "most important and least recognized need of the soul" while being at the same time secondary to the need for order. For it is only through having roots that one finds a *meaningful* order. One only finds Being through history. This is a very incarnational philosophy indeed.

This much solves the exegetical problem of how Weil can say that both order and rootedness play a primary role in the life of the soul. It gives some sense of what she means. But, it does not solve a much larger philosophical problem that would seem to involve a large portion of Weil's thinking. The problem is put again by Winch, who notes that "the fascination of the thought that everything belongs to a single all-embracing system of necessities was something Simone Weil never freed herself from."[9] Although we may have shown how she thinks rootedness is related to order, and that any order, to be meaningful, must be related to the actual lives of those who live with it, Weil herself did see the idea of order as very important because it suggests to the soul an image of the order of the universe. Is that a good idea? Is it even a coherent one? Winch suggests she may be confusing some very different senses of order and necessity. She seems to be taking a notion that properly applies to things *within* nature and applying it to nature as a whole. Nature as a whole needs to be thought of as something other than another example of what goes on within it.

Weil does, even in her latest writings, talk this way; it is no use to pretend she does not. Even in *The Need for Roots*, she clearly wants to reintroduce notions of order such that the universe is a macrocosm to the polis's microcosm, which in turn is a macrocosm to the soul's microcosm. She does subscribe to the idea of an all-embracing order to life, and she wants to recommend it to people who have lost their way in the cosmos. But, politically, this would of course seem to lead us right back to our original problem with order. We have only advanced to the degree that it seems to be in tension with some historical factors in Weil's thinking.

However, something much more profound is happening in Weil's thinking in *The Need for Roots,* and much of it has to do with a unique resurrection of the microcosm/macrocosm argument of classical political philosophy. Rather than suggesting that there is a single order to the universe that is repeated at larger and smaller levels—that is, that order comes from the notion of a repeated action applied to wider and wider spheres[10]—Weil sees as the order of the universe something more like "an order of orders." This "order of orders" fully recognizes—and needs—the very different sorts of orders. The beauty of the universe, which she thinks obvious, is the harmony of all the orders that go to make it up. She wants us somehow to emulate that beauty.

This idea of various orders is implied in the very notion of the idea of rootedness. If Weil held it in anything like the way I have suggested, then she was very clearly aware of the nature of human sociableness and realized that it could not be reduced to an incommensurate form of thought, say, mathematics. To get at humans, one had to go by way of their roots; one cannot avoid them, except at great peril, she recognized.

If this is the case, then what can it possibly mean to suggest, as she does, that the order of the world, the beauty of the world, "can sustain us in our efforts to think continually about . . . human order" (NR 11)? It could mean that Weil has reverted back to a simple mathematical model and does think, despite what she says about roots, that all orders are the same. Or, it could mean that she believes that the distinctive and previously largely unrecognized organic, social nature of human thought *is* nourished by thought of the world's beauty, and vice versa. Unless human thought finds some way of connecting itself to something bigger than itself, something that gives a sense of value (and this is what the world's beauty does), human thought will lose depth and dimensionality. I am proposing that it is the latter. It is not because the two sorts of order, social and cosmic, are so similar on the face of things that they are linked, but rather they are linked because one can more easily and more deeply think the one by having the concept of the other. Which is to say, one needs to think analogically here. The idea has an initial plausibility for the simple reason that any order, including the order of the universe, is an order *of* something, as Weil herself knew.[11] If you do not know the elements that go into it, then you are quite likely to misconceive the order.

But once again there is more to it than that, which may best be explained through the use of an illustration. As is well known, ancient and medieval political philosophers often relied on some version of the macrocosm/microcosm argument. This can be said to result in an image of the universe of meaning consisting of a series of concentric spheres, the diameter of any one representing its greater or lesser ability to comprehend the others. For non-Christian philosophers such as Plato there would have been three concentric spheres: the individual soul would have been the smallest and would have been encompassed by the world of the polis, which in turn would have been encompassed by the universe. For Christian thinkers such as Augustine and Aquinas, the universe would further have been encompassed by God. The point of this image is that as the soul, for example, finds its place in the polis, it also finds a place of meaning in the universe and, if one is a Christian, within God's providence. One can also read it in the opposite direction: God gives meaning to the soul through the universe and the polis. The image is one of interlocking spheres that give meaning to each other. This image was particularly effective in the Middle Ages as, for whatever reason, the various institutions in which human life took place, that is, church and state, were far more interdependent, sharing in many ways a common symbolism and set of lived expectations.

The Renaissance saw the beginning of the disappearance of this image. Several factors contributed to this: the medieval synthesis began to break apart, so there was little outward sign of an interlocked harmony; the institutions that depended on the image for their authority—and that gave it authority—lost credibility; nominalism called into doubt the sort of thinking that could articulate the image in any meaningful way. But whatever the reason, the result is fairly clear: the *series* of linked concentric spheres was lost. But it was the series as a whole and their linkage; various aspects actually remained in play, but without the mediating influence of the other key parts. We find in Machiavelli, on the one hand, the loss of God and a purposeful nature, both replaced by something quite different and purposeless, namely, fortune. This, of course, alters the relation between the remaining elements, humans and society. Now society points to nothing beyond itself; it is a human creation and can be altered without reference to eternal standards. Indeed, it must to make the most of fortune. On the other hand, we find in somebody such as Luther the retention of God as purposeful, but the loss of society and human thought as anything capable of pointing to God, resulting in the soul standing alone before God, with society largely irrelevant or indifferent. In either case, despite what is often said, human beings now become the center of value. They are not part of a larger whole. As this happens, there is no reason to think that they will not repeat the process within human communities as well.

This is to paint the picture of the origins of modern thought, particularly social thought, in very broad strokes. Still, it is in such a direction as this that modern thought ventured forth. With society no longer a mediator between the soul and God, a thinker such as Hobbes could see social thinking as strictly a matter of mathematical and physical principles. Similarly, liberal societies that leave the individual to choose his or her own good have also left behind the mediating role of the social. The human world has shrunk, and its aspirations are more and more self-referential.

Weil wanted to recover this older image or something akin to it. She wanted society to contribute to our greater depth, our life within an eternal mystery. She wanted a sense of social differences that is both fully respected *and* balanced within a larger, communal whole. Despite using very deliberate mathematical metaphors to make her case, as she does in her theory of the *metaxu*, in the end it is not the mathematical method she celebrates but the recovery of a sphere of human thought that is being lost. She would, I suspect, feel confirmed in this were she able to look at Western societies in the twenty-first century, which are very good at applying algorithms to social life but are cut off from the universe. The recovery she wants is not the repeated application of a method; it is the insight that human life has not been understood very well because an important element was missing, namely, the larger whole in which we live and move and have our being. It is the insight that a mere repeated application of a method kept one on the same plane all the time; the problem was how to move to a different plane—and to see *all* the planes on which human life is lived. Social life thus became a mediating term for Weil again on the microcosm/macrocosm model because it allowed her to think better about God and the soul. Because it was, in fact, an order of a very different sort, it caused her to think about order itself in a very different way, even though she retained some of the old imagery to talk about it. And, one suspects, she did not see a mathematical model so much as a tool to provide a method—an analogy, a way of relating different things.

Let me put this somewhat differently. What Weil finds valuable in her theory of the *metaxu*, which is based on a mathematical analogy, is that it allows a way of describing and talking about what she regards as fundamental relationships between very different, even incommensurate, spheres of life. The point of doing so is to emerge from a limited point of view to a fuller one, where we can read that "The order of the world is the same as the beauty of the world. All that differs is the type of concentration demanded. . . . It is one and the same thing, which with respect to God is eternal Wisdom; with respect to the universe, perfect obedience; with respect to our love, beauty; with respect to our intelligence, balance of necessary relations; with respect to our flesh, brute force" (NR 295).

The soul's need for order is a need for a sense of a world that is broad and inclusive, a world where differences come together in some sort of balance. To satisfy it, it is undoubtedly necessary to plan, order, and legislate things in a society so that there are no irreducible conflicts between obligations. Nevertheless, the larger necessity is to conceive of order in such a way that it can encompass very different sorts of things within its ken. The need for order is not a logistical need but a conceptual one. And that, in turn, is a need to relate oneself differently to the world and society. It is a need to find in the culture of which one is a part[12] a way of thinking of the very diverse—and often incommensurate—aspects of human life as still cohering within the parameters of an individual human life, and, conversely, for individual lives to find themselves as somehow fitting into a world of plural values and meaning. If the need for order is a need for ordered being, it is also a need for thinking about being differently than we presently do. One important example of how Weil thinks this can be done can be seen in the very fact that her list of needs of the soul is given in such a way that a just order is the result of balancing contrary needs. They do not compete but are resolved on a higher plane.

But it is here that the need for roots is crucial to understanding this sort of order. It is in the recognition that we thrive by virtue of having roots that one also recognizes exactly what the problem of order is. For the relation of roots to order is not simply finding an order that is historically meaningful to a people; it is recognizing that the problem of order is also a problem of seeing a people related to each other and to the universe and God through social and historical relations, past and present. And it is a problem of having an order that will let a people see themselves in that way. Their roots go to their identity, and their identity is what, in the end, lets them be related to, not distant from, others in the world.

CHAPTER TWELVE

A THEORY OF CULTURE
Inspiration and Its Outworkings

For Simone Weil, the great revolution in her late social thought consists in the way that she came to think of social entities. In her earlier writings, fueled by her disappointment over her experiences with political movements, she tended to dismiss most social groupings and institutions, including the Church, as best analyzed by a consistent and thorough application of Plato's metaphor for society as a great ravenous beast of whimsical humor. Yet, in her very last writings, while she was in London writing for the Free French, Weil shows a remarkable change. In these writings, her treatment of nations, social groupings, and cultures tends to the positive—with certain reservations, of course. In *The Need for Roots,* the nation is not an absolute good, and yet it is something very important for human life. It is "food for the soul," a recognition that many goods for human life, including those that allow human spiritual development, can only be had within a community. So communities are important for spiritual life and can and ought to be mediators of the divine. Continuing this insight, she adds that cultures give us access to the spiritual treasures of the past, and that we therefore dare not lose our roots in them. Those roots are our access to the eternal. She even goes so far as to claim that "culture is the formation of attention"—not attention's enemy. In "A War of Religions," she adds that the issue of religion is actually inescapable within societies and that, therefore, all cultures have a religious basis of one sort or another. What needs thinking about is what that basis actually is.[1] Since she thinks that getting the right one is truly important, her recommendations for a newly constituted French government include a demand that a newly constituted France be a transcendently rooted society and that its leaders even subscribe to a sort of credo. Only those who can do so are to be trusted with leading the souls of the nation's citizens.

For many readers who live in the liberal societies of the West, this is strong and even offensive language. The path to good politics, it is thought, should include casting off religious mooring; religion works against good, inclusive politics. Mary Dietz, more than twenty-five years ago, argued that, at best, Weil's work is "beset by a tension between the political and the spiritual characterized by an almost palpable sense of urgency to reconcile the two."[2] Dietz thought that Weil in her later writings did have a more positive view of politics than she had earlier, but, as we have seen, she also believed there remained something fundamentally antipolitical in Weil. This, she thought, was due to Weil's mysticism, which "grants no value or meaning to either individual autonomy or collective, public action";[3] like other mystics, she writes, Weil "encourages a genuine passivity in this world."[4] This does not mean that Weil had nothing interesting to say about politics; she did. So the wonder is the degree to which she *resisted* the pull of the mystical in her later works and achieved some political insights. The problem, Dietz claims, is that Weil's religious sensibilities often short-circuit the attention to history and to specific negotiations within time, the ongoing push and pull of human interaction, that is the real nature of politics.

As we have just seen, it is not the case at all that Weil avoided history, even while looking toward the eternal. Weil did not think that there was an irreconcilable antithesis between the two. Rather, she believed in a tight relation between a properly mystical understanding of religion and the sort of politics that she proposed in *The Need for Roots* and *Écrits de Londres*; neither was meant to stand alone. This meant not only that good societies need somehow to grow roots that will allow their people to draw sustenance from the transcendent, but also that religion for its part cannot be world denying and must be worked out within communities, and in ways that, although they ultimately bear a relation to explicit religious issues, do not always wear that relation on their face.

To say this much is to uncover a vital dynamic in Weil's later political and social writings, and it shows that a good deal of her continuing relevance is in posing a challenge to societies in which the organization of social life has become unlinked from any question of the transcendent. Or, *too* linked, as when values of the middle realm become sacralized and the transcendent loses any ability to genuinely inspire a culture too busy with idols to listen to anything else.

But this challenge has to be more than rhetorical. There has to be some sense that finding the right links is possible and that doing so raises a meaningful question. I think there is such a sense, and it can be seen in Weil's belief that lasting cultures are the concrete, historical outworkings of an original religious inspiration. That is not only a backward-looking theory; it lays the plans for how it is possible, and also desirable, to think about the relation of the historical and the eternal. Weil's mysticism is meant not to deliver us from history but to be worked out in history.

At the outset, I want to issue a caveat. Despite the fact that I present something like a Weilian theory of how religion operates historically through culture, Weil herself did not systematically or in one place work out in any detail the sort of narrative that I am going to ascribe to her. However, she makes a number of striking and original comments in her last writings that, when a connecting line is imaginatively drawn through them, allow us to construct a narrative framework or outline that gives them enough coherence to proceed to an analysis of the various parts and how they might work together.

Perhaps the most striking aspect of her thinking on the issue is that she seemed to believe that cultures are the concrete outworkings of an original revelation. What this "original revelation" means in the first place and what it means for there to be outworkings were not, to her mind, anything like deductions from an original sacred proposition or received doctrine. Doctrine itself is simply an articulation of that revelation. Luther once described Scripture as the cradle that holds the child. You have to look in the cradle for the truth, but you should not mistake the cradle for the living child. The original revelation that Weil seems to have in mind, rather, is more like an insight into the deep relation between matter and necessity, and necessity and the divine love that necessity ultimately obeys, and the role that the human mind plays in those relations. That insight centers and inspires a culture. It is then worked out in various ways within a culture; or, more exactly, the cultural activities of a society *are* activities that have this insight at its center, and this insight is what ultimately makes all these different activities cohere. The point can be rather exactly illustrated by a claim that Weil makes in one of the fragments from the London period:

> Science is an effort to perceive the order of the universe. It follows that it is a contact between human thought with eternal wisdom. It is something like a sacrament. In all the peoples of antiquity—except the Romans, of course—lived the thought that inert matter, by its submission to necessity, gives man the example of obedience to God. This thought permits embracing in a single act of the mind science as an investigation of the beauty of the world, art as the imitation of the beauty of the world, justice the equivalent of the beauty of the world in human affairs, and love towards God insofar as he is the author of the beauty of the world. Thus is recovered a unity lost for centuries. (SWW 119)

If, however, this original revelation is the cohering center of cultural activity for any given society, different societies may, given their historical circumstances, work this out differently. Each may come to stress one thing more than another. Weil claims that all peoples of antiquity (excepting the Romans, of course) knew one special thing about God.[5] For example, the Jews knew about the unity of God; the Greeks, concerned as they were about the distance between divine fullness and human misery, sought the bridges, the *metaxu*, that exist between divine fullness and emptiness. One presumes that it would possible to see, therefore, as Weil suggests, a sort of transcendental unity of cultures that, within their particular circumstances, pursued an understanding of the relation of matter and necessity. The distinctive lives of different cultures would therefore be not a set of contradictory principles, but complementary outworkings of similar revelations. Showing something like this seemed to be the driving motivation for Weil's extensive research during the last couple of years of her life into the folklore of different cultures.

The claim of an original revelation behind the growth of a culture is an historical claim. As such, it demands historical evidence and investigation. However, such an idea also has philosophical import that may well be more significant for understanding what Weil is getting at. It is most important when anyone asks why this narrative makes any difference to thinking about the nature of culture now and its relation to the supernatural. Indeed, Weil seems to think that the importance of the historical narrative is chiefly in illustrating the possibilities of that present relation.

It is quite clear that this relation of matter to necessity and necessity to divine love is not, for Weil, something that can be determinately captured in a proposition. It is conceptually unlike the propositions generated by anybody or any culture that has this revelation. Why? Because, Weil claims, it is "outside"; Weil regularly talks about the relation as being "outside" the world of time and space. For example, in the essay "Is There a Marxist Doctrine?" she argues, "If we examine closely not only the Middle Ages of Christendom but all the really creative civilizations, we notice how each one, at any rate for a time, had at its very center an empty space reserved for the purely supernatural, the reality that lies outside this world. Everything else was oriented towards this empty space" (OL 167–68).

The point of this sort of talk has nothing to do with locating the supernatural in anything like a physical space. Its point, as suggested in chapter 10, is more like what Wittgenstein suggests in pointing out that certain concepts are not in a logical space but actually define it. To have this "revelation," then, even if it might subsequently be enshrined in, say, a religious doctrine, is really something more like having an understanding of how everything else is to be understood and used. Its "outsideness" is not meant to negate the importance of this world, nor is it some place to escape to. It is more like a vantage point on what is important in this world. In a helpful analogy already used here in chapter 2, Weil talks of the supernatural's relation to matter as being like the fulcrum of a balance. That point of balance—and it is a mere point—is not part of the system it balances, but it is crucial for the relation of the forces that are balanced around it.[6] Thus she claims, "The true knowledge of social mechanics implies that of the conditions under which the supernatural operation of an infinitely small quantity of pure good, placed at the right point, can neutralize gravity" (OL 167). To have this sort of concept is to see how things hang together. To have it, for example, might be to see as important, as Weil claims the Greeks did, discernment of the bridges, the *metaxu*, that exist between human misery and divine fullness, or to see, as the psalmist did, that "the earth is full of the glory of God." As Weil comments, "According to the conception of human life expressed in the acts and words of a man[,] I know . . . whether he sees life from a point in this world or from above in heaven." She concludes, "The Gospel contains a conception of human life, not a theology" (FLN 146, 147).

Weil provides an important cultural illustration of just what she had in mind when she talked about this fulcrum. In two essays on the lost culture of Languedoc, Weil praises its people for their sense of balance, a sense that she thinks is admirably evidenced in Romanesque architecture.[7] But it is especially evidenced in their rejection of force as a way of life. For the people of Languedoc, forces had to be balanced morally, not overwhelmed by other forces. According to Weil, this is particularly seen in the way that Catholics and Cathars interacted and interceded for each other when the country was attacked in a crusade to wipe out the Cathars. *Neither* people was the heart and soul of the Occitan civilization; together they balanced each other, and both had a sense of balance. The culture was the two sides together, balanced against each other by their consent to something outside the system, consent to which held the system together. This also says something about Weil's concept of order: it is not a restraint so much as something intended to foster interaction and harmony.

This should help us to get much closer to what she thinks is the relation between the supernatural and human cultures. An original revelation here is not revealing the hitherto unknown concept of a *thing*, or even a proposition, so much as it is a transforming way of thinking about things, or even a way of standing in the world, and thus a way of being in relation to everything else. Although the idea of an original revelation is, of course, a historical claim about origins, Weil is not particularly interested in using it to *ground* any cultural norms or to exclude others. The notion of an "original revelation" is meant not so much to explain subsequent history as to point to the deepest character and the defining moral and spiritual horizons of a people within which cultural relations are formed and understood. So, far from using the supernatural to devalue such relations, they can be seen to be important precisely because for human beings, who live out their lives in such relations, these relations can be the human connection to the supernatural. As Weil observes, "Earthly things are the criterion of spiritual things." Like a sacrament, in which supernatural grace is embodied in a material element and does not come as something separate from it, so, too, the supernatural is present precisely in its historical and social outworkings, including in material culture.

Putting things this way also helps us to see something more about what such a revelation entails. If having it is more like an ability to see value, at least of a certain kind, in the world, having it is therefore also a matter of putting oneself, or finding oneself, in a certain relation to the world as a whole. If the original revelation consists in understanding the submission of matter to necessity and necessity to divine love, and in understanding that submission as a model for human obedience to God, then understanding the revelation consists in the action of one's consent to God by consenting to the necessity that God ordained to rule matter, including social matter.

Consider a parallel to illustrate the point of how "understanding" is used here. Augustine famously argued that "unless you believe you will not understand." The heart of his claim lies in that understanding in religious matters is dependent not on credulity but on putting oneself into a relation of trust and assent. It *is* the understanding that comes from love, friendship, and gratitude, and vice versa. What one thinks— and Augustine defines faith as "thinking with assent"—as one lives life with this internal relation is then what I am calling the outworkings of revelation. What one thinks and indeed what one feels, especially with regard to moral, social, and spiritual matters, are the expressions and articulations of this internal relation. They have their sense within it and make little sense independent of it.

Such understanding is not episodic nor simply ejaculatory. It does not come primarily in flashes, although there may be a few flashes along the way; it has a history. For while such thinking goes on within the moral and spiritual horizons established by the relation to the supernatural, at few points could one trace any given concept or idea *directly* to the supernatural. Thinking builds on thinking, and in this sense, that internal relation, that consent to the necessity that obeys God, has for any given individual a history that helps to make sense of such thinking. It has a history, and it has the possibility of a future, too.

Weil argues that unless a desire of the soul "passes through the flesh by means of actions, movements and postures that naturally correspond to it, it hasn't any reality for the souls. It dwells there only as a phantom" (SWW 100). For example, if one wants to be brave or to defend one's country against an invader, that desire and that self-image of bravery are mere phantoms if that one does nothing about it. Such patriotism tends to phoniness. The way that one really becomes brave is by first going to the recruiting office, then undergoing basic training, and then facing enemy fire, and perhaps even finally by going on a perilous mission. In this process one consents at each step to the danger that bravery needs to be willing to face. So, one is in one sense always assenting. But the understanding of it, the understanding of bravery and the actual bravery, depend on a series or a history of small consents to danger. This is true for any sort of genuine moral or spiritual apprenticeship. The point then is this: the outworkings of an internal relation are not simply manifestations of a static relation to the supernatural; what is said and done is a matter of repeated and consistent assent, and each new expression and action often builds on what has gone before it. This does not mean that one ever fully grasps the supernatural. It is transcendent and forever working within the finite limitations of human life, and within the history of human beings.

But, if in this way, individuals can have a history of assent, then their expressions and articulations of faith can build on each other. So, in an analogous way, can cultures as a whole. The thinking that goes on in any given culture, while it may have its own spirit, *is* the thinking of individual men and women in conversation with each other. Whatever moral and spiritual horizons there are and whatever opportunities one encounters in any culture are something like the nested consents—or refusals—of the souls who have lived in that culture. The sense of justice, for example, of any given culture is the justice that it has exercised historically and concretely. To the degree that consent to the internal relation souls have to the divine good through their acceptance of necessity remains alive, the culture remains morally and spiritually alive. To the degree that it has been lost, the moral traditions become so much dead weight, or they become incoherent, as, for example, Alasdair MacIntyre, in *After Virtue*, has claimed has happened in the liberal traditions of the West.

What this means most importantly for Weil's thinking is that human spirituality depends upon this historically nested consent and does not operate outside it. Grace can strike us suddenly, yet the access of souls to a lot of grace is primarily through history; what grace they have is played out historically. Thus she claims in the essay "East and West: Thoughts on the Colonial Problem,"

> If man is in need of help from outside himself, and if it is agreed that this help is of a spiritual kind, then the past is indispensable because it is the storehouse of all our spiritual treasure. It is true that the operation of grace can, ultimately, put man in direct contact with another world; but it is only the radiance from the spiritual treasures of the past that can induce in the soul that state which is the necessary condition for receiving grace. That is why *there is no religion without a religious tradition.* (SE 207)

Given this understanding of the relation of souls to God through what is historically conditioned, it is easy to understand precisely why Weil, in *The Need for Roots*, insists on the importance of rootedness in general for the well-being of human souls. Such rootedness does not respond just to a mere psychological need to feel a part of a place and to have a sense of identity in time and among others; it is the very means by which the human soul has an active relation to the heart of existence and to the God who creates it. It is through the centuries of nested consent that one develops the possibility, through one's own consents in a society, of consenting to the necessity that rules matter and to the divine love that persuades necessity. To take the past away from a people, as happens in the case of colonialism, is to take away that possibility. It is to take away the very forms of spiritual life, some of which may not necessarily be explicitly religious, that bear a connection to a soul's final end.

We may well conclude, given this Weilian theory, that in her latest political writings Weil took human history seriously, despite the timeless quality of many of her pronouncements. Even her religious views take human religious faith as thoroughly ensconced within history, for they always function within a tradition. There is not necessarily any impossible tension between Weil's mysticism and her political thinking. Indeed, one can even see that in human life, insofar as it is inescapably material and historical, the two cannot be divorced. That surely is *her* point, one that is a deliberate critique of modern, uprooted Western societies.

Still, the problem is not entirely settled. Close examination of Weil's specific religious ideas reveals elements—and Dietz insists on this—that make one continue to suspect that she is moving in antithetical directions at the same time. The problem lies with the very Weilian notion of decreation (Dietz uses the term *dépouillement*), for decreation is the unmaking of the person. Such would seem to involve taking away many, if not most, of the social goods and arrangements at the very heart of politics. The problem is, in short, as Dietz and others think, "that its ultimate form is death."[8]

The problem is demonstrated and underlined in the final pages of *The Need for Roots*. There Weil recommends that the spiritual core of any society, but especially French society after the war, be labor. Why? Because "physical labor willingly consented to is, after death willingly consented to, the most perfect form of obedience" (NR 281), and because "physical labor is a daily death" (NR 286). Weil is clear and consistent here. By consenting to labor, one submits to necessity and thereby begins and sustains the process of decreation. This seems an easily earned point for Dietz's position.

Some of this is a matter of the language that Weil is using. She uses language in a highly paradoxical way, a rhetorical strategy that is often needed to shake readers from running lethargically in worn and common conceptual ruts. Weil uses *death* here in such a way. Thus, in the first place she is not talking directly about physical death or even ontological obliteration; she is talking about something analogous that bears some proportion to physical death but is also its own phenomenon. So, what experiences death is, at least in the first instance, a certain sort of self-image and self-placement at the center of the universe. This is no mean thing, especially in social and political action, but it need not defeat either social or political action. Good social and political action in far too many instances could well use the death of the ego of many of those who plan and execute social policy.

There is more to it, too, as this death is crucial for finding true life, for opening the moral and spiritual space for a different kind of life. At the same time as she talks about "death" of the self or decreation, Weil is trying to develop a different and, she thinks, truer sense of what life really is. This sort of move is not at all unusual in Christian thinking, mystical or not, nor is it unusual in many other religions, such as Buddhism. Weil found Christ's admonition, "Unless a grain of wheat falls into the earth and dies, it remains just a single grain; but if it dies it bears much fruit" (John 12:24) worthy of continual meditation. The death Weil is talking about is a way to finding real life. Since the sort of daily death she commends is also clearly connected to the idea of submitting oneself to necessity, there is also a sense that it is a personal repetition of the same sort of insight in which cultural life began. If so, then just as cultural life is the outworking in history of that original revelation, it would stand to reason that an individual soul's submission to necessity signals not a withdrawal from the world of time and necessity, but a working out of that relation in time, subject to necessity. One ought to suspect that there can be no real change, no real transformation in culture or politics, unless this kind of death is taken seriously.

The paradoxical language of mystics, as Michel de Certeau pointedly argues,[9] is frequently a critique of the surrounding culture, especially when that culture has become restrictive and psychically damaging—in short, when *it* begins to mistake the ways of death for life. *Its* normal use of language is what is damaging, and it is only by startling paradox that it may be called upon to right itself again. Such language is not at all antipolitical; it is actually highly charged, politically, and usually regarded as threatening the political status quo and therefore dismissed as being destructive. There is little doubt that such a critique was part of Weil's larger agenda in *The Need for Roots*. It is no mean thing to challenge the imperiousness of the language of "rights." It is the language which we use to affirm life, and yet it is, in fact, usually contentious and often violent, and not ultimately life-giving. It is something that shrinks our moral horizons and being. That doesn't mean such language doesn't have a place, but it needs something bigger to find that place and be effective in it.

This helps locate Weil's project. What needs investigation is the question of whether there is any sense in which that project is actually more life-giving than what it critiques. One way of doing this is to think about how Weil thinks about the human soul, for, as we have already noted, all political theories of any coherency have at their base an understanding of what human beings are and what the good for humans is. The point of any constructive political theory is to advance that good. Therefore, it is important to get some sense of the spiritual nature of human beings that Weil is trying to press upon her readers.

Once again it would seem that we are not on promising ground since Weil tells us that what is most important about a human being is not any particular aspect, not even an integrated personality, but rather the "impersonal." This is utterly consistent with her insistence on decreation. But it again seems to discount the worth of any negotiations about social goods, which so often are meant to serve the personality, at least in liberal democracies. As they are discounted, so too it would seem that politics is discounted.

Once again, however, it is necessary to bear in mind Weil's deliberately paradoxical and provocative way of approaching the problem. For her, as seems clear in "What Is Sacred in Every Human Being?," the point of insisting on the idea of the impersonal is to get her reader to rise beyond the limitations of personal language. Such language inevitably limits and reduces the human being to mere aspects of his or her being. What is particularly worrisome is that it keeps one from hearing those whose lives are marginal, who have nothing, especially the power of articulating their distress, that can command the respect of others. So, insisting on the impersonal is at once a demand for a certain unlimited impartial justice—and that is the only kind that really deserves the name, isn't it?—and also a recognition that the human being *simpliciter*, without determinate conditions, is always deserving of this sort of respect. One's own respect for the good demands respect for the other's desire for good as a whole. It does not rest in any specific good, although respect for them, as Weil makes clear in *The Need for Roots*, has to take place in specific concrete responses.

The problem, of course, is determining what those specific responses are to be. Let us consider one more text from the London period, namely, the essay "Are We Struggling for Justice?" (SWW 120–30), as it fills out Weil's understanding of the human being in the relevant social, moral, and political terms. If "What Is Sacred in Every Human Being?" demands a non-reductionistic approach to the human, "Are We Struggling for Justice?" pins down just what exactly this means with regard to human action, namely, that in all things we are to seek the consent of others. If we truly respect others as a whole, we will ask them if they consent to be involved in any of our actions that may affect them. Asking recognizes their essential freedom. If this is violated, whether by force or by manipulation, then their aspirations for the good may be damaged. Weil notes forcefully, "Human consent is a sacred thing. It is what man grants to God. It is what God comes in search of when like a beggar he approaches men" (SWW 122). It is the respect for humans found in asking for their consent that constitutes justice, both divine and human. It is therefore consent that above all constitutes the specific link between Weil's religious and political views, for it is a concept that is both religious and political. It is religious insofar as human spirituality is a matter of obedience to God, but, as Weil sees it, this is a willed obedience to God. God does not force but persuades, and comes like a beggar asking us to love him. That is God's respect for us. To consent freely, for our part, then, is to consent to God's providence, that is, to the world of necessity that he has made and to our position in it. We are not consulted on its design; we are, however, as spiritual creatures—and this is the very meaning of being a spiritual creature—given the opportunity to accept it willingly. A similar sort of respect Weil thinks ought to be at the heart of justice in human institutions. Indeed, the realm of human justice with respect to how it deals with human consent is one of the most important outworkings of the original revelation.

How so? Respecting the free consent of others is a form of one's own consent to others' existence as creatures of God, to a world not of one's making, and so it is also a form of consent to God himself. It is respect for their otherness, which one does not create or control. It is also a very specific consent to God, who creates them and the world and its order. It is a consent to not be the center of the universe. This sort of consent is at the heart of Weil's understanding of decreation (and not vice versa), for justice like this, which cedes our place as the imagined center of the universe, undoes the self that is formed by the play of social forces that makes the "I" the moral focus of the world. But it is also clear that if this "I" is undone, such undoing is in the service of a radical *disponibilité* to the world. It is the sort of attention that allows us to take a world into ourselves and to be united to it in a sort of indissoluble friendship. This is, then, ultimately less a matter of decreation than of re-creation. That is, indeed, a mystical idea, but it is also one that can be concretely political and give a politics a very specific flavor.

Clearly, Weil's mysticism is not necessarily antipolitical and certainly not life-denying. Her mysticism does not pull one away from the world of daily activity; it is only practiced within that world. Weil is not moving away from the quotidian world but is looking for ways to move toward it.

Recognizing this as the direction of her thought does not leave us without tension, however. As American theologian David Tracy has suggested, Weil, in approaching human affairs in the way she does, wants us to see that there is an inescapable element of tragedy in them.[10] One's relation to God and the world is worked out in the world of human affairs, but that relation can never be fully and exhaustively worked out there. Weil recognizes this when, for example, she points out that although consent is a sacred thing, it is an impossible expectation to think that in all human affairs we can always ask the permission of others before involving them. We frequently *presume* they agree. But even when we are right, and even when they don't mind, we don't really pay attention to them and focus on the project instead. Weil notes, "This is necessary. If it were otherwise, things would not get done, and if things did not get done we would perish. But because of this, action is tainted by sacrilege. For human consent is a sacred thing" (SWW 122).

The tragedy involved here is that of an inevitable failure of the ideal and the actual to fit together. It is also the consequence of taking seriously the idea that human beings have souls, which much of contemporary philosophy and politics does not.[11] This is an important political recognition that many political philosophies derived from the Enlightenment project do not get. Political failure in the case of, say, Hobbes, or Kant, or Rawls is a failure of rationality, a failure to appreciate and apply consistently the rules that provide for justice in human affairs. That sort of failure is not tragic; it is the result either of stupidity or limited knowledge; it is in principle remediable by further reasoning. For Weil, however, morals and politics are not the sorts of things that are best described by fundamental rules and principles. Nor is politics a matter of calculating how best to direct the traffic of competing desires and social goods; it is not a matter of designing a social machine. Rather, morals and politics are activities of the human being as she seeks to bring herself into some kind of relation with the world and with God. What is tragic is that in seeking to do so, one cannot, even with goodwill and foresight, avoid certain kinds of dilemmas in which the concrete, but necessarily limited, goods we are seeking are mutually exclusive. In pursuing a transcendent good in a world of limited goods, it is a frequent measure of human experience to find frustration. Strong temptations to idolatrous actions and self-assertion are also present due to the inevitable anxiety that comes from an unclear future. It is also to find that things can go terribly wrong, and one can commit idolatrous mistakes in seeking something of lasting worth in a world of limited being. They can go wrong because of evil intent; they can also go wrong because of unseen human reactions and chains of events. There is *no* guarantee of safety, and there are no guaranteed outcomes.

That is something to recommend Weil's political philosophy as a realistic political philosophy, even if it is not apparently optimistic. It particularly stands as an important and trenchant critique of Enlightenment political projects, which, even when they themselves have not been particularly sanguine about human nature, have thought they could provide rational and technical fixes for them without having to fix that nature. Weil's thought therefore first stands opposed to any project where it is assumed that a perfectly rational management of human interactions can be achieved or that the human being can be either fixed or satisfied by external order without any attention to internal order. In the current state of political philosophy, of course, that is hardly a novel thought. But it also stands opposed to the looser prudential or pragmatic management of conflicting human ends and desires that pretends to a justice no deeper than fairness and evenhandedness. It opposes it insofar as it seeks to recognize that the issue of justice is deeper than any pragmatic management ever tries to go and that the failure of justice is a failure to realize a transcendent good that ultimately surrounds human life and nourishes it. In this sense, the use of the term *tragic* is not an academic one, but denotes the pity that failures in human life deserve, the failure of the soul that desires good but does not find it, even though it is often offered luxurious substitutes.

The designation *tragic*, especially with respect to its classical dramatic overtones, goes well beyond what may simply be called "the too-bad." As in tragic drama, a politics that recognizes tragedy not only recognizes the foolishness of arranging society and politics into anything resembling a machine for producing or protecting human happiness, but also puts the moral center of politics and social life squarely in the realm of character. Just as classical tragic drama tests and proves and develops—and sometimes destroys—the moral character of those who are stung by tragic developments beyond their control, so too a political philosophy that admits tragedy will be most concerned with character. In this respect, it is hardly surprising to note that Weil's politics is far less concerned with, say, the elimination of the poor, as she thinks both communism and capitalism try to do, than it is with finding a way to treat the poor with honor and respect instead of contempt. It is a matter of begging their consent—not to degradation, but, as she saw in the Occitan concept of *parage*, to necessity. Everybody will obey somehow and somewhere; the moral concern is how this can be done without force or degradation.

But this also reveals the positive heart of Weil's political vision. It is ultimately a politics of generosity and of self-giving. It is not, though, so much the generosity that flows from largesse, thus depending on certain kinds of economic production; rather, its generosity consists in hospitality, in welcoming others. Its giving is its ability to take in and to admit others to a common, balanced life of mutual respect. The point of decreation in Weil's mystical writings is ultimately to allow the creation of a self that has made the world its own body, so that what exists there is not foreign to it, whether it is joyful or sorrowful. Similarly, within her politics she consistently envisions a society in which the sort of character that is developed in its citizens, and which is most crucial to the well-being of both individuals and society, is one of *disponibilité* to others and to the world. It is, for example, by acting on one's obligations to others, and doing so without narrow self-interest, that Weil thinks the human soul is best shaped and formed. That may not be a self that is particularly well-formed to pursue certain sorts of social goods; it is well-formed, however, to welcome reality and to give itself to it freely and, ultimately, even with a sense of joy.

If this assessment is accurate, then certain specific things have to be seen as central to Weil's understanding of politics. In conclusion, to give some sense of these concrete expectations, I simply list the four most important.

First, the central individual virtue in a Weilian society is attention and the seeking of consent that follows upon it. Its central enemy is distraction—the sort of *divertissement* that Pascal warned about—that keeps us from looking at ourselves or really looking at others.[12] As one of the better Weil scholars, Rebecca Rozelle-Stone has pointed out we are a distracted nation. The advancement of studies on the rearrangement of our brain patterns due to our incessant watching of computer and phone screens indicates that we are fast losing in a material way even the potential to pay attention. We have reason to worry. The central task of a culture as a whole is to form our ability to pay attention and even to give us something to pay attention to. But that also means that within the educational system we need to take seriously the moral development of a certain kind of respect for what is not always in one's narrow interests. Our current politics is the reaping of a decided failure in this area. Weil said that with respect to thinking, she wanted her mind to be like water, that is, something that would automatically give each thing its proper weight. That is more than intellectual; it is the spiritual ability to consent to a reality and an order of reality not of one's making.

A good part of this development of attention surely has to come in education and has to do with the mind. But, second, the sort of spiritual attention that interests Weil needs to be developed through the opportunities that cultures allow for generosity and through the examples they can provide of generosity and attention. These opportunities for generosity need to involve people directly. Certainly, humans have needs that if not met cause them to have seriously diminished lives, and, as Weil understands things, it is a political necessity to make sure that food, shelter, and medical care are available. She would not have been impressed with a political culture that argued that it is simply up to individuals to provide this. Nevertheless, the sort of socialism that provides for human needs but does not engage its citizens morally in that provision will sooner or later develop citizens who have a galloping sense of entitlement, but little sense of the omnipresence of the neighbors that they ought to love. Like the rich young lawyer who asked Jesus "Who is my neighbor?" because he wanted to find the *limits* of his obligations, those who are not habitual givers tend to look for ways to limit the category of those to whom they are obligated. It is in giving, as Evagrius and many other ancient desert fathers thought, that one overcomes selfishness. A culture that depends on generosity therefore needs to offer concrete ways to be generous. It also needs to make sure that there is as little social disincentive for giving as possible.

Third, this is a politics that exists within a spiritually rooted culture. Above all, being rooted spiritually here means a continual consent, a continual giving of oneself to the forms and orders that the past has used to consent to necessity, even if those are frequently adapted to changing circumstances. Indeed, true rootedness, truly drawing life from a culture's resources, may well mean a certain originality and creativity. And it also means that one's present consent shares the same attitude as the original consent, not from pragmatic considerations, but from a sense of needing to rely on something outside oneself for help, and from a sense of respect for existence. And, as with the Occitan concept of *parage*, being truly rooted makes this sort of spiritual obedience something that, if it goes some distance in decreating us, does *not* humiliate us. That is possible when consent to the forms and orders of the past includes the possibility of using them imaginatively, to be an expression of thought and dignity.

Fourth, and finally, this is a culture whose central political and social virtue is in providing a certain kind of order. When Weil named "order" as the chief and most important need of the soul in *The Need for Roots* she had a very specific idea of order in mind, namely the order of balance. Political orders can be systematic, whether rationalistic or authoritarian, and they can be simply imposed. When they are, they are usually felt to be artificial; they are certainly sustained by power and the threat of violence, sometimes even rather effectively. (The political order of the former Yugoslavia is an excellent example. Once the strongman was removed, the order disappeared.) However, in a Weilian politics, the sort of order that ought to be achieved is the one that comes about, as she believed she saw in the case of Occitan culture, from the internal moral willingness of its people to put themselves in balance with everybody else, and from their willingness to be balanced by others. This balance, insofar as it is only possible by attention and consent, is in human social life the expression of the justice that rules necessity. It is the social outworking of lives lived attentively.

CHAPTER THIRTEEN

SEARCHING FOR A NEW SAINT BENEDICT

Attention and the Formation of Community

In an oft-quoted sentence, Simone Weil declares, "Today it is not enough merely to be a saint, but we must have the saintliness demanded by the present moment, a new saintliness, itself without precedent" (WG 99). It is not enough, she adds, to cite saintliness of former days; we live in unprecedented times and need something new. Still, if this saintliness is new, it is to be in service of reestablishing a sort of eternal proportion and order that has been lost in the present. She thus continues, "A new type of sanctity is indeed a fresh spring, an invention. If all is kept in proportion and if the order of each thing is preserved, it is almost equivalent to a new revelation of the universe and of human destiny. It is the exposure of a large portion of truth and beauty hitherto concealed under a thick layer of dust" (WG 99).

This is inspiring. If Weil's times were unprecedented, ours seem even more so. This is what we need. But what exactly would such a saint of genius look like? According to Weil, such saints would be able "to give full love to God and at the same time to exercise their obligations to all that is smaller in the universe" (WG 98). Saint Francis and Saint John of the Cross were like this, she says, and then adds, significantly, that this is "why they were both poets" (WG 98). Weil is quite clear that the new sanctity needs to make explicit what may have been only implicit in the earlier sanctity. This is, in fact, her great concern in a work such as *The Need for Roots*. What I want to concentrate on in this chapter, however, is what is implied in the suggestion that Francis and John of the Cross were poets and what that has to do with the formation of communities, especially with respect to how Simone Weil thought healthy communities were formed and how they live in such a way as to give health and holiness to their citizens. By doing so we should gain a clearer understanding of what exactly it was that she was making explicit, for we gain an understanding of the crucial practices that she thought were central to the formation of a moral community.

In order to do so, however, I do not want to begin with Simone Weil or with Francis or John of the Cross. Rather, I want to start by noting what another philosopher, Alasdair MacIntyre, has said in invoking another saint, Benedict, in the present state of moral crisis.

MacIntyre, in his seminal work in 1981 on moral philosophy, *After Virtue*, decries the chaos of contemporary moral philosophy. That chaos, he argues, is the result of several factors: the inheritance of numerous incommensurate moral traditions and the failed secular attempt to bring them together, a failure that is inevitable since so many of them have their homes in religious milieus. What we have lost in this chaos, he thinks, is any sense of a moral tradition, but specifically the tradition of the virtues that depend on moral narratives embedded in the life and thought of ongoing communities. As a result, we have also lost any vital sense of community itself. He concludes,

> What matters at this stage is the construction of local forms of community within which civility and the intellectual and moral life can be sustained through the new dark ages which are already upon us. And if the tradition of the virtues was able to survive the horrors of the last dark ages, we are not entirely without grounds for hope. This time, however, the barbarians are not waiting beyond the frontiers; they have already been governing us for quite some time. And it is our lack of consciousness of this that constitutes part of our predicament. We are waiting not for a Godot, but for another—doubtless very different—St. Benedict.[1]

What is so significant about Saint Benedict? MacIntyre does not say much. He merely points to him as an example of someone who, like other men and women of goodwill, turned away from "the task of shoring up the Roman *imperium* and ceased to identify the continuation of civility and moral community with the maintenance of the *imperium*. What they set themselves up to achieve instead—often not recognizing fully what they were doing—was the construction of new forms of community within which the moral life could be sustained so that both morality and civility might survive the coming ages of barbarism and darkness."[2]

Benedict is a wonderful example to which to point for this purpose. In a time of failing institutions, particularly moral institutions and the communities in which they were embodied, the community of Saint Benedict was an alternative. If, initially, Benedict's followers simply turned away from the *civitas* and retreated to the deserts of unsettled Europe to form very different sorts of communities, and to drink deeply from spiritual wells while isolated from the failing imperium, they also gained a moral energy that sent them throughout the continent. As each Benedictine community braved its isolation, in time communities grew up around the monastery. And, most important, as each community grew, it was also taught by the monks. By teaching and by clearing a space for human life, the Benedictines not only civilized Europe but also imparted a new and vital moral tradition, a new moral way of living.

We are taught this much as a matter of course in any number of histories, and Benedict's choice to start over has come to stand for an alternative. MacIntyre made it so; more recently Rod Dreher, in *The Benedict Option*, has argued, taking his cue from MacIntyre, that our national life is no longer capable of supporting a life of faith.[3] He believes that people of faith need to flee to live in their own communities, and only there will they find what they need. We will consider his version in due course, although at this point it does need to be stressed that fleeing the barbarians is one thing, and forming a community is quite another. For, once Benedict has been invoked, what is not so clear is *how* Benedict formed a community with this kind of moral energy, vision, and vitality. Dreher doesn't pursue that angle, and Benedict never explained how to do it. Benedict was not a philosopher, and he did not leave behind any sort of treatise of social or political theory. All that we have is his Rule. Yet, reading this, even if its striking sanity and moderation is explained to us, still does not give us many clues as to how it could generate the sort of community it did. It is surprisingly lacking in any sort of general description as to why it is better than any other way of organizing a community, a lack that is particularly troublesome if we want to mine it for insights on how to establish and organize a new moral community that is not a monastic community. The best we may come up with is that the Rule was universal in the West and obedience to it was meant to be unswerving. Because it was universal, whatever came out of it had a home wherever else there were monasteries, and in time they were everywhere. Because obedience to it was so important, this universality was possible. But obedience and universality by themselves do not explain why these communities were *attractive*—after all, any number of morally bankrupt totalitarianisms of the twentieth and twenty-first centuries have also insisted on obedience and universality. Nor does the Rule's moderation explain much by itself, since liberal societies have always valued moderation. So, it is not easy for us to explain how it *morally* influenced a wider civilization or how it might be translated to any other sort of community. It may well seem that its genius is buried deep within its own monasticism.

A good part of the problem of making the translation to our time, however, may be because we seek rules to establish a community in the Rule. In contemporary moral philosophy, rules function as law-like generalizations for morality. If not exactly recipes for it, they are not unlike recipes, either. So, we are often looking for certain law-like generalizations inducted from the specific points of the Rule. We will have, as I have already suggested, a very difficult time in finding ones that are useful and translatable to our time if we go about things this way. What may be far more helpful in finding and translating Benedict's genius in establishing a moral community is if we look for it in what John Henry Newman called "the idea of monasticism," even if monasticism itself no longer seems to be a widely viable option. So, again delaying talking about Weil, I want briefly to look at what Newman thought was the genius of Benedict.

In "The Mission of St. Benedict," Newman, like MacIntyre, notes the monastic impulse of the late ancients:

Serious men not only had a call, but every inducement which love of life and freedom could supply, to escape from [the all-encompassing social system's] presence and its sway.

Their one idea then, their one purpose, was to be quit of it; too long had it enthralled them. It was not a question of this or that vocation, of the better deed, of the higher state, but of life and death. . . . Early monachism was flight from the world, and nothing else.[4]

More specifically, Newman continues, "monachism was, as regards the secular life and all that it implies, emphatically a negation, or to use another word, a *mortification*; a mortification of sense, and a mortification of reason."[5] This is to say, the flight from the world was not simply physical; it was a desire for peace and simplicity, a desire to be rid of systems and rules and complex and conflicting goals and conclusions. The state of mind they sought was one that "lets each work, each place, each occurrence stand by itself,—which acts towards each as it comes before it, without a thought of anything else."[6] It was a state of mind that dwelt in the eternal.

This state of mind, and how it was shaped and developed in the Benedictine communities, Newman describes as "poetical," and it is as poetical that he wants to talk about the creation of community by Benedict and his followers. By this he does not mean that Benedictine communities chased after romantic idylls. Poetry here is to be understood as something to be distinguished from the scientific, the analytic and investigative state of mind such as one finds in the Scholastics who followed. The poetical state of mind "demands, as its primary condition, that we should not put ourselves above the objects in which it resides, but at their feet; that we should feel them to be above and beyond us, that we should look up to them, and that, instead of fancying that we can comprehend them, we should take for granted that we are surrounded and comprehended by them ourselves."[7]

It is this poetic state of mind that helps us understand the growth of Benedictine communities. They were not the planned outgrowth of one mind, not even Benedict's. The sort of mind that could look ahead carefully and tactically, plotting social and psychological cause and effect—as Hobbes tried to do under the influence of the Cartesian system—was not Benedict's, nor was it Benedictine. The immensely vital growth of these communities was far more organic, the shooting forth of some immense energy that came from within the state of mind that it cultivated. It is also this state of mind that lay at the heart of the Benedictine method of teaching, for that teaching was centered in reading, listening, and meditating, a continuous *lectio divina* to be sharply contrasted again with the Scholastic methods, or even with Saint Ignatius's very detailed and methodical spiritual exercises. It was not methodical, even if it was disciplined. Like Aristotelian *phronesis*, it depended upon personal moral example and influence.

Newman's description helps us better understand the particular genius of Benedict and how he formed a moral community of wide and lasting influence. How it does so can be seen in how we should understand the Benedictine ora et labora. It was not that Benedict scientifically balanced work and prayer, giving each its due and proper place. The central overriding consideration was *always* prayer and meditation; this was the opus Dei at which he aimed. The role of work, Newman claims, is simply then to enable prayer, and it plays the role of a mortification that enables the attentive quietness of mind that is prayer. The whole point of work was to prepare the mind for prayer.[8] The work did not have to be great; it had to be simple and consuming. Manual labor certainly did that; so did reading to oneself and others, and so did copying the Scriptures and Church fathers. The Benedictines in this sense never planned to civilize the wilderness of medieval Europe. But they did form a community based and focused on a quietness that then allowed particular virtues to arise: hospitality, literacy, tolerance, civility, and charity, and that allowed a community to thrive, and they were certainly civilizing virtues. But these were not created, suggested, or invented by the Rule as moral rules to establish community where there was none before; the Rule simply lets attention be focused. The virtues arise quite naturally. As they arise, they can be taught, sometimes as explicit rules, but most often by "personal influence," as Newman thought, and as a way of life. So, if the monastic impulse as Newman describes it was to flee a decaying and overly complex and incoherent world, its simply disciplined quest for quiet was nevertheless creative because it let the world that God had created speak once more. And that, above all, was what created a lasting moral community and tradition.

There are many important ways in which Weil is *not* like Benedict. She did not form a community herself, nor did she write a Rule for an already existing community with its own inherent spiritual impulses that simply needed wise discipline. Her—and our—age lacks even the physical space to which to flee from the present imperium. Weil in any case did not seem to have any impulse to do so, and, indeed, the very idea would have seemed to her to be irresponsible—although, it should also be stressed, she did think France at the end of World War II had a unique opportunity to fill a blank moral space in new ways. Furthermore, unlike Benedict, she was a philosopher and did seem to have something like a political and social theory. By her own definition of a "new saintliness," it was, in fact, necessary to have one, at least insofar as, she argued, it was no longer possible to leave spiritual, social, and ethical matters at a level of implicit understanding. They had to be made explicit, and that was a central aspect of her new saintliness.

Still, Benedict's achievement may be very helpful in casting light on Weil's later writing on communities, especially *The Need for Roots*. It can illuminate the approach Weil takes in thinking about moral communities. It is also helpful in letting us see the *how* of that approach.

Earlier we saw that in her later political and social thinking Weil was, in effect, "retheologizing the political." I argued that, while much political thinking and philosophy assumes that the public space of social life, the space that politics addresses, is a morally neutral space sharply delineated from the private, where our thinking about our ultimate goods and desires actually goes on, it is, or should be, also a task of political philosophy to investigate how that space itself is conceived. One of the chief ways that Weil is a political and social philosopher is in challenging the idea that such a space is or ought to be neutral, as did Arendt. Rather than conceiving communal life as a neutral space where we negotiate our private conceptions of the good but leave their privately conceived substance alone, she saw the space of politics as fundamentally moral and hence an important place where our very conceptuality and activities concerning the human good are formed and played out, and where the moral self is also shaped. In this, she, like Arendt, borrowed heavily from the ancients. This was a matter of "retheologizing the political" because Weil saw such moral space as always sub specie aeternitatis. In this case, then, many of her particular suggestions about the shape of politics in France after the war were less the substance of her political vision than tentative suggestions of how life conceived and lived in this way might look. She thought they were open to revision; she did not think them to be steps in a recipe. But if they were not, of course, that leaves unanswered the question of how exactly she thought such a community could be formed. What are the most basic activities and practices that make her projected community into a moral community? What is the practical heart of this community? What, concretely, is its moral vision? What is *not* tentative in her practical recommendations?

It is here where the comparison with Benedict is most helpful, for his vision, at least as Newman understands it, sheds light on Weil's understanding of what the most important and fundamental moral activities of the community are. These, I claim, are twofold: her understanding of work as the spiritual core of any society and her belief that a community should grow organically out of the relation between the human and the divine that is forged in work.

In the concluding two sentences of *The Need for Roots* Weil claims, "It is not difficult to define the place that physical labor should occupy in a well-ordered social life. It should be its spiritual core" (NR 288).[9] In saying this she concludes a line of argument begun several pages earlier about providence, that is, the order of the universe, and our varying conceptions of it over the course of time in history and science. We have come, she argues, to see the universe not as an ordered whole where God "has so beautifully set out all the parts of the universe" (Aquinas); rather, it is brute, cold matter to be dominated, rather like a master dominates a slave. Theologically, we come to view God's providence in nature like the relation between the Roman emperor and the dominated empire and have subsequently idolized force. In our history, both our acting out of it and our writing of it, we have glorified this domination. In science we have not sought for truth, which is also beauty. But we have sought technical mastery over nature as scientists have excluded beauty and goodness from their consideration of it. Even those "pure scientists" who do not look for technical application are often not motivated by anything more than prestige and prizes, the social forms of force.

But why should work reverse this trend? What does it do to set a society straight? Work, and here Weil means the physical work that wears us down, makes us realize that we are not masters of the universe; it teaches us obedience just as nature obeys God, the good. But it teaches us the nature of obedience as well. Nature does not obey God as a superior force—that would be to make God a part of the universe and not its informing and indwelling wisdom. It obeys God's wisdom, which in Plato's phrase, "persuades Necessity." The sort of obedience that nature displays is found in its beauty as a whole. So, just as nature obeys God and finds the order that makes it beautiful, so, too, should we obey God in a similar way. It is as the psalmist suggests:

> To you I lift up my eyes, O you who are enthroned in the heavens!
> As the eyes of servants look to the hand of their master,
> as the eyes of a maid to the hand of her mistress,
> so our eyes look to the Lord our God, until he has mercy upon us.
>
> Psalms 123:1–2

Work teaches us to look by destroying our pretensions to be masters and keeps us from idolizing force and misunderstanding God, as if God were simply another, larger natural force and not Wise. By making physical work the spiritual center of a society, by valuing it, we learn the universe and its order. Like the ancients, Weil believes that the human order can arise from the natural order—if we look.

In order to understand Weil's claim, it is perhaps helpful to see where she differs from Arendt's understanding of work. Like Arendt, she differentiated between labor and work and ultimately distinguished both from the highest human activity of free human interaction in the *agora*. But, as French Weil scholar Robert Chenavier has correctly suggested, if Weil sees physical labor as wearing us down, that is not all it does. Chenavier argues that for Arendt, "work is only a sort of metabolic exchange between man and nature."[10] For Weil, on the other hand, work is also an art. It is not so much, as Arendt might argue, that Weil, like Marx, has confused the worker and the work. Rather, the work is the worker in this case, although, strictly speaking, the worker is God's work.

For Weil in *The Need for Roots*, the point of work is precisely to wear the worker down so that she or he might obey necessity just as matter does, for work is "daily death" and will turn us ultimately into inert matter. That, at first, does not sound very encouraging. But it gains considerable positive sense if the decreation of the self that work produces is understood in the same way that Newman has suggested, that work was an act of mortification for the Benedictine community. The point is not to wear us down *simpliciter*, but to transform us into a willing intermediary between God and all that we come into contact with. By driving away our fantasies, we have to focus—or, rather, we have the opportunity to focus—on what we really are and on what each thing is, unimpeded by our wishes and desires. Work gets us to pay attention, and it is attention that is of prime interest for Weil. In Benedictine terms, work, physical work, for Weil is the prime example of how we come to pray, and prayer, not the act of laboring itself, is the opus Dei.

It is the relation of work to attention, and hence to prayer, that can distinguish work from servile labor, even when it is grueling and grinding. Without attention, or the hope of attention, work of all kinds would always be servile. So it is also *only* in relation to attention that work can be the spiritual center of a society. But when it is so related, it can become the center by serving as an exemplar for all other kinds of work, including intellectual work, which also ought to have attention as its goal, as she suggests in "The First Condition for the Work of a Free Person" (LPW 131–44), where she outlines numerous ways in which, through intermediary symbols, work can be so directed. When work is related to attention, work becomes a sort of "supernatural poetry." She means the same sort of poetry that she found in Saints Francis and John of the Cross.

This helps us to better understand the point of the first part of *The Need for Roots* and brings us closer to seeing how Weil thinks moral communities are formed. In the opening section of *The Need for Roots*, Weil stresses the moral primacy of obligations over rights. In doing so, she has made an important contribution to moral philosophy. But we need to understand exactly what obligations are for her. They are not moral rules in anything like the contemporary sense of "rules." They are not laid on us externally, nor are they, like the principles of the Kantian conscience, arrived at by reason alone, an attempt at self-consistency. They are a first-person activity, a way of seeing, although one can and ought to spell them out when possible. They are a function of attention—no one who understands an obligation can understand it as *not* applying to himself or herself. Thus, work, that is, willing obedience to the universe, not only teaches us how to pay attention to God, to pray and "to look to the hand of one's master," it also teaches us how to pay attention to the needs of our neighbors. It is by doing so that a moral community may be formed.

There is, of course, a great deal of complexity to be encountered in trying to form such communities, and dealing with that complexity is a good part of Weil's enterprise in *The Need for Roots* and her later political writings. I shall not attempt to unravel it here. What does need to be dealt with at this point, however, is once again the charge that what Weil proposes is not only faintly ludicrous but also not really political, simply an offshoot of her "mysticism." Indeed, it appears ludicrous precisely because it is mysticism out of place. She has taken moral activities from the first-person mode and transferred them to the wider public sphere, where they are politically and practically inappropriate. So it is claimed. Because they fit that sphere so ineptly, so out of proportion to the size and sort of what are usually conceived to be the tasks of the public sphere, the whole project, while admirable, seems almost clownish.

I have already suggested that much of Weil's significance as a political philosopher is precisely in challenging the assumed lines between the public and the private. The public needs to be enlarged so that the good is not simply private and there is actually a space for genuine moral human interaction. This is a theological challenge to political philosophy, arguing that no significant human activity can be neatly sectioned out from the all-embracing good and the more it is, the less significance it comes to have. The realm of the private simply cannot hold it. But Weil is also issuing a more concrete moral challenge as well. Her philosophy of work and her social philosophy are not only idealistic suggestions for how a moral community might be formed; the positive suggestion is also linked to a critique of what the public sphere has become. Because work has become so degraded in liberal societies, where discussions of any overarching good are excluded, she offers an alternative. Work, even intellectual work, and even the highest sort of theoretical intellectual work, becomes degraded to a mere "metabolic exchange between man and nature" when the public sphere no longer discusses the good, leaving it to private conscience. Here she would certainly agree with Arendt's argument in *The Human Condition* that human work in modern liberal societies has been lowered to the level of utilitarian labor, that thinking has become a servant of doing instead of contemplation, and that "contemplation itself has become altogether meaningless."[11] But she goes farther than Arendt in suggesting that work can be linked to contemplation and is indeed, when properly conceived, the prime exemplary means for understanding what contemplation is.

If there is this disagreement between the two philosophers, agreement can be found again in what meaningful human activity is. Where liberal political theory, from Locke to Rawls, while admirably guarding the integrity of the individual, has gone wrong is that in protecting the individual, the individual has become isolated and alienated. While attempting to protect one's most important beliefs and values, liberalism actually insulates individuals and their most important beliefs from each other, for, in forming the social contract and shaping political society, it is precisely these beliefs and values which have been put into the private and protected that do *not* come into play. Political society, meaning to protect them, leaves them out. Ironically, this means that the negotiations in the political realm are not moral negotiations themselves—that is, the free interplay of moral beliefs and values that subsequently shapes human agency. Both Weil and Arendt would argue that the highest human activity is this interplay, and to exclude it is to force human activity to lower spheres of existence. If, therefore, there is to be meaningful moral activity, it has to arise and be worked out in an *agora*. One needs space in which to act on obligations, and one needs to be actively engaged with others in order to confront necessity.[12]

We can now to see how Weil can conceive that the linking of work and attention can be formative of a moral community, and why her later social writings are not simply private moral and mystical experience idealistically writ large on the stage of national political life. Attention, to be sure, belongs to the individual. But the capacity for it is not formed in isolation, nor, once formed, is it speculative dreaming. It is formed in contact with nature and with others. Nor does it act in isolation; in its continuance and growth it both creates and demands a moral space with others. It is precisely paying attention to another and taking him or her into one's life. This does not happen when work is aimed simply at production; mere production drives the person into the realm of the purely private. But it may happen when the individual is forced to confront necessity in nature and in other human beings. A community organized so that this confrontation is conceived in such a way that attention, and not production, is the primary aim is a community in which, according to Newman, each thing is let stand as it is, in which there is genuine moral contact and interaction between human beings. Within such a community, attention may arise. Not only may it arise, but attention becomes its substance, and the growth of the community may then occur organically. It is not a planned community, but it is a community that can grow. That such a community did at one time arise, and that it is therefore not impossible to conceive one arising, is clear in the Benedictine example.

This is Weil's logic for the formation of moral communities. In concluding, I would like to address two issues, unfortunately just briefly, and then to make some brief comments on how very different her proposal is from Dreher's Benedict option.

The first is the practicality of this vision. Pointing to the Benedictine example may be instructive, but *The Need for Roots*, of course, is not a proposal for any sort of return to the past. It takes place, and consciously so, in the twentieth century, a century with no deserts, in which society is much larger and already weighed down by its forms of life, seemingly without much possibility of undoing them and starting over anew. Weil understood this very well. But it is important to keep in mind that *The Need for Roots* is not a generalized proposal for a new society, that is, for a utopia, although as we have seen, her writing may well fit into a utopian genre as critique. In writing it, Weil believed that France after the war had a unique opportunity to begin again and to reorganize social relations in a way that was not possible at any other time. That France did not avail itself of this opportunity means the time was lost.

Nevertheless, if the opportunity as a whole was lost, Weil's most important suggestions are not for the creation of a society as a whole and in all parts as from a tabula rasa by a general authority. Indeed, I do not think Weil's vision ultimately depends on this general authority. In *The Need for Roots,* the vestiges of her syndicalism have evolved into a sort of communitarianism. Social life as a whole and its growth, as in Benedictine communities, comes not from the top down but rather from the bottom up. Social life as a whole comes from vitality in small communities and regions, which then in their interactions in society and the nation as a whole recreate it. The society as a whole is a "community of communities," in the words of American philosopher Josiah Royce. The role of general authority, had her proposals been enacted, would have been limited to restraining the forces that might overwhelm community life and leave it sapped of its vitality. In this sense, while the larger social realm remains threatening to communal life, communal life does not depend on it. The small communities that Weil envisioned where work could be turned into attention are not impossible, although they are severely threatened.

The second issue is that even if we can dismiss the charge that Weil's vision was an attempt to make society as a whole a mystical society, still, that vision really is religious from beginning to end. If Weil, unlike Arendt, believed that work of all sorts can be linked to attention, and that labor was in fact exemplary in this regard, it was because of what she, from very early on, believed to be an original compact between the mind and the universe. This compact is revealed when the mind freely submits itself to necessity, almost always in some sort of decreative suffering, whether seen in tragedy or in figures such as Christ. She further believed that this revelation was always at the core of any civilization and civilizations were an organic outgrowth of social forms centered in it. The deep problem of contemporary society is that the contact with necessity has been lost, at least in any revealing way; its restoration is imperative in order to have a moral society—thus her claim that work must be central to the spirituality of a society.

Here is also where she has so much more to give to thought than Dreher does. There is a lot to take very seriously in his critiques of contemporary society, which does make the life of the spirit difficult and, in that regard, frustrates human development. His critique of contemporary education is forceful and not to be taken lightly. But, in the end, he makes no positive proposal for how to create a society. There is a lingering and fairly overt sense of resentment at the lost privilege of American Christianity. There is a proposal to withdraw, but not how to reform the life of Christian churches and communities, which themselves have contributed to the cultural malaise. There is not much sense of how to do anything for the larger communities. Isolated communes are not enough to make the spirit alive within a contemporary community, including their own.

Weil's insistence that there must be a spirituality to contemporary society and that work is at its core is a strong one. But, in increasingly pluralistic and divided societies, this seems deeply problematic. There is little doubt that Weil's proposals for France saw France as a Christian society or, at least, one whose leaders recognized a transcendent good. That is not possible for France now, nor is it possible for the United States, except perhaps by developing a very generalized "civil religion." In the United States, we have long talked about the "Judeo-Christian tradition," although those are in fact two traditions. As Muslims increasingly become a part of U.S. society, we hear talk about the "Abrahamic religions." Still, that is so abstract and generalized as to be worthless as a genuine unifying principle. It is, in fact, giving up on one.

That problem remains, and I do not know how it is soluble, if it is at all. However, my one suggestion is that if the apparent difficulties for society in general have increased, the possibility that small communities might be formed and reformed around the sort of "original revelation" that Weil claimed still remain. I cannot speak for Jews and

Muslims, but I can suggest that this may be the most crucial task for the Christian churches in the future, which in Benedict's time and later in the Renaissance and Reformation, always managed to find ways of living together where the dehumanizing demands of the imperium are set aside and a genuine human community can be formed. If it is genuine, and if other communities in the society have anything genuine about them, *then* perhaps we can meet them in a community of communities. Perhaps the churches can be the leaven in the loaf, or the salt of the earth, which is really what those Benedictine communities were. But that will only happen when we ourselves restore that original compact within our own communities, for that is the only way we can develop the attention to see what is important and vital in others.

CHAPTER FOURTEEN

MORAL CLARITY IN WAR

War is not very often thought about except when the times press it upon us. Moral and political philosophers do not usually spend a lot of time on it until they see a present need to include it; otherwise, it is not on their usual list of topics. Yet, it is a regular feature of human social life. Simone Weil lived and wrote in a time of war, and it would be a mistake not to treat her writing about war, especially her singular essay, "The *Iliad*: Poem of Force" as a part of her moral and social thought. It is also a very specific topic, not simply a theoretical one, in which it is possible to see how so much of her thought comes to bear on a difficult, distinct issue of human social and moral life. Issues such as "nature" and "supernature" and politics as the care of souls are very much in the front of Weil's thinking. They make some very concrete differences.

I will discuss Weil's thinking about war in relation to a debate about war that occurred at the beginning of the United States' decision to go to war in Afghanistan and Iraq after the events of September 11, 2001. It is the most recent time in which Americans vigorously debated the issues of war and thus is our freshest take on the issue.

In a controversial article titled "Moral Clarity in a Time of War," published in *First Things* in January 2003, Roman Catholic moral theologian George Weigel undertook to clear some of the fog that surrounds war. Admirably, he begins by rejecting the notion that war is utterly a fog that "takes place beyond the reach of moral reason, in a realm of interest and necessity where moral argument is a pious diversion at best and, at worst, a lethal distraction from the deadly serious business at hand."[1] Instead, he insists, "Nothing human takes place outside the realm or beyond the reach of moral reason. Every human action takes place within the purview of moral judgment."[2]

Weigel insists that it is important to pay attention to the venerable just war tradition developed in the West. That tradition is, he argues, an important public resource, for it allows moral debate to take place on both the decision to engage in war in the first place and how war is conducted. It is a tradition that, unlike the irrationality theory of war, allows us to raise these sorts of questions:

> Who has the authority to wage war? The President? The President and the Congress? The United States acting alone? The United States with a sufficient number of allies? The United Nations?
> Is it ever right to use armed force first? Can going first ever be, not just morally permissible, but morally imperative?
> How can the use of armed force contribute to the pursuit of peace, freedom, and order in world affairs?[3]

The just war tradition that allows us to ask these questions and debate them openly, Weigel contends, has been largely forgotten, especially by religious leaders. It is worth noting that this point had existential bite at the time because many Catholic and mainline Protestant clergy were voicing serious doubts about one or both of the war enterprises of the United States. He wanted to raise a number of issues deriving from the just war theory that he believed needed serious attention, and, it seems clear enough, he wanted to use just war theory to argue for both the Afghanistan and Iraq wars.

The first of these issues is that "the just war argument recognizes that there are circumstances in which the first and most urgent obligation in the face of evil is to stop it. Which means that there are times when waging war is morally necessary to defend the innocent and to promote the minimum conditions of international order."[4] This recognition of the just war tradition is thus actually a "sustained and disciplined intellectual attempt to relate the morally legitimate use of proportionate and discriminate military force to morally worthy ends."

It is, in short, a "theory of statecraft." More strongly, it is not a method of casuistry, which is to say, war is not an exception to and a violation of the normal state of affairs, but, as Carl von Clausewitz writes—and Weigel explicitly invokes him—"the extension of politics by other means." Such a view may sound cynical, but, to give Weigel his due, his point was not to encourage war but to argue that, within the just war tradition, were we to recognize that war is an extension of politics, we would need to see war as centered squarely within the moral parameters of political consideration. This avoids putting politics itself under the fog of war. It is part of moral and political philosophy.

Second, he continues, *bellum* is a use of armed force for public ends by public authorities. It is a tool that can be used by those who have an obligation to defend the security of the nation, and, one may well add, this obligation lies at the heart of even Lockean social contract theory when it tries to explain the legitimacy of a government at all.

It is this point that was particularly controversial in Weigel's case. Based on it, he argues that those who have argued that the just war tradition contains a presumption against war or a presumption against violence are quite wrong. To give him the most generous reading possible, I take him not to be saying that there is a presumption or preference for war or violence, but rather that those who take war as an exception to and violation of the rules and practices that make for peace put war back into the sphere of irrationality, as something that cannot be debated and therefore should be avoided at all costs. To a degree, he surely has a point, at least with respect to the arguments of many pacifists who, by making peace an either-or issue, must surely take themselves out of any debate about getting into war, or even about the means used in a war, since for them the whole thing has passed out of the realm of the moral. Were we to apply this either/or logic of pacifism consistently, we could never think about things such as the Geneva Convention or ever conduct war-crimes tribunals. Sin is sin, and being a different kind of sinner does not make one a more qualified judge or better in the eyes of God.

Nevertheless, this surely is a crucial and eminently debatable point in Weigel's case. It is debatable from an Augustinian perspective insofar as Augustine's own responses to the question posed to him of whether a Christian may ever take up arms or, more precisely, whether a soldier can be a Christian, revolve around issues such as fighting only when attacked, using no more violence than is necessary to bring the aggressor to a desire for peace, and not using violence against noncombatants. In short, Augustine, in his sketchy answers about the issue, seems to think that war is what necessity drives us to from peace, that peace is what is to be returned to, and that the less violence used in prosecuting a war, the better. So, for Augustine, there is at least that kind of presumption against violence; Augustine does seem to make war an issue of necessity and not simply the extension of quotidian politics. But, for Augustine, the second, deepest issue of peace was whether and how a combatant could keep his soul. That issue is really the constant, overarching concern of his reflections. That this is the case can be seen insofar as his reflections are a personal response to a friend who asked him exactly that sort of question.[5]

Augustine's concerns surely are at the heart of what it may mean to talk about moral clarity in war. They require us to ask: is moral clarity in war, or in a time of war, a matter of statecraft, or is it a matter of keeping one's soul? However, we will leave that aside for a moment to make Weigel's position clearer. Perhaps Weigel would not really have been against the first Augustinian sort of presumption of peace, even if he were to put a different spin on it than I have. In any case, his chief point was, citing Augustine himself, that the sort of peace involved is a public and political issue, a matter of *tranquillitas ordinis*. That is to say, it is a worldly peace. It is not, he pointedly says, "a matter of the individual's right relationship with God, nor is it a matter of seeking a world without conflict."[6] It is simply the order created by the "political community and mediated through law." He goes on to say, "This peace of *tranquillitas ordinis*, this peace of order, is composed of justice and freedom. The peace of order is not the eerily quiet and sullen 'peace' of a well-run authoritarian regime; it is a peace built on foundations of constitutional, commutative, and social justice. It is a peace in which freedom, especially religious freedom, flourishes. The defense of basic human rights is thus an integral component of 'work for peace.'"[7]

This *tranquillitas ordinis* is important, and, as he rightly suggested, all the more so in a time when the worldly order is threatened by aggressive and virulently antirational forms of violence. There is, thus, he argues, a moral obligation to rid the world of this threat to the peace and security of all. "Peace," he notes, "rightly understood, demands it."

Indeed. Still, Weigel seems to have taken a position somewhat akin to Luther's "two kingdoms" theory by splitting off the world's peace from the individual's right relationship with God in the course of his strong defense of the government's rather singular right to wage war as a matter of policy. The context of his argument is important to remember, as his article was a defense against the clerics and theologians who were so vocal in condemning the war in Afghanistan and the looming war in Iraq as unjust. Weigel contended that war was a matter of statecraft, and that clerics do not own the just war tradition and have largely forgotten what it is really about, namely the *tranquillitas ordinis*, the City of Man, and *not* the City of God. Where this "Lutheran" two-kingdoms defense is troublesome is that, while it does, on the one hand, actually allow for a certain kind of moral discourse about war that the irrationalist "fog of war" theory does not, on the other hand, if clerics and theologians had naively pushed a sense of peace that was inappropriate and unreasonably demanded that the government exhaust every last resort before it declared war, still, their application of the standards of the City of God was not wildly inappropriate—nor could it ever be for Christians who have to fight and are traveling to that city. While there may well be a worldly peace that both the citizens of Rome and the citizens of the City of God may enjoy and profit from, real *moral* clarity about war isn't something that can be hived off neatly from that transcendent peace. In this regard, Weigel's position seems to have an underlying assumption that is not so much Luther's as that of the neo-Thomists who so neatly divided nature and supernature, giving human life two different ends. This argument we have already seen in chapter 7. But if one does not separate nature and grace so neatly, then, theologically, that heavenly peace needs to serve at least as a sort of measuring stick, or perhaps better put, as a place of perspective and imagination that is far more self-reflective than Weigel's position allows. So I shall now argue by turning to Simone Weil's essay "The *Iliad*: Poem of Force."

As odd as it may appear to say, there could be a great deal of agreement between Weil and Weigel. The reason, though, that it would seem to be odd and counterintuitive is because in that essay Weil uncompromisingly portrays blind, mindless force as the real hero of the *Iliad* and, by implication, of wars in general. There are among the participants no moments of profound moral reflection, nor does there seem to be any room for it. Those who are on the receiving end of force are made into things, transformed into stones, sometimes while they still breathe. But even the wielders of force, Weil contends, come under mindless force as it maddens them. Though they foolishly think that they possess it, it possesses them and blinds them to the fact that they are under force, a fact usually brought home to them sooner rather than later on the battlefield. On the surface, Weil would appear to be a proponent of the irrationality thesis about war and, indeed, a very eloquent spokesperson for it. If force is the real hero of war, then it would follow that there is no moral clarity in war. The portrayal of war in the *Iliad* essay is as something utterly irrational, since it is mindless force that directs it; moreover, war takes away the humanity of those who engage in it. It would seem only logical, then, to conclude that the essay, in portraying the irrationality of war, is an apologia for peace and that the only rational thing, the only way to maintain rational and moral reflection, would be to stay out of war at all costs.

But to take the essay this way would be to put it at odds with a good deal of the rest of what Weil was thinking and doing at the time (1940) that she wrote it. She did have explicit pacifist commitments during the 1930s, and she did not change her views until the "last resort" had been exhausted and Hitler invaded Czechoslovakia. But change her views she did. She was bitterly disappointed when Paris was not defended by arms. She worked eagerly with the Resistance movement, although she herself did not bear arms. She never spoke against the justice of the Allies in fighting Hitler. She even wanted to become a frontline nurse. Nobody could ever say that she didn't support the troops. Furthermore, in *The Need for Roots* she grants governments powers commensurate with declaring war. And, finally, in her reflections on the *Bhagavad-Gita*, she certainly seems supportive of Arjuna's fighting in the war and finds his resolution to fight after being confronted by Krishna to have been a matter of the highest moral purity. So, there would seem to be nothing in Weil's larger views or practices to indicate that she would be opposed in principle to a position such as Weigel's.

But she is a very different sort of thinker than Weigel on what counts as moral clarity and at what depth it needs to be found, and, hence, about the nature of war itself. For her, the issue is far less one of whether or not war can be declared—it already had been and was over for a lot of France when she wrote this essay; for her, it is far more an issue of how one can avoid losing one's soul to force and violence; of how, in the midst of war, one can have any sort of moral center left in order to reflect and to act morally. That she was interested in this sort of issue can be seen in her chief rationale for her frontline nurses project. Whether it was practicable or not, the point of it was to show instances of selfless care and compassion and thereby to show above all that the Allies were fighting for something quite different than the Nazis. It was meant to show this to the Allies themselves just as much as it was to show it to neutrals and the Nazis.

Read from the perspective of this question, Weil certainly sets herself a tall order, if, in the end, she thinks she is going to offer any sort of hope for finding moral clarity in war. Her analysis of the soul's domination by force and of force's destruction of the sort of reflection needed for moral clarity is uncompromising. Force is, as she boldly asserts, the real hero of the Trojan War, or any war for that matter.

Force, of course, destroys reflective equilibrium in those who are its most direct objects. The obvious example is that of the one who is killed, for "when exercised to the full [force] makes a thing of a man in the most literal sense, for it makes him a corpse" (IC 24). But, moreover, force can make a thing of a man while he still lives. Considering the suppliant trying to touch Achilles' knees, kneeling to keep the bright lance from being thrust, she observes, "even though he still breathes, he is only matter, still thinking he can think of nothing" (IC 26). Force in such cases "wipes out all interior life" (IC 30).

Far more to the point, however, is Weil's contention that "as pitilessly as might crushes, so pitilessly it maddens whoever possesses, or believes he possesses it" (IC 31). In large measure this is due to the lack of space for reflection that comes when, in violent anger, one's superior force finds no resistance in one's victim, and thus violent desire moves to fulfillment immediately: "He who possesses strength moves in an atmosphere which offers him no resistance. Nothing in the human element surrounding him is of a nature to induce, between the intention and the act that brief interval where thought may lodge. Where there is no room for thought, there is no room for justice or prudence. This is the reason why men of arms behave with such harshness and folly" (IC 34).

So, even in those one might believe to be the least desperate and most in control of their own wills and thoughts, there is no thought and no moral clarity. They are blind—blind certainly to the humanity of their victims, but also to their own humanity, and especially to the fact that they do not possess force unequivocally. They see no possibility that force's favor is easily reversed; they fail to see how easily and quickly they themselves may become its victims as, in the narrative of the *Iliad*, inevitably happens. The victor of one day is chased across the field of battle the next.

As a result, they make stupid and foolish decisions. Weil suggests that at the end of the first day of fighting recounted in the *Iliad* it is possible that the Greeks might have been able to snatch Helen and return home. But that is not a decision they can make, for now "what they want is no less than all. All the riches of Troy as booty, all the palaces, the temples and the houses as ashes, all the women and all the children as slaves, all the men as corpses" (IC 36). Yet, two days later, having overplayed their hand, they are driven back to their ships. On the Trojan side, Hector on that first day believes that his side is defeated and there is no hope; two days later, when the tide has turned, he will no longer be satisfied with having the Greeks leave. He wants to burn the ships. And, because of the delay, the Greeks chase him across the plains of Ilium the next day. And so it goes on.

Thucydides' reflections on the decisions made during the Peloponnesian War parallel Weil's on the *Iliad*, and they can serve to underline them and her contention that this sort of issue was a matter of extended reflection in ancient Greek culture. The failure of Athens and Sparta to manage and to hold to an armistice, even though it was clearly in their respective best interests to do so, especially after ten years of war, is a case in point. So, too, is the disastrous Athenian decision to invade Syracuse just when Athens was recovering from the earlier losses of the war and an infestation of plague.

Incisively, Thucydides early on in his account analyzes war's power to induce madness: "In peace and prosperity both state and individuals are actuated by higher motives, because they do not fall under the dominion of imperious necessities; but war which takes away the comfortable provisions of daily life is a hard master and tends to assimilate men's characters to their conditions."[8] He further adds how foolish men in war become, especially when revenge is an issue, by observing that in so many decisions

> If malignity had not exercised a fatal power, how could any one have preferred revenge to piety, and gain to innocence? But when men are retaliating upon others, they are reckless of the future, and do not hesitate to annul those common laws of humanity to which every individual trusts for his own hope of deliverance should he ever be overtaken by calamity; they forget that in their own hour of need they will look for them in vain.[9]

Weil, for her part, affirms that the necessity that "belongs to war is terrible, wholly different from that belonging to peaceful works" (IC 40). But for that very reason it is easy to fall under the dominion of war's necessity since, in a time of peace, "danger is an abstraction, the loves which one takes seem like toys broken by a child no more important; heroism is a theatrical pose soiled by artificial braggings. If added to this, an influx of vitality comes to multiply and inflate the power of action, the man believes that, thanks to divine intervention, he is irresistible, providentially preserved from defeat and from death. War is easy then, and ignobly loved" (IC 40–41).

Thus, according to Weil, moral clarity can be lost even before hostilities begin and can be lost easily even in a just cause, even in a case where one's own defense is at stake. For this reason, clarity about rightness and wrongness in war is not sufficient for the sort of clarity that lets one keep one's soul. However, with this said, what is needed at this point is a far more precise sense of what exactly constitutes moral clarity, since for Weil it is not exhausted by questions of self-defense nor by the question of moral right.

Weil suggests that violence's hold over both victim and wielder makes force and violence appear as an external enemy, a third combatant in any conflict. This externality easily lends itself to the idea of a "destiny beneath which the aggressors and their victims are equally innocent, the victors and the vanquished brothers in the same misfortune" (IC 39). But there is another, better way of describing what is going on, Weil thinks, than the idea of destiny. Force, never possessed by either victor or vanquished, operates indifferently to both. It is not capricious, but operates according to a strict equilibrium. Over time, force is a matter of balancing scales, allowing for a sort of retribution "which punishes automatically the abuse of strength." It is this sort of balance, and the human ignorance of it, that, Weil says, was the principal subject of moral meditation for the Greeks. She has good evidence for this: one sees it in the tragedies, one sees it in Thucydides. Numerous philosophers pondered this balance and how to achieve it in the soul and read it in the world.

Recognition of this balance is the key to moral clarity for Weil. How? In the first place, it is a recognition of a fundamental equality of all people under necessity. Weil gives an example of this in citing from Thucydides the Athenian conversations with the inhabitants of the island of Melos whom the Athenians want to join their alliance in the Peloponnesian War. They give the Melians the option of joining them or being destroyed. The Melians respond that this is unjust and the gods will therefore defend Melos. The Athenians simply reply that they see no reason to think that at all. It is a law of nature that the strong command and the weak obey. That, of course, appears arrogant and callous. What Weil finds worth paying attention to in this answer, though, is that at least the Athenians recognize explicitly that if it were the other way around, they, the Athenians, would be subject to the orders of the Melians. That self-recognition, she thinks, is a matter of moral clarity that is just below charity.

It is below, though. If moral clarity is at least recognition of equality under force, at its deepest level it is still something more. It also includes pity and a sense of compassion for the other, and even a sense of bitterness about "the subordination of the human soul to might." She argues, "the understanding of human suffering is dependent upon justice, and love is its condition. Whoever doesn't know just how far necessity and a fickle fortune hold the human soul under their domination cannot treat as his equals, nor love as himself, those whom chance has separated from him by an abyss" (IC 53).

Moral clarity is thus a recognition of human equality before force, but particularly a recognition of it when one is not forced to recognize it. It is a recognition, for example, when wielding force, that the victim is not a different species. As she concludes, "Only he who knows the empire of might and knows how not to respect it is capable of love and justice" (IC 53).

But how is moral clarity like this even possible, especially in a time of war? It is clearly on a level that Weigel does not consider. Should anybody? Weil has so thoroughly put humans in war under the empire of force that it would seem impossible that they could ever achieve the needed reflective equilibrium to see their own position and their shared humanity with the enemy with any clarity at all. Even in the deliberations during peace that take place before war, she has suggested that peace itself may keep them from seeing what they are really getting into, and after that it is too late.

Yet, she does think that it is possible. This is why she is not a proponent of the irrationality thesis. Her evaluation of the *Iliad* as a "miraculous object" (IC 52) is a contention that the human soul, in this case Homer's soul, is capable of seeing the range of force's hold on humanity and of seeing it with equanimity. None in the *Iliad*, Greek or Trojan, is despised by the author. One could not tell from his narration which side he might have been on. There is also a bitterness over affliction, no matter whose it is, heightened by Homer's ability to see and to show the sweetness of both Greek and Trojan life, to which he occasionally alludes both before and outside the battles. This same spirit and light and justice, she says, infuses the gospels. What Homer has done is take away the idolatry inherent in war and show how one might be saved even in it. She notes, "The false God changes suffering into violence; the true God changes violence into suffering. . . . In a poem like the *Iliad*, there is a transmutation of violence into suffering by the poet. There is a participation in the work of redemption" (NB 242).

Weil also makes it clear that she thinks that this clarity and transformation is miraculous, the result of grace. That, however, is *not* another form of irrationality, nor is this assessment a moral deus ex machina. It, rather, should draw the attention of the reader of the *Iliad* or the gospels to the fact that cultures, in possessing texts such as the *Iliad* and the Gospels, and individuals, in reading them, do have the resources to shed light on what needs to be thought about before one enters war and to witness to what moral clarity is in war. That sort of witness is precisely what clergy and intellectuals ought to be talking about, and it is what gives them any moral authority whatsoever. Which is not to say that that is what they are actually talking about, for they can be foolish and naive, just as Weigel thinks they are. To be these sorts of witnesses, they, too, have to take seriously that human life is under necessity and that wars do arise—an insight that separates an Augustine from many of his would-be followers. Too often, they ignore that insight—but they don't always ignore it. Sometimes they really do get it right.

By way of providing an example of just what doing this might look like, I cite a sermon preached at the outset of the Iraq War by a colleague who occupied the pulpit of a large and prominent New York church. In an aggressive defense following a *Wall Street Journal* critique that the American clergy were naive and misguided in their opposition to the war, my colleague, who had himself flown numerous combat missions in Vietnam, argued that the administration had no experience of war; they were the ones who were naive about what they were getting into. They were the ones who did not understand the effects of force and violence on humans and the loss of moral reflection that one encounters in war. Furthermore, he noted how, during his military days, the chaplains, who should have deepened the understanding of the soldiers and given them clarity, did little more than urge them on to their bombing because God "was with them." They did so with absolutely no sense that they saw the enemy as worthy of being reflected on morally. Had the chaplains given even a glimmer of this, my friend noted, "we might have had some respect for them." In this critique of the chaplains' messages there was no thought whatsoever that the pilots would have walked away from their missions if they had been encouraged to take a broader view, that a broader and more balanced view would have made them poor warriors. What might have happened, he suggested, is that the pilots would have had an opportunity to grapple and to make a fuller peace with what they knew they were doing. The same point is made in the *Bhagavad-Gita*. After Arjuna is confronted by Krishna before battle, he does not balk from his duty as a warrior; he is, however, able to do it without hatred or desire for revenge or gain. That surely is a sort of heavenly peace even in the time of war, a peace that Weigel seems to think irrelevant. Augustine, for his part, says quite pointedly, "Let necessity slay the warring foe, not your will."[10]

However, it also needs to be noted that this witness is only half the issue. This witness is a moral clarity *about* war. As such, it is important in deliberations in time of peace, when there is time for reflection; it is also an important witness to everybody in a time of war. But what about achieving moral clarity *in* war if one is in the heat of fighting it? How, when actually wielding force or being the victim of it, can one know how properly to respect the empire of force? How is one to take to heart the witness?

It would, of course, be foolish to expect a soldier about to make a decision to kill or to be killed to look for the room and time needed for ethical reflection. Conscience, as Hamlet observed, can kill resolve and action. But there is another way to look at the question. It can be seen in the (attempted) example of Weil herself in her frontline nursing project. I also note that raising this example in this context may help us understand what exactly she was trying to do.

In that project, Weil had hoped to provide a witness to show that the Allies were fighting for reasons morally superior to those of the Nazis, that compassion and a willingness to sacrifice oneself for a moral cause were in the front of Allied war efforts, and that the ideals touted in times of peace had not been lost. Personally, however, for Weil herself it also involved a sense that if this war had to be fought, then one needed to make oneself subject to the necessities that it involved. This involved a sense that moral clarity was not simply about force but something to be achieved through enduring force, just as Christ's union with the Father was perfected on the Cross, when the weight of sin and necessity had crushed him.

There is much to be said about Weil's thinking here. Positively, as Alexander Irwin has thoroughly examined it, for Weil there is certainly a sense that by consenting to harsh necessity one could find clarity, even, or especially, in violence. Violence could be a transforming moment. Moreover, the "gesture would fuse religious meaning and political efficacy in an art of poetic, performative power."[11] Belief would be incarnated in action and made real. A great deal of ink has been spilled on these issues in Weil's thought, especially insofar as they have been seen to tend toward a sort of self-immolation on her part. I will not deal with these here. But two things do need highlighting about the importance of Weil's view, and they are both profound and less controversial. First, in embodied action, including suffering or action where suffering is a real possibility and the mind cannot flee from it by fantasy, we can reach moral clarity. We may in facing death and our own vulnerability also *fail* to reach clarity, and in some truly chilling ways. But to recognize that failure does happen should also make us recognize how very important it is, when confronting violence and necessity, that we do gain clarity. This is, therefore, an absolutely crucial confrontation for a moral being. There is in actual confrontation with necessity and thus with one's own vulnerability and death something, Irwin correctly observes, that "tests human values and commitments more rigorously than any other phenomenon and thus reveals truth with unexcelled clarity."[12] As Weil puts it, "Reality appears only to him who accepts death" (OC 6.4, 334). Any thinking on war, whether from pulpit or podium, that does not allow or encourage gaining this sort of clarity can be a quick way to guarantee the loss of souls. Simply getting clear on the right to use violence, as Weigel argues for, without at the same time making it clear how dangerous it is to use it, may then ultimately press rightness into the service of something other than goodness. It can be a quick way to a bad decision and loss of clarity.

The second thing that needs highlighting is a corollary to the first. It is about modern warfare, which has increasingly been conducted at a distance and by technological means. At the time the Iraq and Afghanistan wars began, in the early 2000s, many had reached a point where they thought we could dream of conducting a soldierless war, a war of precision bombing and shock and awe. It was how the United States had conducted its most recent war, in Bosnia, and initially meant to conduct the war in Iraq. But to achieve this is to become spectators of violence, thinking it does not affect us and that we have been delivered from necessity. Setting aside the fact that such tactics have rarely been as effective as their planners would like, as long-term involvement in both Afghanistan and Iraq proved, the problem is that the very attempt of modern warfare to minimize risk to one's own soldiers, while admirable, also runs the moral risk of letting one believe that one's side is not vulnerable. It can keep one from ever being tested morally or having, through harsh experience, to reflect on and witness to violence. It can keep one, as Kant thought, in a purely commercial frame of mind, seeing war strictly within capitalist terms. This lack of reflection may happen not only when war is simply viewed from a distance, but also whenever, in war, might is disproportionately distributed between the two sides. Apparently the Greeks and Trojans were at about the same strength, and that fact could make the lessons of the *Iliad* much more immediate. For the truly powerful, the nature of force and its tendency to establish equilibrium will not be seen quickly. It can occur only by reflection over a long time, if at all. If Weil is right and there is truly a balancing scale of force, at least in the long term, then the failure to be exposed to violence and to feel one's own vulnerability is something that can madden us and lead us into believing that we are not subject to necessity. That, in turn, can ultimately make us more defenseless and not less. And it surely can cause us to lose important capacities and experience needed for moral clarity in war and elsewhere, especially the clarity that is needed for broad moral compassion. Those capacities and experience are also crucial for being able to achieve compassion in times of peace, even the *tranquillitas ordinis*.

CONCLUSION

Central to the thought of Simone Weil is the belief that the values by which we live our lives are not all on a level. There are base values—the values of naked power, unvarnished egotism, pleasure, the avoidance of pain. These are the things that brute necessity sets out for us, and to embrace them is to have failed to rise above brute necessity. The person who lives by them has a Hobbesian life, one that is disappointed as inexplicably and as often as it is enjoyed. It is a life that is dictated by necessity, although those who live this way may well not have the insight to recognize that they are not in control of their own lives. A sort of moral gravity dictates what they do and believe. Weil once suggested, "Those whom we call criminals are only tiles blown off the roof by the wind and falling at random. Their only fault is the initial choice by which they became those tiles" (SWW 49). But there are also what might be called civilized values, values that belong to what she calls the "middle realm," such as rights, democracy, and personality. These values rise above brute force, as they depend upon a sort of controlled distribution of force that helps to equalize the inequalities between human beings. To many minds, justice is a matter of extending this realm. It provides a sort of balance of forces and of people, much as the market provides balance for those buying and selling in it. But that is to say that these more elevated values depend for their play upon a sort of social force and do not rise entirely above what necessity can give us. We might believe they do, but that would be a mistake. At most, with them, we can rise to the level where we can have some sort of perspective on necessity. Should any human being see that these values may well hint at an impersonal equality between human beings, he or she rises to a moral level that is above force, above the belief that might is coextensive with right, to a sort of understanding that there is nothing particularly special about oneself and others have rights and personalities too. Yet, to Weil's mind, that does not go far enough. It certainly does not go far enough to save us, especially those who are afflicted and crushed by force. We can also become complacent and think that we are freer than we really are, more just and high-minded than we really are. We are unaware that there is anything above us. Then there are the values of a transcendent realm, values signaled by words such as *God*, *truth*, *justice*, *love*, and *good*. Those alone put us, who are otherwise and always creatures of necessity, on the other side of necessity. Those values alone give us the lives we are destined for. Those alone will make for compassion and justice when procedural justice and systems fail us.

There is no doubt that Weil came by this sort of thinking about value early and that she owed it to Plato. The contempt for "the Great Beast" and the aspirations to the good that is "beyond Being, exceeding it in dignity and power" appear throughout her works, early to late. She also regularly draws on Plato's allegory of the cave to stress the need to turn around and emerge from one point of view to a higher one.

Anybody who talks this way is clearly going to challenge directly what Charles Taylor has talked about as the triumph of the hollow men and the victory of flatness in human life. We see that challenge issued in several places: where we have reduced the inner life to biological determinism, or behaviorism, or to just inner gazing and a rich fantasy life, is one place. There are others: where we treat religion as little more than impulse control, a form of self-affirmation, or a political tool used by political tools; where we never talk about science in relation to the beauty of the world or as how human thought situates itself by an image that it creates of the cosmos; where we have continually deconstructed meaning; in our loss of tragedy and comedy, both of which, at any depth beyond the ironical, need soul. There is no doubt that Weil challenges all these things, culturally, personally, and politically.

That she does so is surely a good part of her continuing attraction to those who read her. But she also thinks about value in some very distinctive ways, ways that indicate that she is not simply reacting to the ennui and frustrating meaninglessness of contemporary thought. These ways are signaled, we will recall, in how she describes her third and most significant religious experience. It was in this experience, she says, "that Christ took possession of me." She notes that, up until it happened, she had thought of the problem of God as something that could not be solved, and so she left it alone. But once it did happen, it did not exactly solve the problem of God, at least intellectually. She hadn't seen the possibility of a "real contact, person to person, here below between a human being and God. . . . Moreover, in this sudden possession of me by Christ, neither my sense nor my imagination had any part; I only felt in the midst of my suffering the presence of a love, like that which one can read in the smile on a beloved face. . . . Yet, I still half refused, not my love but my intelligence" (WG 69).

What she had encountered, the good she now confronted, the good that confronted her, was unlike anything that she had thought about before. If she half refused her intelligence but committed her love, it was because she now saw that intelligence wasn't the way one approached this good, although once one had been touched by it, intelligence would be inexorably set in a certain direction. She also does not talk about this experience of God as taking away her suffering; it is something that occurs within it and alongside it.

The vital point to be taken away here is that the God she experienced, the good she now was transfixed by, was utterly unlike any that she had thought about. It was on an entirely different level. The values signified by the words *God*, *justice*, *love*, and *truth* are not just the values of other levels magnified. God is not a natural being, just bigger and more powerful, nor is a transcendent good a good that compensates for evil. Any good that compensates or consoles for evil or suffering may have something going for it, but it is not a transcendent good that demands our all, no matter what. Anything else is on the level of necessity, and it has limits. This sort of good does not.

That Weil believed that helps explain her resistance to any talk about religious matters, such as an afterlife, that could be turned into a good that is merely compensatory. She did not want to make a mistake; there is a sort of horror at the thought of idolatry. That is the negative side of things. On the more important, positive side, though, that such thoughts about God and goodness had entered her mind, she realized, required a different way of thinking about value. It meant that one needed to pay attention and wait to be revealed to. It also meant that love preceded intellect, and that love is not an emotion but a personal stance toward what is before one.

This is what is particularly distinctive about her thinking. The mystery of the good within which we live requires a certain subjectivity, as Kierkegaard also thought. One cannot *only* talk about the transcendent without thereby making it into an amplified natural good. Nor can one think it out and then *apply* it. If one has any true sense of God, one has to change and approach things differently. One has in this way to take seriously that the good crosses the void that we otherwise experience as existing between goodness and our necessity. Taking it seriously is then a matter of letting it dwell within us. This is why love precedes intellect, without being anti-intellectual. Some kind of inner life is required. Without it, the hollow men will always triumph.

Max Weber is regularly cited as having said that the modern world is a disenchanted one. It is a world without mystery, a world increasingly defined by its technology, one that inevitably will become more and more secular. Such disenchantment can well be given as the reason for the contemporary world's flatness. It usually *is* given as that reason. The remedy, however, is not simply to reintroduce enchanting things: more mystery, more God, more poetry. All of those things, unless they go hand in hand with an inner turn, with a certain subjectivity, will simply be gassy versions of the same things that make for flatness. Taylor has suggested that part of our problem is that the modern self is a "buffered self." It stands apart at a critical distance from what it is engaged with; we understand ourselves at a remove and treat ourselves objectively, thinking about ourselves in the third person. We do not engage in first-person thinking.

That is where Weil is such an important challenge and has an authenticity that few thinkers exhibit. That she seriously and insightfully talks about God, and justice, and truth is very much to her credit in a world where those things are not talked about much at all. But *how* she talks about them is even more important, for simply adding them to the conversation is not enough. We who are talking won't get what they mean because of who we have become. There has to be a change in us in order for us to say that we take them seriously. That change cannot merely be, as Weil said, a matter of "adding God onto everything." It requires a change in our stance. Clearly, she altered her stance.

Knowing that about Weil helps us understand better what she is trying to say and what her challenge is. For example, her late political and social writings are striking because they are *not* meant as an improvement on our current discussions. They are meant to make us look at our social being in a very different way and to find entirely different kinds of solutions, not just improved ones, to our current malaise. They are meant to get us to see, for example, that, morally, obligations precede rights, that is, that rights have little weight without our willing the good of those whose rights we should respect, and that the culture fails the souls that live in it, if it does not somehow orient them beyond the social. It gets us to see that we have to commit ourselves to the good of others in our social organization. There are no algorithms that will do it for us.

That is where Weil's philosophical and religious and social thinking are all of a piece. The inner turn and the mysticism of her philosophical and religious thinking are not off to the side of her thinking about the quotidian matters of politics. They form the person who would actually do something important for our life together.

NOTES

Chapter One

1. Simone Pétrement, *Simone Weil: A Life*, trans. Raymond Rosenthal (New York: Pantheon Books, 1976), 341.
2. Ludwig Wittgenstein, *The Big Typescript: TS 213*. ed. and trans. C. G. Luckhardt and M. A. E. Aue (Chichester, U.K.: Wiley-Blackwell, 2013), §86, 300E.
3. Pascal David, "'Philosophie, Chose Exclusivement en Acte et Pratique': L'Écriture Philosophique des *Cahiers* comme Exercice de l'Absence," *Cahiers Simone Weil* 31, no. 2: 119–52.
4. See Pétrement, *Simone Weil: A Life,* 220.
5. With a variant at OC 6.1, 139–40. English translation: FLN 4.
6. David, "'Philosophie, Chose Exclusivement en Acte et Pratique,'" 138.
7. See chapter 6, "Spiritual Apprenticeship."
8. This is in all likelihood the best explanation for her oft-debated letter "What Is a Jew? A Letter to the Minister of Education." In it, Weil wants to know why she has not been given a new teaching post. She surmises that it is because of the statute that disqualifies Jews. She goes on with biting sarcasm to highlight the incoherencies of the statute. Some have seen the letter as self-serving, as she uses its logic to argue that it shouldn't apply to her. Others have seen it as heroic and critical of the regime that made up such a statute. Yet, if she was trying to be brave, it may well be an example of not seeing how truly dangerous these people were and how risky it was to point out their idiocy. As her niece, Nicolette, opined to me, it was a trait that she shared with her brother, who mocked his captors when he was a prisoner of war, never really appreciating that he was within an ace of getting shot (SWR 79–81).
9. Terry Eagleton, *Radical Sacrifice* (New Haven, CT: Yale University Press, 2018), 4.
10. Eagleton, *Radical Sacrifice,* 7.

11. Iris Murdoch, "The Idea of Perfection," in *The Sovereignty of the Good* (New York: Schocken Books, 1971), 35.

12. Martin Heidegger, *What Is Called Thinking?*, trans. F. D. Wieck and J. G. Gray (New York: Harper & Row, 1968).

13. Pierre Hadot, *Philosophy as a Way of Life* (Oxford: Blackwell, 1995), 107.

14. Jean-Yves Lacoste, *From Theology to Theological Thinking* (Charlottesville: University of Virginia Press, 2014), 28.

15. See, in particular, Michel Henry, *Incarnation: A Philosophy of the Flesh*, trans. K. Hefty (Evanston, IL: Northwestern University Press, 2015).

16. Joseph Rivera, *The Contemplative Self after Michel Henry: A Phenomenological Theology* (Notre Dame, IN: University of Notre Dame Press, 2015), 219–20.

17. Rivera, *The Contemplative Self after Michel Henry*, 225. The interior quotation comes from Rowan Williams.

Chapter Two

1. Michael Foster, *Mystery and Philosophy* (London: SCM Press, 1957; repr., Westport, CT: Greenwood Press, 1980).

2. Antony Flew and Alasdair MacIntyre, eds., *New Essays in Philosophical Theology* (London: SCM Press, 1955).

3. To be sure, the volume contained essays by able defenders of religion. Yet, it still seems that even they were being asked to respond to a formidable case laid against religion, and that the burden of proof was being laid on them.

4. Foster, *Mystery and Philosophy*, 11.

5. Foster, *Mystery and Philosophy*, 18.

6. Foster, *Mystery and Philosophy*, 17.

7. Foster, *Mystery and Philosophy*, 20.

8. Foster, *Mystery and Philosophy*, 27.

9. Foster, *Mystery and Philosophy*, 88.

10. Foster, *Mystery and Philosophy*, 88.

11. For a full analysis of Weil's concept of mystery and how it differs from a logical contradiction, see my "Contradiction, Mystery, and the Use of Words in Simone Weil," in *The Beauty That Saves: Essays on Aesthetics and Language in Simone Weil*, ed. John M. Dunaway and Eric O. Springsted (Macon, GA: Mercer University Press, 1996), 13–30.

12. Charles Taylor, *A Secular Age* (Cambridge, MA: Harvard University Press, 2007), 734.

13. E.g., in "Letter to a Priest," in GTG §26, 27, 28; NB 238–39.

14. For a fuller discussion of this, see my *Christus Mediator: Platonic Mediation in the Thought of Simone Weil* (Chico, CA: Scholars Press, 1983); "Contradiction, Mystery and the Use of Words in Simone Weil"; and Vance Morgan, *Weaving the World* (Notre Dame, IN: University of Notre Dame Press, 2005).

15. See my "Divine Necessity: Weilian and Platonic Conceptions," in *Spirit, Nature, and Community: Issues in the Thought of Simone Weil*, by Diogenes Allen and Eric O. Springsted, 33–51(Albany: State University of New York Press, 1994).

16. "With respect to the completed systems constructed with the intention of eliminating all the essential contradictions of thought, we see that they do have value, but only as poetry" (LPW 36).

17. Taylor, *A Secular Age*, 771.

18. Taylor, *A Secular Age*, 737.

19. Susan Sontag, "Simone Weil," in *Against Interpretation* (New York: Farrar, Strauss & Giroux, 1961), 50.

Chapter Three

1. Emmanuel Gabellieri, *Être et Don: Simone Weil et la Philosophie* (Louvain: Éditions Peeters, 2003).

2. See, e.g., "Divine Love in Creation," IC 89–105.

3. I argue this at length, giving full textual support, in my *Christus Mediator*. I repeat the argument in *Simone Weil and the Suffering of Love* (Cambridge, MA: Cowley Publications, 1986; repr., Eugene, OR: Wipf & Stock, 2010) and integral parts of it regarding the concepts of "necessity" in Allen and Springsted, *Spirit, Nature, and Community*, chapter 3.

4. Hans Urs von Balthasar, *Mysterium Paschale*, trans. Aidan Nichols (Edinburgh: T&T Clark, 1990), 65.

5. Jacques Cabaud, *Simone Weil* (London: Harvill Press, 1964), 212.

6. Inese Radzins, "Truly Incarnated: Simone Weil's Revised Christianity," in *The Relevance of the Radical: Simone Weil 100 Years Later*, ed. A. Rebecca Rozelle-Stone and Lucian Stone, 230–31 (New York: Continuum, 2010). What is incoherent here is the claim that the universal and divine Word is more truly incarnate than "the Word [that] became flesh and dwelt among

us" when the latter is precisely what the Incarnation means. To deny the latter makes it impossible to understand what the former might possibly mean as being more "truly incarnated." But that is simply on the face of things. More deeply and much more troubling is that a cosmological and universal Christianity, as Radzins describes it, is in fact an *excarnated* Christianity, one that is gnostic, and metaphysical in the worst sense of that term, little more than a just-so story. It lives in the head, not the body.

7. Peter Winch, *Simone Weil: "The Just Balance"* (Cambridge: Cambridge University Press, 1989).

8. Winch, *Simone Weil*, 211. See chapter 9 here for a fuller discussion of Winch's position.

9. Kathryn Tanner, *Christ the Key* (Cambridge: Cambridge University Press, 2010), 8.

10. Tanner, *Christ the Key*, 12.

11. Tanner, *Christ the Key*, 13.

12. Tanner, *Christ the Key*, 36.

13. Tanner, *Christ the Key*, 52.

14. Tanner, *Christ the Key*, 59.

15. Tanner, *Christ the Key*, 62.

16. Tanner, *Christ the Key*, 102.

17. Tanner, *Christ the Key*, 105.

18. I note carefully that this is not meant as a proof of the Incarnation, or that certain human experiences must be seen as necessary consequences of it. This is simply a grammatical account of the concepts in play.

19. Tanner, *Christ the Key*, 254.

20. Tanner, *Christ the Key*, 257.

21. Tanner, *Christ the Key*, 261.

22. On this point, see Diogenes Allen and Eric O. Springsted, "The Enigma of Affliction," in *Spirit, Nature, and Community*, chapter 3, 97–110.

23. For a full discussion of this theory, see chapter 6.

24. The Church "should never have excommunicated any except the Docetae, those who deny the Incarnation" (GTG 107).

Chapter Four

1. André Naud, *Les Dogmes et le Respect de l'Intelligence: Plaidoyer Inspiré par Simone Weil* (Quebec: Éditions Fides, 2002). For further explication of Naud

and his thinking about Weil, see Lawrence Schmidt's "André Naud: From Vatican II to Simone Weil," *Philosophical Investigations* 43, nos.1–2: 115–21.

2. This is crucial for her argument. It is particularly modern, and therefore her position takes the modern on as it presents itself. Ancient and medieval versions of the intellect, however, may be different, not distinguishing sharply between love and intellect. Ultimately, they accomplish the point she wants to make. German Catholic philosopher Josef Pieper suggested that it was Kant who made the modern distinction. He writes, "For Kant, the sum of man's intellectual knowledge is exclusively discursive, that is, noninuitive. Thus, in Kant's view, human knowledge is essentially realized in the acts of researching, relating, comparing, differentiating, inferring, proving—in all manner and form of active intellectual exertion. By contrast, intuition is a receptive, accepting, and passive attitude of the soul. According to Kant, however, intuition is limited only to the realm of the senses." Pieper, "Philosophical Education and Intellectual Labor," in *For the Love of Wisdom: Essays on the Nature of Philosophy*, ed. Berthold Wald, trans. Roger Wasserman (San Francisco: Ignatius Press, 2006), 14.

3. See chapter 9 for a further discussion of this distinction, one that is especially relevant to values in the social realm.

4. Borrowing a term from John Henry Newman, who also emphasized such a distinction, it might be better to say that what Weil is after is "certitude" as an attitude of the soul (if we are careful to avoid a psychologically reductive use of the term) as opposed to the "certainty" that is a characteristic of propositions.

5. This is the recommendation: for five hundred years the Western Church has been split in an act of violence. A great deal has been accomplished in the last fifty or so years to help heal it. Yet, the Roman Church still officially bars communion to non-Catholics until the many doctrinal issues dividing the Protestant and Roman Catholic churches are resolved. But perhaps this is to go at it backward. Perhaps those issues can only be resolved by peoples who stand on their baptism in Christ and are fed at the same table. Perhaps it is a common Eucharistic participation of those who are baptized and who confess the Real Presence of Christ and who are willing to work for unity that will reduce the violence of the split.

6. In this respect, to a degree, but only a very limited one, what she has in mind bears some similarities to Aquinas's concept of faith (see *Summa Theologiae* 2, 2, qq.1–16). For Aquinas faith is a full and complete assent to the will to God, with the intellect lagging behind. This is to say that the will does not assent because the intellect has established its object with certitude. The will

(whose object is the good) therefore leads, and the intellect follows, which reverses the normal course of things for Aquinas. However, once the will has assented, the intellect then thinks the object of faith and works out its details and can bring itself to more and more intellectual certainty, guided by grace, of course. Weil also seems to think that the intellect is guided by grace and that it can think through more fully something grasped by the will. However, where she differs from Aquinas—and this is an important point—is that since he sees faith as an intellectual virtue and being as prior to goodness, he therefore needs to talk about how faith works as an intellectual virtue (even if he is also beholden to Augustine's primacy of the will). He needs to see the intellect as being filled in, as it were. Here is where Weil genuinely differs, for she is headed in a very different direction with the intellect. Consistent with her view of spiritual life in general, she wants to talk about the role of the intellect as a matter of how it participates in the increase of attention, which is also to say how it, as a natural faculty, ultimately is decreated, ceding its own function to attention as attention yields the self to the object of love. She is indeed admirably consistent in thus making intellect serve and obey attention and not putting it into some dialectical bargain with attention. However, these differences probably also need to be adjusted in light of the fact that Aquinas has a somewhat broader use of "intellect" than the modern sense of "discursive intellect."

7. In this regard Weil may hold a view similar to that of John Henry Newman, who assumed that drawing a conclusion and assenting to it were two different mental operations. This also seems to be a Stoic position.

8. It is probably not too much to say that in this case one doesn't really think anyhow. To accept, say, on authority that there is a proof (or five of them) of the existence of God is to have missed both the intellectual and spiritual value of thought.

9. In an essay on the Occitan civilization of the Romanesque period, Weil praises it for having developed a conception of justice that is, in langue d'oc, called *parage*. She describes it thus: it "makes the servant equal to the master through voluntary fealty and allows him to kneel and obey and suffer punishments without losing any self-respect" (SE 39). It is "obedience without self-abasement" (SE 41), the sole condition of legitimate order. What she is aiming at here can without difficulty be described as *parage* with respect to the intellect.

10. Yet, as Kierkegaard observed of someone attending a play who could only see the actors, the person who was not deceived is the one who is worse off.

11. E.g., "The connection between humility and true philosophy was known in antiquity. Among the Socratic, Cynic, and Stoic philosophers it was considered part of their professional duty to put up with insults, blows, and

even slaps in the face without the slightest instinctive reaction of offended dignity. Since Christian apostleship was a similar or identical profession, Christ's precept to his disciples to 'turn the other cheek' should be seen in this way, as an obligation pertaining to a particular function, and not as an obligation of Christian life" (FLN 335–36). (NB: One suspects that the last qualification has something to do with the fact that Weil was working for the Free French at the time and deeply regretted her prewar pacifism.)

12. See, for example, his "Love the Safeguard of Faith against Superstition," in *Fifteen Sermons Preached before the University of Oxford between A.D. 1826 and 1843* (Notre Dame, IN: University of Notre Dame Press, 1997). Newman says of faith that it has its own way of dealing with facts—"the reaching of the mind itself towards them. . . . They go out of themselves to meet Him who is unseen, and they discern Him in such symbols of Him as they find ready provided for them" (225). But if it is not a matter of reason, then what keeps faith from superstition? "The safeguard of faith is a right state of heart. This it is that gives it birth; it also disciplines it. This is what protects it from bigotry, credulity, and fanaticism" (234).

Chapter Five

1. For example, in talking about the degradation of an ancient ceremony of cremation, which she thinks must originally have symbolized how supernatural fire transports a thing from this world to the next, she acerbically comments, "As the result of a decadence of thought, this ceremony came to be taken as the condition of the thing for which it was a symbol; exactly as baptism became, for narrow Catholics like Augustine" (FLN 248).

2. Charles Taylor is a surprising source for this in *The Sources of the Self* (Cambridge, MA: Harvard University Press, 1989), chapter 7.

3. See, e.g., Phillip Cary, *Augustine's Invention of the Inner Self: The Legacy of a Christian Platonist* (New York: Oxford University Press, 2000). For recent work on the concept of the self in Augustine, see also Jean-Luc Marion, *In the Self's Place: The Approach of Saint Augustine*, trans. Jeffrey L. Kosky (Stanford, CA: Stanford University Press, 2012), and Willemien Otten and Susan E. Shreiner, eds., *Augustine Our Contemporary: Examining the Self in Past and Present* (Notre Dame, IN: University of Notre Dame Press, 2018).

4. On "inner and outer" in Augustine, see Denys Turner, *The Darkness of God: Negativity in Christian Mysticism* (Cambridge: Cambridge University Press, 1995).

5. Evagrius Ponticus, *Chapters on Prayer*, no. 60, in *The Praktikos and Chapters on Prayer*, trans. J. E. Bamberger (Kalamazoo, MI: Cistercian Publications, 1981).

6. See Turner, *The Darkness of God*, chapter 1, "The Allegory and the Exodus."

7. Plotinus, *Enneads*, trans. A. H. Armstrong (Cambridge, MA: Harvard University Press, 1966), vol. 2.15:285.

8. See Augustine, "On the Advantage of Believing," 13, in *On Christian Belief* (Hyde Park, NY: New City Press, 2005).

9. Augustine, *The City of God against the Pagans*, trans. R. W. Dyson (Cambridge: Cambridge University Press, 1998), 8.3.

10. Augustine, *The City of God*, 8.4.

11. Cary argues that unlike Augustine's "inner space," which is a place of light and vision, Locke's inner space is dark and we are locked into it with little chance of escape: "Plato's picture is intellectual vision, pure and simple, Plotinus's is intellectual vision construed as inward turn, Augustine's is intellectual vision resulting from a turn first in then up, and Locke's picture is of a self with no direct intellectual vision of anything but its own private inner world, seeing only the images of things outside." *Augustine's Invention of the Inner Self*, 5. See also 122–24.

12. This essential self-involvement also gives a very different way of understanding what exactly the Platonic search for "essences" amounts to. It is not an attempt to peer behind phenomena to discover a permanent something that is more really the thing than its appearances suggest, a something that can then be treated in much the same way as the appearances were treated. It is to stand before and take in things in a very different way, in the light of a necessarily self-involving good.

13. One can see this illustrated, for example, in Aldous Huxley's *Brave New World*. Often regarded as a velvet version of oppressive totalitarianism wherein controlling authorities efface real individuality, it in fact portrays the most individualistic world of all—and in that lies its totalitarianism and passivity. People get everything they want and by genetic manipulation are fortunate enough to not want anything they cannot have. Social control and the loss of soul are achieved not by external forces bearing down on the inhabitants of this utopia but rather by guaranteeing the parameters of choice. Here is the nub of Weil's point about the world we construct being passive. In choosing in certain ways, particularly ways that avoid the pain that openness to others might bring, we lose the self and any sense of familiarity with a larger world. But once those inner

resources disappear, so too does the possibility of any real originality. Our images, our goals and aspirations, are what we grasp from the outside. This is also a point Alexis de Tocqueville made about the philosophical effects of equality. When everyone believes the self to be self-sufficient and nobody else's opinions to be of any more worth than one's own, one will never consult another. But where then does one get principles, the indispensable beginning points of thought? From the mob, which alone is big enough to command his respect, Tocqueville suggests.

14. In Huxley's *Brave New World*, imagine how impossible it would be to discern the artificiality of that world, at least from the inside, were it not for characters such as Mustapha Mond who live in a different world and can therefore limn the artificial one. Although Mond is hardly a figure of grace, his otherness is the only thing that can bring one to consciousness of the problem. Without him, any who felt out of joint with the world might well think themselves the problem with such a perfect world.

15. Josef Pieper, *Leisure, The Basis of Culture* (South Bend, IN: St. Augustine's Press, 1998; originally published 1948), 10–11.

16. Pieper, *Leisure*, 15.

17. This is Augustine's point in "On Free Choice of the Will." Evil is a matter of trying to live in a world that is not of God's making and with an order of our own.

Chapter Six

1. Ludwig Wittgenstein, *Philosophical Investigations*, rev. 4th ed., trans. G. E. M. Anscombe, P. M. S. Hacker, and Joachim Schulte (Chichester, UK: Wiley-Blackwell, 2009), §107: "We have got on to slippery ice where there is no friction and so in a certain sense the conditions are ideal, but also, just because of that, we are unable to walk. We want to walk: so we need *friction*. Back to the rough ground!"

2. I quote the first edition: Joseph Dunne, *Back to the Rough Ground: 'Phronesis' and 'Techne' in Modern Philosophy and Aristotle* (Notre Dame, IN: University of Notre Dame Press, 1993), 5.

3. Alasdair MacIntyre, in chapter 1 of *After Virtue* (Notre Dame, IN: University of Notre Dame Press, 1981), points out that should we ever fail to teach modern science to only one generation, even if all our textbooks were to be fully accessible to the generation after that one, whatever they did with those textbooks would not, could not, be science as we know it.

4. This observation should give away the type of philosophy of education that permeates online learning. It is precisely what Dunne criticizes. If technique, and control, and mere factuality are what is to be learned, why not do it without a real teacher? Blessedly, at least, to date, no one appears to have tried to teach anyone virtue online.

5. On the argument of this paragraph and its roots in Wittgenstein, see Peter Winch, "The Expression of Belief," in *Proceedings and Addresses of the American Philosophical Association* 70, no. 2: 7–23.

6. NB: Simply to use symbols and technology to advance our pleasure and avoid pain, however, is not by itself to have moved up to a different *reading*. To be genuinely scientific, a different frame of mind is required.

7. See also OC 6.2, 353.

8. "The difference between [force and education] is that people do not associate themselves with the former (they only react) whereas they do associate themselves with the latter" (NB 25).

9. The Greek term means "in between." Weil borrowed it from Plato's *Philebus*, when he talks about all the things intermediary between the one and the many and necessary for moving between them.

10. I might note here that, although Weil does not develop things in this way, one might well say that Christian faith as participation in the body of Christ—sacramentally, morally, and communally—is to make Christ's body one's own body and to read the world through it.

Chapter Seven

1. Hilary Putnam, *Jewish Philosophy as a Way of Life* (Bloomington: Indiana University Press, 2008), 6.

2. Henri de Lubac, *The Mystery of the Supernatural*, trans. Rosemary Sheed (New York: Crossroad, 1998; first pub. 1965), 53.

3. See John Milbank, *Theology and Social Theory: Beyond Secular Reason* (Oxford: Blackwell Publishers, 1990).

4. Deirdre Carabine, "The Fathers: The Church's Intimate, Youthful Diary," in *The Beauty of Christ: An Introduction to the Theology of Hans Urs von Balthasar*, ed. Bede McGregor, O.P., and Thomas Norris (Edinburgh: T&T Clark, 1994), 90, quoted in Tamsin Jones, "Dionysius in Hans Urs von Balthasar and Jean-Luc Marion," in *Re-thinking Dionysius the Areopagite*, ed. Sarah Coakley and Charles M. Stang (Malden, MA: Wiley-Blackwell, 2009), 214.

5. As is related in Exodus 3, in the story of God's revealing God's name to Moses.

6. De Lubac similarly thought that to rid ourselves of pure nature was to recognize "the call of Love" (*The Mystery of the Supernatural*, chapter 12).

Chapter Eight

1. Pétrement, *Simone Weil: A Life*, 475. Biographical facts are taken from this source.

2. Pétrement, *Simone Weil: A Life*, 475.

3. See Maritain's *Les Droits de l'Homme et le Loi Naturale*, which was published in New York in 1942. I cite the English translation, *The Rights of Man and the Natural Law* (London: Geofrey Bles, 1944), 57.

4. See Maritain, *The Rights of Man*, 37.

5. On the earlier work uncovering Maritain as the object of Weil's critique, see Simone Fraisse, "Simone Weil, la Personne et les Droits de l'Homme," *Cahiers Simone Weil* 7, no. 2 (June 1984): 120–32, as well as Eric Springsted, "Rootedness: Culture and Value," in *Spirit, Nature, and Community*, ed. Allen and Springsted, 178–79 (Albany, NY: SUNY Press, 1994).

6. In French, these were mostly concentrated and originally published in *Écrits de Londres et Dernières Lettres* (Paris: Gallimard, 1980) and are now collected in OC 5.1. In English, they were scattered throughout SE and OL, with some later published in SWW.

7. Maritain, *The Rights of Man*, 37.

8. Maritain, *The Rights of Man*, 57.

9. Maritain, *The Rights of Man*, 34, 35.

10. Fraisse, "Simone Weil, la Personne et les Droits de l'Homme," 123–24.

11. This issue in particular admirably illustrates Weil's approach to Maritain's book, as discussed in the next few paragraphs, and her own, very different approach to these issues in general. Maritain spends considerable time defending the dignity of labor and liberating it from the conditions of slavery and servitude (Maritain, *The Rights of Man*, 50–60). Weil wouldn't disagree as far as that goes. However, unlike Maritain, who thinks we ought to aim at progressive liberation from material necessity (22, 27) and subjugate nature (26), she thinks that the value of labor is that it allows one to obey necessity and is a "possibility of gaining access to an impersonal form of attention" (LPW 112). So, when Maritain outlines the rights of the working person (61–62), he

chiefly considers issues of property such as a just wage, ownership, insurance, and other benefits. To Weil, choosing to talk to workers about the size of their salaries, as Maritain does, smacks of haggling with the devil over the right price for one's soul (LPW 112–13).

12. Maritain, *The Rights of Man*, 6.

13. She did not succeed with her colleagues in London, though. I have heard the story told that the Free French dropped copies of *The Rights of Man* into occupied France as a propaganda exercise. I have not been able to confirm this, but the irony is so great that the story bears repeating. Fortunately, Weil had died by the time this happened. It would have killed her.

14. Although he was not aware at the time that Weil had Maritain in her sights in this essay, Stanley Hauerwas uses Weil's thinking about rights in "What Is Sacred in Every Human Being?" to help make his own case of the inappropriate use of rights in moral thinking and theology. See his "How to Think Theologically about Rights" in *The Work of Theology* (Grand Rapids, MI: Eerdmans, 2015).

15. For more detail, see footnote 13 in chapter 9.

16. Stanley Cavell, *The Claim of Reason* (Oxford: Oxford University Press, 1979), 361.

Chapter Nine

1. Rainer Maria Rilke, "Interiors, II," in *The Inner Sky: Poems, Notes, Dreams*, trans. and ed. Damion Searls, 13 (Boston: David R. Godine, 2010).

2. Michael Sandel, *What Money Can't Buy: The Moral Limits of Markets* (New York: Farrar, Strauss & Giroux, 2012).

3. See my "Having an Inner Life" in *Philosophical Investigations* 43, nos. 1–2: 142–57.

4. Sandel, *What Money Can't Buy*, 51.

5. Sandel, *What Money Can't Buy*, 8.

6. Sandel, *What Money Can't Buy*, 9.

7. Sandel, *What Money Can't Buy*, 9.

8. Sandel, *What Money Can't Buy*, 64–65.

9. Sandel, *What Money Can't Buy*, 113.

10. Recall: "There is something wrong in the vocabulary of the stream of modern thought called 'personalist.' And in this domain whenever there is a grave error in vocabulary it is hard to avoid grave errors in thought" (LPW 104).

11. Sandel, *What Money Can't Buy*, 203.

12. In *What Money Can't Buy*, Sandel does not spell out what exactly these human values are. He has, however, dealt with them in works such as *Justice: What's the Right Thing to Do?* (New York: Farrar, Straus and Giroux, 2010) and *Liberalism and the Limits of Justice* (Cambridge: Cambridge University Press, 1998). In what follows, I do not see any reason to suggest that Sandel would be opposed to the additional distinctions Weil draws.

13. The relevant argument on which I draw may be found in her essay "Is There a Marxist Doctrine?," written at about the same time as "What Is Sacred in Every Human Being?" Marx, she argues, had the great insight that there is such a thing as "social matter," which is analogous to physical matter. It is not subject to the laws of mechanics, but it is an interplay of social forces. It has laws like mechanics has laws. Arguing, as did Plato, that the necessary is distant from the good and that necessity is not a machine for producing goodness, she asks, "If Marx is right, then how can justice ever occur?" Plato and she saw the possibility of exceptions, moments of grace, but these are in some sense from outside the collective. Plato saw the need for something from without the system. Marx did not, and he thought that something like the morality of professional groups, a morality of social opinion, could produce justice. But these, too, she argues, are subject to the same forces in the end. This was pretty obvious in those who had achieved the supposedly enlightened workers' and revolutionary consciousness. She says, "The characteristic common to all these moralities, and to every kind of social morality, was formulated by Plato in definitive terms: 'They call just and beautiful things that are necessary, for they do not know how great in reality is the distance which separates the essence of the necessary from that of the good'" (OL 182–83). We should also consider her comments in a similar vein in the also contemporaneous essay "Are We Struggling for Justice?" She argues there that true morality requires the consent of those whose lives are brought into the sphere of our actions. Of course, in the quotidian world, one can't go around asking permission of everybody for everything. We accept social morality and need it to move ahead. Still, we cannot ignore consent, for consent is essential for justice, and it is important for a just society to find ways by which people can give their consent. Money and other forms of coercion are violations of it. This is why markets can corrupt and do so deeply. "Consent is neither to be bought or sold. Consequently, whatever the political institutions, in a society where monetary transactions dominate most of social life, where almost all obedience is bought and sold, there can be no freedom" (SWW 127).

14. See, e.g., Michael Walzer, *Thick and Thin: Moral Argument at Home and Abroad* (Notre Dame, IN: University of Notre Dame Press, 1994).

15. Alexis de Tocqueville, "Principal Causes Which Tend to Maintain the Democratic Republic in the United States," in *Democracy in America*, trans. Henry Reeve, rev. Francis Bowen (New York: Vintage Books, 1945), 1:298–342.

Chapter Ten

1. Plato, *Laws,* 650b, in *The Collected Dialogues*, ed. Edith Hamilton and Huntington Cairns (Princeton, NJ: Princeton University Press, 1961).
2. John Rawls, *Political Liberalism* (New York: Columbia University Press, 1993), 223.
3. Ludwig Wittgenstein, *Philosophical Remarks*, ed. Rush Rhees, trans. Raymond Hargreaves and Roger White (Chicago: University of Chicago Press, 1975), 85.
4. Wittgenstein, *Philosophical Investigations*, §124.
5. Martin Heidegger, "Letter on Humanism," in *Martin Heidegger: Basic Writings*, ed. David Farrell Krell (New York: Harper and Row, 1977), 232.
6. Milbank, *Theology and Social Theory*, 15.
7. See Mary G. Dietz, *Between the Human and the Divine: The Political Thought of Simone Weil* (Totowa, NJ: Rowman and Littlefield, 1988).
8. See my "Rootedness: Culture and Value," in *Spirit, Nature, and Community*, ed. Allen and Springsted.
9. Winch, *Simone Weil: "The Just Balance,"* 211.
10. Winch, *Simone Weil: "The Just Balance,"* 199.
11. Leo Tolstoy, *Resurrection*, in *The Complete Works of Tolstoy* (n.p.: Golgotha Press, 2010), 2694.
12. Allen and Springsted, *Spirit, Nature, and Community*, 89.
13. Augustine's *The City of God* is again an appropriate example of just what this might mean, as the concept of Christian revelation with which Augustine works is a matter of seeing pagan Roman history in a very different light than the Romans had been wont to see it. It is a matter of seeing the concepts of history and nature themselves in a very different light than they had been seen before.

Chapter Eleven

1. It is for these reasons that Weil concerns herself to the great degree that she does with science in later sections of *The Need for Roots*. The problem of

modern science is that it has obscured the moral resources of the order of the world and the beauty it gives rise to. It is unconnected to our moral being. Her essay on modern science, "At the Price of an Infinite Error: The Scientific Image, Ancient and Modern" (LPW 155–98), bears heavily on this topic as well.

2. David McLellan, *Simone Weil: Utopian Pessimist* (London: Macmillan, 1989), 258.

3. "Although Weil is an extremely idiosyncratic thinker, it would not be misleading to characterize her later political thought as conservative. She was certainly implacably opposed to the ideas of change and progress so firmly entrenched in the world views of bourgeois democracy and its offspring, classical Marxism. This opposition was firmly rooted in the Platonic belief in the existence of absolute, eternal values opposed to, or at least entirely separate from, the way of the world. Throughout history, Platonism has had two sides to it: a radical one that appeals to eternal and absolute values as against those of the status quo and a conservative one in that Platonism's eventual goal is a static society governed by an elite of the wise and the good. The proposal for rule by philosophers in Plato's *Republic* exhibits both these facets, and Weil's ideas are an attempt to adapt the principles of the *Republic* to twentieth century France." David McLellan, *Unto Caesar: The Political Relevance of Christianity* (Notre Dame, IN: University of Notre Dame Press, 1993), 21–22.

4. *Blackwell Encyclopedia of Political Thought*, ed. David Miller, Janet Coleman, William Connolly, and Alan Ryan (Oxford: Basil Blackwell, 1991), s.v. "utopianism."

5. *Blackwell Encyclopedia of Political Thought*, s.v. "utopianism."

6. Winch, *Simone Weil: "The Just Balance,"* 85.

7. Michael Walzer, *Spheres of Justice: A Defense of Pluralism and Equality* (New York: Basic Books, 1983), 8–9.

8. "What is indispensable for this task is a passionate interest in human beings, whoever they may be, and in their minds and souls; the ability to place oneself in their position and to recognize by signs thoughts which go unexpressed; a certain intuitive sense of history in process of being enacted; and the faculty of expressing in writing delicate shades of meaning and complex relationships" (NR 199).

9. Winch, *Simone Weil: "The Just Balance,"* 65.

10. See Winch, *Simone Weil: "The Just Balance,"* 65ff, on this notion of a repeated operation as the base of the idea of an all-embracing necessity.

11. See Weil's 1933 letter to Alain, in which she notes, "Descartes never found a way to prevent order from becoming, as soon as it is conceived, a thing

instead of an idea. Order becomes a thing, it seems to me, as soon as one treats a series as a reality distinct from the terms which compose it, by expressing it with a symbol; now algebra is just that, and has been since the beginning (since Vieta). It is only the use of analogy that offers a way of conceiving a series without separating it from its terms" (SL 3).

12. See "Culture is the formation of attention" (SWW 119).

Chapter Twelve

1. See my "The Religious Basis of Culture: T. S. Eliot and Simone Weil," *Religious Studies* 25: 105–16.
2. Dietz, *Between the Human and the Divine*, 106.
3. Dietz, *Between the Human and the Divine*, 124.
4. Dietz, *Between the Human and the Divine*, 125.
5. See SE 45: "Every country of pre-Roman antiquity had its vocation, its revelation referring, not exclusively but mainly, to one aspect of supernatural truth."
6. T. S. Eliot just has to be quoted in this context:

> At the still point of the turning world. Neither flesh nor fleshless:
> Neither from nor towards; at the still point, there the dance is.
> But neither arrest nor movement. And do not call it fixity,
> Where past and future are gathered. Neither movement from nor towards,
> Neither ascent nor decline. Except for the point, the still point,
> There would be no dance, and there is only the dance.

"Burnt Norton II," in *The Complete Plays and Poems 1909–1950* (New York: Harcourt, Brace & World, 1971).

7. "A Medieval Epic Poem" and "The Romanesque Renaissance," SE 35–72.
8. Dietz, *Between the Human and the Divine*, 120.
9. Michel de Certeau, *The Mystic Fable* (Chicago: University of Chicago Press, 1995).
10. David Tracy, "Simone Weil: The Impossible," in *The Christian Platonism of Simone Weil*, ed. E. Jane Doering and Eric O. Springsted (Notre Dame, IN: University of Notre Dame Press, 2002).
11. "Tragedy invokes the possibility of irretrievable loss whereas for postmodernism there is nothing momentous missing. . . . The postmodern subject is

hard-pressed to find enough depth and continuity in itself to be a suitable candidate for tragic self-dispossession. You cannot give away a self you never had. If there is no longer a God, it is partly because there is no longer any secret interior place where he might install himself. Depth and interiority belong to a clapped-out metaphysics and to eradicate them is to abolish God by rooting out the underground places where he has been concealing himself." Terry Eagleton, *Culture and the Death of God* (New Haven, CT: Yale University Press, 2015), 186.

12. I note here Rebecca Rozelle-Stone's excellent "Le Déracinement of Attention: Simone Weil on the Institutionalization of Distractedness," *Philosophy Today* 53, no. 1: 100–108. Her title is indicative of her important argument. She argues that considerations of the modern problem of distractedness neglect issues of morality and agency in their discussions. Drawing on Weil's concepts of attention, the imagination, and "the need for roots," she looks at what she terms the "institutionalization of distraction" in the modern world. In particular, she offers an in-depth analysis of the two "poisons" identified by Weil as giving rise to uprootedness: money and education.

Chapter Thirteen

1. Alasdair C. MacIntyre, *After Virtue* (Notre Dame, IN: University of Notre Dame Press, 1981), 245.
2. MacIntyre, *After Virtue*, 244.
3. Rod Dreher, *The Benedict Option* (New York: Sentinel, 2017).
4. John Henry Newman, "The Mission of St. Benedict," in *Rise and Progress of Universities and Benedictine Essays* (Notre Dame, IN: University of Notre Dame Press, 2001), 374–75.
5. Newman, "The Mission of St. Benedict," 374–75.
6. Newman, "The Mission of St. Benedict," 376.
7. Newman, "The Mission of St. Benedict," 387.
8. The master of novices at the Benedictine monastery of Christ in the Desert once explained to me the importance of all monks taking two hours in the afternoon for *lectio divina*, a habit that certainly put work projects in the monastery in second place. He noted, waving his hand all around him at the buildings of the monastery, that without this daily practice, "all this is not worth anything."
9. As it is currently published. The work is unfinished, and current publication omits a number of lines after these quoted in which Weil starts to

develop the thought further. These have been added in the *Oeuvres Complètes* version.

10. Robert Chenavier, *Simone Weil: Une Philosophie du Travail* (Paris: Cerf, 2001), 487.

11. Hannah Arendt, *The Human Condition* (Chicago: University of Chicago Press, 1958), 292.

12. I would cite Marcel Gauchet's argument in *The Disenchantment of the World* (Princeton, NJ: Princeton University Press, 1999) as well. Gauchet argues that as humans create their own space for protection (a space that arises precisely because they have a religion), they begin to lose contact with the same nature that threatened them, and they also begin to lose contact with each other, which ultimately means that they lose the very sources they need for religion.

Chapter Fourteen

1. George Weigel, "Moral Clarity in a Time of War," *First Things* (January 2003): 20.
2. Weigel, "Moral Clarity," 20.
3. Weigel, "Moral Clarity," 20.
4. Weigel, "Moral Clarity," 22.
5. In response to Boniface's inquiry whether a soldier can be a Christian, Augustine says that he can, and that the soldier's job is an important one. Nevertheless, one cannot forget what it means to be a Christian. Clearly this has implications for how one approaches war. He writes, "Therefore when you are preparing for battle, think first that even your bodily strength is a gift of God. In this way, you will not think of using the gift of God against God. When fidelity is promised it must be kept, even to an enemy against whom war is being waged. . . . The will should be concerned with peace and necessity with war, so that God might liberate us from necessity and preserve us in peace. Peace is not sought in order to provoke war, but war is waged in order to attain peace. Be a peacemaker, then, even by fighting, so that through your victory you might bring those whom you defeat to the advantages of peace. . . . If human peace is so sweet for attaining the temporal well-being of mortals, how much more sweet is divine peace for attaining the eternal well-being of the angels! Let necessity slay the warring for, not your will. As violence is returned to one who rebels and resists, so should mercy be to one who has been conquered

or captured, especially when there is no fear of a disturbance of peace." Augustine, "Letter 189: To Count Boniface," in *The Confessions and Letters of St. Augustin*, vol. 1 of *A Select Library of Nicene and Post-Nicene Fathers*, ed. Phillip Schaff (Grand Rapids, MI: Wm. B. Eerdmans, 1974), 554.

6. Weigel, "Moral Clarity," 24.

7. Weigel, "Moral Clarity," 24.

8. Thucydides, *The History of the Peloponnesian War*, trans. B. Jowett (New York: Random House, 1942), Book 3:82.

9. Thucydides, *The History of the Peloponnesian War*, Book 3:84.

10. Augustine, "Letter 189: To Count Boniface," in *The Confessions and Letters of St. Augustin*, 554.

11. Alexander Irwin, *Saints of the Impossible* (Minneapolis: University of Minnesota Press, 2002), 187.

12. Irwin, *Saints of the Impossible*, 196.

BIBLIOGRAPHY

Works of Simone Weil

The works of Simone Weil in English can be found in the list of abbreviations in the front of the book.

Cited and Selected Secondary Works on Weil

Allen, Diogenes, and Eric O. Springsted. *Spirit, Nature, and Community: Issues in the Thought of Simone Weil*. Albany: SUNY Press, 1994.
Bell, Richard. *Simone Weil: The Way of Justice as Compassion*. Lanham, MD: Rowman & Littlefield, 1998.
———, ed. *Simone Weil's Philosophy of Culture*. Cambridge: Cambridge University Press, 1993.
Blum, Lawrence A., and Victor J. Seidler. *A Truer Liberty: Simone Weil and Marxism*. London: Routledge, 1989.
Cabaud, Jacques. *Simone Weil*. London: Harvill Press, 1964.
Chenavier, Robert. *Simone Weil: Une Philosophie du Travail*. Paris: Cerf, 2001.
Dargan, Joan. *Simone Weil: Thinking Poetically*. Albany: State University of New York Press, 1999.
David, Pascal. "'Philosophie, Chose Exclusivement en Acte et Pratique': L'Écriture Philosophique des *Cahiers* comme Exercice de l'Absence." *Cahiers Simone Weil* 31, no. 2: 119–52.
Dietz, Mary G. *Between the Human and the Divine: The Political Thought of Simone Weil*. Totowa, NJ: Rowman and Littlefield, 1988.
Doering, E. Jane. *Simone Weil and the Specter of Self-Perpetuating Force*. Notre Dame, IN: University of Notre Dame Press, 2010.
Doering, E. Jane, and Eric O. Springsted. *The Christian Platonism of Simone Weil*. Notre Dame, IN: University of Notre Dame Press, 2002.

Finch, Henry L. *Simone Weil and the Intellect of Grace*. New York: Continuum, 1999.
Fraisse, Simone. "Simone Weil, la Personne et les Droits de l'Homme." *Cahiers Simone Weil* 7, no. 2 (June 1984): 120–32.
Gabellieri, Emmanuel, ed. *Cahier L'Herne: Simone Weil*. Paris: Éditions de L'Herne, 2014.
———. *Être et Don: Simone Weil et la Philosophie*. Louvain, Belgium: Éditions Peeters, 2003.
Irwin, Alexander. *Saints of the Impossible*. Minneapolis: University of Minnesota Press, 2002.
Janicaud, Joël. *Simone Weil: l'Attention et l'Action*. Paris: PUF, 2002.
Little, J. P., ed. and trans. *Simone Weil on Colonialism: An Ethic of the Other*. Lanham, MD: Rowman & Littlefield, 2003.
McCullough, Lissa. *The Religious Philosophy of Simone Weil: An Introduction*. London: I. B. Tauris, 2014.
McLellan, David. *Simone Weil: Utopian Pessimist*. London: Macmillan, 1989.
———. *Unto Caesar: The Political Relevance of Christianity*. Notre Dame, IN: University of Notre Dame Press, 1993.
Morgan, Vance. *Weaving the World*. Notre Dame, IN: University of Notre Dame Press, 2005.
Moulakis, Athanasios. *Simone Weil and the Politics of Self-Denial*. Translated by R. Hein. Columbia: University of Missouri Press, 1998.
Naud, André. *Les Dogmes et le Respect de l'Intelligence: Plaidoyer Inspiré par Simone Weil*. Quebec: Éditions Fides, 2002.
Perrin, J. M., and Gustave Thibon. *Simone Weil as We Knew Her*. Translated by E. Craufurd. London: Routledge, 2003.
Pétrement, Simone. *Simone Weil: A Life*. Translated by Raymond Rosenthal. New York: Pantheon Books, 1976.
Rhees, Rush. *Discussions of Simone Weil*. Albany: State University Press of New York, 1999.
Rozelle-Stone, A. Rebecca. "Le Déracinement of Attention: Simone Weil on the Institutionalization of Distractedness." *Philosophy Today* 53, no. 1: 100–108.
Rozelle-Stone, A. Rebecca, and Lucian Stone, eds. *The Relevance of the Radical: Simone Weil 100 Years Later*. New York: Continuum, 2010.
———. *Simone Weil and Theology*. London: Bloomsbury, 2013.
Ruhr, Mario von der. *Simone Weil*. London: Continuum, 2006.
Saint-Sernin, Bertrand. *L'Action Politique selon Simone Weil*. Paris: Cerf, 1988.

Schmidt, Lawrence. "André Naud: From Vatican II to Simone Weil." *Philosophical Investigations* 43, nos. 1–2: 115–21.

Sontag, Susan. "Simone Weil." In *Against Interpretation,* 49–51. New York: Farrar, Strauss & Giroux, 1961.

Springsted, Eric O. *Christus Mediator: Platonic Mediation in the Thought of Simone Weil.* Chico, CA: Scholars Press, 1983.

———. "Contradiction, Mystery and the Use of Words in Simone Weil." In *The Beauty That Saves: Essays on Aesthetics and Language in Simone Weil,* edited by John M. Dunaway and Eric O. Springsted, 13–30. Macon, GA: Mercer University Press, 1996.

———. "Having an Inner Life." *Philosophical Investigations* 43, nos. 1–2: 142–57.

———. "The Religious Basis of Culture: T. S. Eliot and Simone Weil." *Religious Studies* 25: 105–16.

———. *Simone Weil and the Suffering of Love.* Cambridge, MA: Cowley Publications, 1986; reprint, Eugene, OR: Wipf & Stock, 2010.

Vëto, Miklos. *The Religious Metaphysics of Simone Weil.* Translated by Joan Dargan. Albany: State University of New York Press, 1994.

Weil, Sylvie. *At Home with Andrè and Simone Weil.* Translated by Benjamin Ivry. Evanston, IL: Northwestern University Press, 2010.

Winch, Peter. *Simone Weil: "The Just Balance."* Cambridge: Cambridge University Press, 1989.

Works Cited and Used

Aquinas, Thomas. *Summa Theologiae.* 5 volumes. Westminster: Christian Classics, 1981.

Arendt, Hannah. *The Human Condition.* Chicago: University of Chicago Press, 1958.

Aristotle. *The Nicomachean Ethics.* Translated by David Ross. Oxford: Oxford University Press, 1925.

Augustine. *The City of God against the Pagans.* Translated by Robert W. Dyson. Cambridge: Cambridge University Press, 1998.

———. *Confessions.* Translated by Henry Chadwick. Oxford: Oxford University Press, 1991.

———. *Homilies on the Gospel of John 1–40.* Translated by Edmund Hill. Hyde Park, NY: New City Press, 2009.

———. *The Confessions and Letters of St. Augustin*. Vol. 1 of *A Select Library of Nicene and Post-Nicene Fathers*. Edited by Phillip Schaff. Grand Rapids, MI: Wm. B. Eerdmans, 1974.

———. *On Christian Belief*. Hyde Park, NY: New City Press, 2005.

———. *Political Writings*. Translated by Michael W. Tkascz. Indianapolis: Hackett, 1994.

———. *Teaching Christianity*. Translated by Edmund Hill. Hyde Park, NY: New City Press, 1996.

———. *The Trinity*. Translated by Edmund Hill. Hyde Park, NY: New City Press, 1991.

Balthasar, Hans Urs von. *Mysterium Paschale*. Translated by Aidan Nichols. Edinburgh: T&T Clark, 1990.

Cary, Phillip. *Augustine's Invention of the Inner Self: The Legacy of a Christian Platonist*. New York: Oxford University Press, 2000.

Cavell, Stanley. *The Claim of Reason*. Oxford: Oxford University Press, 1979.

Certeau, Michel de. *The Mystic Fable*. Chicago: University of Chicago Press, 1995.

Chrétien, Jean-Louis. *The Ark of Speech*. Translated by Andrew Brown. London: Routledge, 2004.

———. *The Call and Response*. Translated by Anne A. Davenport. New York: Fordham University Press, 2004.

de Lubac, Henri. *Augustinianism and Modern Theology*. Translated by Lancelot Sheppard. New York: Crossroad, 2000.

———. *The Mystery of the Supernatural*. Translated by Rosemary Sheed. New York: Crossroad, 1998. First published 1965 by Aubier.

Dreher, Rod. *The Benedict Option*. New York: Sentinel, 2017.

Dunne, Joseph. *Back to the Rough Ground: 'Phronesis' and 'Techne' in Modern Philosophy and Aristotle*. Notre Dame, IN: University of Notre Dame Press, 1993.

Eagleton, Terry. *Culture and the Death of God*. New Haven, CT: Yale University Press, 2015.

———. *Radical Sacrifice*. New Haven, CT: Yale University Press, 2018.

Eliot, T. S. *The Four Quartets*. In *The Complete Plays and Poems 1909–1950*. New York: Harcourt, Brace & World, 1971.

Evagrius Ponticus. *The Praktikos and Chapters on Prayer*. Translated by John E. Bamberger. Kalamazoo, MI: Cistercian, 1981.

Flew, Antony, and Alasdair MacIntyre, eds. *New Essays in Philosophical Theology*. London: SCM Press, 1955.

Foster, Michael. *Mystery and Philosophy*. London: SCM Press, 1957; reprint, Westport, CT: Greenwood Press, 1980.
Gauchet, Marcel. *The Disenchantment of the World*. Princeton, NJ: Princeton University Press, 1999.
Hadot, Pierre. *Philosophy as a Way of Life*. Oxford: Blackwell, 1995.
Hauerwas, Stanley. "How to Think Theologically about Rights." In *The Work of Theology*, 191–207. Grand Rapids, MI: Eerdmans, 2015.
Heidegger, Martin. "Letter on Humanism." In *Martin Heidegger: Basic Writings*, edited by David Farrell Krell, 213–66. New York: Harper and Row, 1977.
———. *The Question Concerning Technology and Other Essays*. Translated by William Lovitt. New York: Harper & Row, 1977.
———. *What Is Called Thinking?* Translated by Fred D. Wieck and John G. Gray. New York: Harper & Row, 1968.
Henry, Michel. *I Am the Truth: Toward a Philosophy of Christianity*. Stanford, CA: Stanford University Press, 2003.
———. *Incarnation: A Philosophy of Flesh*. Translated by Karl Hefty. Evanston, IL: Northwestern University Press, 2015.
Huxley, Aldous. *Brave New World*. New York: Harper & Row, 1932.
Janicaud, Dominque, Jean-François Courtine, Jean-Louis Chretien, Michel Henry, and Jean-Luc Marion. *Phenomenology and the "Theological Turn": The French Debate*. New York: Fordham University Press, 2000.
John of the Cross. *The Collected Works of St. John of the Cross*. Translated by Kieran Kavanaugh and Otilio Rodriguez. Washington, DC: ICS, 1973.
Jones, Tamsin. "Dionysius in Hans Urs von Balthasar and Jean-Luc Marion." In *Re-thinking Dionysius the Areopagite,* edited by Sarah Coakley and Charles M. Stang, 213–24. Malden, MA: Wiley-Blackwell, 2009.
Kant, Immanuel. *The Critique of Pure Reason*. Translated by Norman K. Smith. London: Macmillan, 1968.
———. *Practical Philosophy*. Translated by Mary J. Gregor. Cambridge: Cambridge University Press, 1996.
Lacoste, Jean Yves. *From Theology to Theological Thinking*. Charlottesville: University of Virginia Press, 2014.
Louth, Andrew. *Discerning the Mystery: An Essay on the Nature of Theology*. Oxford: Oxford University Press, 1983.
MacIntyre, Alasdair C. *After Virtue*. Notre Dame, IN: University of Notre Dame Press, 1981.

———. *Ethics in the Conflicts of Modernity.* Cambridge: Cambridge University Press, 2016.
Marcel, Gabriel. *Being and Having.* New York: Harper & Row, 1965.
———. *The Mystery of Being.* 2 vols. South Bend, IN: Gateway Editions, 1950.
Marion, Jean-Luc. *God without Being.* Translated by Thomas A. Carlson. Chicago: University of Chicago Press, 1991.
———. *In the Self's Place: The Approach of Saint Augustine.* Translated by Jeffrey L. Kosky. Stanford, CA: Stanford University Press, 2012.
Maritain, Jacques. *The Rights of Man and the Natural Law.* London: Geofrey Bles, 1944.
Milbank, John. *Theology and Social Theory: Beyond Secular Reason.* Oxford: Blackwell Publishers, 1990.
Miller, David, Janet Coleman, William Connolly, and Alan Ryan, eds. *Blackwell Encyclopedia of Political Thought.* Oxford: Basil Blackwell, 1991.
Murdoch, Iris. *The Sovereignty of the Good.* New York: Schocken Books, 1971.
Newman, John Henry. *The Grammar of Assent.* Westminster, MD: Christian Classics, 1973.
———. *Fifteen Sermons Preached before the University of Oxford between A.D. 1826 and 1843.* Notre Dame, IN: University of Notre Dame Press, 1997.
———. "The Mission of St. Benedict." In *Rise and Progress of Universities and Benedictine Essays,* 363–430. Notre Dame, IN: University of Notre Dame Press, 2001.
Otten, Willemien, and Susan E. Shreiner, eds. *Augustine Our Contemporary: Examining the Self in Past and Present.* Notre Dame, IN: University of Notre Dame Press, 2018.
Pieper, Josef. *Leisure: The Basis of Culture.* South Bend, IN: St. Augustine's Press, 1998. First published 1948 by Kösel Verlag.
———. "Philosophical Education and Intellectual Labor." In *For the Love of Wisdom: Essays on the Nature of Philosophy,* edited by Berthold Wald, translated by Roger Wasserman. San Francisco: Ignatius Press, 2006.
Plato. *The Collected Dialogues.* Edited by Edith Hamilton and Huntington Cairns. Princeton, NJ: Princeton University Press, 1961.
Plotinus. *Enneads.* 6 vols. Translated by Arthur H. Armstrong. Cambridge, MA: Harvard University Press, 1966.
Putnam, Hilary. *Jewish Philosophy as a Way of Life.* Bloomington: Indiana University Press, 2008.
Rawls, John. *Political Liberalism.* New York: Columbia University Press, 1993.

———. *A Theory of Justice*. Cambridge, MA: Harvard University Press, 1971.
Rilke, Rainer Maria. *The Inner Sky: Poems, Notes, Dreams*. Edited and translated by Damion Searls. Boston: David R. Godine, 2010.
Rivera, Joseph. *The Contemplative Self after Michel Henry: A Phenomenological Theology*. Notre Dame, IN: University of Notre Dame Press, 2015.
Sandel, Michael. *Justice: What's the Right Thing to Do?* New York: Farrar, Straus & Giroux, 2010.
———. *Liberalism and the Limits of Justice*. Cambridge: Cambridge University Press, 1998.
———. *What Money Can't Buy: The Moral Limits of Markets*. New York: Farrar, Strauss & Giroux, 2012.
Tanner, Kathryn. *Christ the Key*. Cambridge: Cambridge University Press, 2010.
Taylor, Charles. *A Secular Age*. Cambridge, MA: Harvard University Press, 2007.
———. *The Sources of the Self*. Cambridge, MA: Harvard University Press, 1989.
Thucydides. *The History of the Peloponnesian War*. Translated by Benjamin Jowett. New York: Random House, 1942.
Tocqueville, Alexis de. *Democracy in America*. 2 vols. Translated by Henry Reeve. Revised by Francis Bowen. New York: Vintage Books, 1945.
Tolstoy, Leo. *Resurrection*. In *The Complete Works of Tolstoy*. Golgotha Press, 2010.
Turner, Denys. *The Darkness of God: Negativity in Christian Mysticism*. Cambridge: Cambridge University Press, 1995.
Walzer, Michael. *Spheres of Justice: A Defense of Pluralism and Equality*. New York: Basic Books, 1983.
———. *Thick and Thin: Moral Argument at Home and Abroad*. Notre Dame, IN: University of Notre Dame Press, 1994.
Weigel, George. "Moral Clarity in a Time of War." *First Things* (January 2003): 20–26.
Winch, Peter. "The Expression of Belief." In *Proceedings and Addresses of the American Philosophical Association* 70, no. 2: 7–23.
Wittgenstein, Ludwig. *The Big Typescript: TS 213*. Translated by C. Grant Luckhardt and Maximilian A. E. Aue. Chichester, UK: Wiley-Blackwell, 2013.
———. *Culture and Value*. Edited and translated by Peter Winch. Chicago: University of Chicago Press, 1980.
———. *Philosophical Investigations*. Revised 4th ed. Translated by G. E. M. Anscombe, P. M. S. Hacker, and Joachim Schulte. Chichester, UK: Wiley-Blackwell, 2009.

———. *Philosophical Remarks*. Edited by Rush Rhees. Translated by Raymond Hargreaves and Roger White. Chicago: University of Chicago Press, 1975.

———. *Tractatus Logico-Philosophicus*. Translated by David F. Pears and Brian F. McGuiness. London: Routledge & Kegan Paul, 1961.

INDEX

affliction, xix–xx, 5, 33, 43–46, 48, 77, 111, 130, 220
allegory of the cave (Plato), 8, 70, 76–77, 86, 226
Allen, Diogenes, vii, 155–56
apprenticeship, 10, 82, 86, 88–99, 101, 182
Aquinas, Thomas, 106, 171, 235n.6
Arendt, Hannah, 87, 51, 200–203, 205
Aristotle, 3, 75, 79, 121, 124
Arius, 22
Athanasius, 38
attention, 5, 9–10, 12–13, 46, 55–64, 74, 82, 90, 97–98, 101, 110, 112, 188, 191–93, 203–4, 206
Augustine, 14, 62, 68–71, 73, 77, 84, 90–92, 104, 106, 115, 153, 171, 181, 212–13
avatarism, 48–49
Ayer, Alfred Jules, 28

balance, 26, 180, 193, 219, 225
Balthasar, Hans Urs von, 33–35, 48, 107
beauty, 21, 46, 56, 77, 96, 103, 106, 109–11, 114–15, 162, 170, 173, 178, 194, 202, 226

Benedict of Nursia, 195–97, 200–201, 209
Bhagavad-Gita, 215, 222
Buddhism, 112, 185

Cabaud, Jacques, 34
Calvin, John, 41, 56
Caputo, John, 66
Cavell, Stanley, 4, 131
Certeau, Michel de, 185
character, 4, 6–7, 13, 88, 190, 218
Chartier, Émile (Alain), xix, 7–8
Chenavier, Robert, 203
Christ, 10, 22, 33–34, 38–48, 55, 84, 99, 104, 109–11, 150, 207, 222, 227
Christianity, 14, 30, 35–36, 70–73, 82, 85, 107, 208
Christian Platonism, 69–72, 83–84
church, xx, 22, 25, 52–54, 59–64, 68, 175, 235n.5
Clausewitz, Carl von, 212
colonialism, 165, 184
common good, 138–39, 143
community, 91, 175, 195–201, 203–4, 206–9
conscience, 104, 142, 204–5, 222
consent, 47, 110, 183, 187–93
consolation, viii, 12, 97

construction, intellectual, 80–83
contemplation, 13, 15–16, 19–20, 53, 60, 63, 65, 70, 72, 77, 80, 104, 205
contradiction, 22–25, 28, 63–64, 77
convention, 112–13
Couturier, Edouard, 124
Crucifixion, the, 33, 37–38, 41–46, 110
culture, 101, 173, 175, 177–82, 185, 191–93

David, Pascal, 8
death, 29, 41–42, 100, 184–85, 203, 218, 223
deconstruction, 66–67
decreation, 184, 186, 188, 191, 203
de Gaulle, Charles, 123
de Lubac, Henri, 106–7
Derrida, Jacques, 66, 85
detachment, 10, 29, 76
Dietz, Mary G., 152, 176, 184
discipline, 10
disponibilité, 47, 82–83, 98, 188
doctrine, 14, 18, 22, 34, 51–52, 60–61, 63–64, 68–71, 73, 83–84, 148, 177, 179
dogmas, 21, 25
Dreher, Rod, 196, 208
Dunne, Joseph, 87–88

Eagleton, Terry, 12, 246n.11
economics, 135, 191
education, 83, 86–89, 91–93, 95–97, 100, 158, 168, 191–92, 208
enlightenment, 151, 189
equality, 110, 219–20, 226, 239
equilibrium, 26, 219, 224

eternal, the, 15–16, 140, 159–65, 175–78, 198
Eucharist, 102, 112
Eudoxus, 23
Evagrius of Pontus, 70, 192
evil, 32, 97, 102–3, 211, 227
experience, religious, xx, 7, 12, 45, 51, 55, 58, 72–73, 82, 206, 227

faith, 21, 25, 36, 40, 44, 52–55, 59–62, 65, 71–72, 100, 106, 113, 147, 156,181–82, 184, 196, 235
flatness, ix, 16, 20–21, 29, 49, 105, 117, 130, 132–34, 147, 226, 228
force, 24, 33, 45, 53–54, 62, 94–96, 99, 139, 173, 180, 187, 202, 211–12, 215–22, 224–26
Foster, Michael, 17–21, 29
freedom, 61, 64, 121, 129, 150, 160, 187, 198, 211, 213
Free French, 122, 124, 126, 128, 141, 143, 159, 242n.13

Gabellieri, Emmanuel, 32
Gandhi, Mahatma, 12
generosity, 6, 162, 190–92
gifts, 32, 37–40, 42, 62, 84, 98, 100, 107
gnosticism, 28, 48, 70–71, 75
God, 9–11, 14–16, 19, 22, 24, 26–27, 32–34, 36–49, 55–59, 64–65, 67–69, 71–76, 79, 81–84, 86–87, 89, 93, 96–97, 99, 100, 102–17, 124, 127–29, 133–34, 142–43, 146, 150–51, 153, 171–74, 178–83, 187–89,

193–94, 200–204, 213–14, 220–21, 227–28
good, 12, 19–22, 27, 33, 42, 44, 56, 59, 62, 66, 68, 75, 77, 81, 85, 87, 96, 98, 102–4, 113, 115, 122, 130, 133, 160–61, 175, 180, 183, 186–87, 189, 200, 202, 204–5, 208, 226–28
Gospel, 58, 129
government, 212, 214–15
grace, 29, 32–34, 36–43, 45–49, 73, 80, 106–8, 115, 183
grammar, 23, 29, 36, 56, 68, 91, 142, 149
gravity, 34, 106, 154, 180, 225
Great Beast (Plato), 76, 139, 163, 226
Gregory of Nazianzus, 22–23, 42

Hadot, Pierre, 14, 67
Heidegger, Martin, 3–4, 13, 150
Hegel, Georg Wilhelm Friedrich, 13
Henry, Michel, 15
Hippolytus of Rome, 70
history, 6, 24, 35, 107, 151, 155–58, 160–61, 165, 167–69, 174, 176–77, 179, 181–85, 201
Hobbes, Thomas, 172, 189, 199
Huxley, Aldous, 238n.13, 239n.14

idolatry, 220, 228
imagination, 9, 40, 80, 94, 103, 227
imago Dei, 37–39, 47–48, 88
impersonality, 126, 129–31, 186, 226
implicit loves of God, 3, 48, 51, 108–12, 115

Incarnation, the, 32–35, 37–44, 47–48, 59, 85
individualism, 68–69, 127, 139, 166
inner life, 84, 134, 144, 228
intellect, 6–7, 25, 51–66
intimacy, 55, 133, 142
inwardness/inward turn, 14, 68–69, 72, 74, 76, 78, 83, 86, 228

John of the Cross, 50, 83–84, 194, 203
Julian of Norwich, 11
justice, 57, 84, 110, 126, 130, 133–35, 139, 141–43, 146–48, 153–54, 158–59, 178, 183, 186–90, 193, 220, 225–26
just war theory, 211–14

Kant, Immanuel, 73, 79–80, 189, 224
kenosis, 33, 56, 109–10, 114
Kierkegaard, Søren, 35, 228
knowledge, 28–29, 58, 62, 73, 74–76, 79, 81, 83, 89–90, 98, 104
Koyré, Alexander, 124

labor. *See* work
Lacoste, Jean-Yves, 14–15
language, 25–26, 55–57, 62, 91, 113, 132–34, 137, 141–42, 144, 185–86
Languedoc, 180, 236n.9
Leahy, William, 123
Le Senne, René, xix
liberalism, 11, 122, 134, 141–43, 147, 151–52, 165, 172, 176, 183, 186, 205
Locke, John, 54, 121–22, 238n.11

love, 16, 21–23, 25, 33, 43–46, 51, 54–65, 75, 97–98, 108–12, 114–18, 129, 133, 153,178–79, 181, 183, 219–20, 227–28
Luther, Martin, 177, 214

Machiavelli, Niccolò, 172
MacIntyre, Alasdair, 183, 195–97
Marcel, Gabriel, 18, 21
Maritain, Jacques, 121–32, 138–41, 152
marketplace, 56, 133–38, 143
mathematics, 8, 23, 96, 170
McLellan, David, 163–64, 166
metaxu, 33, 46, 49, 69, 89, 99–101, 103, 107, 114–17, 153, 172–73, 178, 180
method, 9, 13–14, 23, 29, 31, 80, 166, 172–73
Milbank, John, 151
Mounier, Emmanuel, 122
Murdoch, Iris, 12
mystery, ix, 17–27, 29–32, 36, 48–50, 55–56, 62–63, 66, 86, 105, 108, 114, 117, 172, 228
mysticism, 8, 50–51, 61–62, 66, 72–73, 78, 80, 82, 151,176–77, 184–85, 188, 204, 207, 229

nations, 159–60, 175
nature, 33, 35, 38–40, 42, 46, 49, 79, 104–8, 110, 112–15, 117–21, 148, 155, 157, 169, 172, 201–3, 205–6, 210, 214
Naud, André, 52, 61
necessity, 13, 24, 33, 43–44, 46–47, 49, 59, 62–64, 96–97, 99, 139, 153–54, 158, 160, 169, 178–79, 181–85, 187, 190, 192–93, 202–3, 206–8, 213, 219, 221–28
needs, 129, 139, 159–62, 174, 192, 204
Newman, John Henry,67, 87, 104, 197–99, 201, 203, 235n.4, 237n.12
Nicholas of Cusa, 75
Nietzsche, Friedrich, 12
nurses project, xxi, 7, 11, 123–24, 216, 222

obedience, 65, 96–97, 116, 173, 178, 181, 184, 187, 192, 197, 202, 204
obligations, 96, 98,101, 126, 128–29, 152, 158–59, 161, 166–67, 173, 191–92, 194, 204, 206, 229
Occitan civilization. *See* Languedoc
openness, 6, 29, 38, 40, 64, 80, 83
order, 104, 160–74, 180, 190, 193
Origen, 70

parage, 190, 192, 236n.9
participation, 37–38, 46–48, 104, 109
Pascal, Blaise, 68, 90, 191
peace, 213–14, 222, 224
Perrin, Jean-Marie, xx, 73
personalism, 122, 124, 126, 129–30, 138
person/personality, 57, 68, 126–30, 141, 186
Pétrement, Simone, 7–8, 123
philosophy, 8–9, 14, 117–20, 23, 27–29, 31, 34–36, 51, 65–67, 70, 72–73, 78–80, 83, 147–48, 197
moral, 80, 195, 197, 204
political, 154, 200, 204, 212
as way of life, 8, 14, 27, 67, 70, 73

phronesis, 87–88, 199
Pieper, Josef, 79–80, 235n.2
Plato, 8, 16, 19–20, 23, 44, 50, 68, 71–75, 78–79, 81–82, 99, 139, 147, 162, 171, 175, 202, 226, 243n.13
Platonism, 68, 70–72, 78, 80, 82
Plotinus, 71, 75
politics, 121, 126, 142, 148–52, 155, 157, 159, 163, 166–67, 176, 184–86, 188–93, 200–201
Popper, Karl, 164
prayer, 15, 36, 64, 70, 112, 199, 203
privacy, 69, 80, 82, 134, 142, 147–50, 200, 204–6
public, 80, 134, 142–43, 147–52, 157, 200, 204–5
Putnam, Hilary, 106

Radzins, Inese, 34–35
rationality, 20, 80, 87
Rawls, John, 148, 189
reading, 10, 24, 49–50, 59, 62–63, 81–82, 89, 93–96, 98–101, 104, 107, 116
reality, 10, 23, 49, 63–64, 66–67, 105–6, 179, 191, 223
reason, 62–63, 72, 75–76, 79, 87–88, 142, 198, 204, 210–11
religion, 18, 30, 32, 51, 109, 112, 148, 151, 175–77, 183, 208, 226
responsibility, 4, 124, 141, 143–44
Resurrection, viii, 12
revelation, 19, 36, 62, 177–80, 187, 207–8
rights, 122, 124, 126, 128, 130–33, 159, 186

Rilke, Rainer Maria, 133
Rivera, Joseph, 15–16
Roosevelt, Franklin D., 123
roots/rootedness, 160, 164–65, 168–70, 174–75, 183, 192
Rousseau, Jean-Jacques, 101, 121
Royce, Josiah, 207
Rozelle-Stone, Rebecca, 191, 247n.12

sacraments, 102–3, 107–9, 112–13, 115–18, 178, 181
sacred, 128, 130, 132, 139–42, 145
sacrifice, 10–12, 41–42, 56, 110–12, 222
salvation, 13, 34, 41, 74, 102, 139
Sandel, Michael, 134–38, 143
Sartre, Jean-Paul, 105
science, 17–19, 30, 32, 50, 93, 107–8, 114–15, 178, 202, 226
secularism, 30, 35, 107, 151, 157, 228
social goods, 134–35, 142, 144, 167, 184, 186, 189, 191
social matter, 129, 243n.13
society, 121–22, 137–38, 144, 160–62, 164, 166–67, 173, 175–76, 178, 183–84, 190–91, 201–3, 205–9
Socrates, 71–72, 90
Sontag, Susan, 31
soul, 46, 58, 67, 78, 131, 139–40, 144, 147, 150, 160–63, 170–71, 175, 186, 189, 218–20
space, 33, 46, 59, 78, 98, 147–58, 179
    moral, 62, 133, 157, 185, 201
    public, 147–52
Stoicism, 76

Strauss, Leo, 151
suffering, 5, 41–48, 96–97, 111, 207, 219–20, 223, 227
supernatural, the, 27, 35, 61, 104–9, 114, 118, 155–57, 179–82, 210, 214

Tanner, Kathryn, 37–45
Taylor, Charles, viii, ix, 20–21, 30–31, 86, 117, 226, 228
technique, 29, 91, 117
technology, 115
theology, 14–15, 19, 21, 34–36, 42, 51, 58, 61, 65–67, 70, 72, 79–80, 106–8, 153, 180
Thibon, Gustave, xx, 5
Thucydides, 217–19
Tocqueville, Alexis de, 143, 238–39n.13
Tolstoy, Leo, 155
totalitarianism, 197
Tracy, David, 188
tradition, 50, 70, 84–85, 88, 90, 165, 183–84, 195, 211
tragedy, 188–90
transcendence, 46, 65, 99, 177, 182, 227
transformation, 8, 30, 86, 88, 112–14, 116

Trinity, 14, 22, 84
truth, 11, 25, 34–36, 54, 57, 59–60, 62, 94, 124

universalism, 34–36
utilitarianism, 137
utopianism, 163, 165–66

value, 10, 27–28, 133–34, 137, 145, 163, 225–27
violence, 212–13, 216, 218, 221–23
virtue, 71, 153, 191, 193, 195, 199

waiting, 13, 65, 80
Walzer, Michael, 167
war, xx, 95, 210–24
Weber, Max, 228
Weigel, George, 210–14, 216, 220–21
Winch, Peter, 35–36, 51, 155–56, 166, 169
wisdom, 67, 73, 78, 82–83, 87
Wittgenstein, Ludwig, 8, 24–25, 29, 36, 87–88, 90–92, 99, 149, 179
work, 97, 99–100, 139–40, 184, 199, 201, 202–8